APOCALYPSE OBSERVED

Apocalypse Observed is a book about religious violence. By analyzing five of the most notorious messianic cults of recent years, the authors present a fascinating and revealing account of religious sects and conflict. The subjects covered include the apocalypse at Jonestown; the Waco siege; the terror campaign of Aum Shinrikyō; the mystical apocalypse of the Solar Temple; and the Heaven's Gate collective suicide.

Through comparative case studies and in-depth analysis, the authors show how religious violence can erupt not simply from the beliefs of the cult followers or the personalities of their leaders, but also from the way in which society responds to the cults in their midst. *Apocalypse Observed* will appeal to anyone with an interest in religious cults and their place in society.

John R. Hall is professor of sociology at the University of California–Davis, and has written widely on the sociology of religion. **Philip D. Schuyler** is associate professor in the department of music, University of Washington. **Sylvaine Trinh** is professor of sociology at Paris-Dauphine University and senior researcher at the Centre d'Analyse et d'Intervention Sociologiques, Ecole des Hautes Etudes en Sciences Sociales, Paris.

D1333954

APOCALYPSE OBSERVED

Religious movements and violence in North America, Europe and Japan

John R. Hall
with
Philip D. Schuyler and
Sylvaine Trinh

London and New York

First published 2000
by Routledge
11 New Fetter Lane, London EC4P 4EE

Simultaneously published in the USA and Canada
by Routledge
29 West 35th Street, New York, NY 10001

Routledge is an imprint of the Taylor & Francis Group

© 2000 John R. Hall, Philip D. Schuyler, and Sylvaine Trinh

Typeset in Goudy
by Curran Publishing Services Ltd.
Printed and bound in Great Britain by
Biddles Ltd, www.Biddles.co.uk

British Library Cataloguing in Publication Data
A catalogue record for this book is available from the
British Library

Library of Congress Cataloging in Publication Data
A catalog record for this book has been requested

ISBN 0–415–19276–5 (hbk)
ISBN 0–415–19277–3 (pbk)

In every era the attempt must be made anew to wrest tradition away from a conformism that is about to overpower it. The messiah comes not only as the redeemer, he comes as the subduer of Antichrist.

Walter Benjamin (1968, p. 253)

CONTENTS

All text is authored by John R. Hall except where otherwise noted.

ILLUSTRATIONS

ILLUSTRATIONS

ACKNOWLEDGEMENTS

The present inquiry has benefitted from the involvement of many individuals. In footnotes at the beginnings of various chapters, we extend our special thanks to people who have contributed to the five case studies on which the book is based. Yet the whole, we hope, is greater than the sum of the parts, and on that score we especially note the help of two individuals. Thomas Robbins has recognized the importance of studying collective religious violence since the mass suicide at Jonestown, Guyana, in 1978, and by his example and his critiques, he has encouraged us – and others – to approach a troubled subject in an engaged yet independent way. No one who approaches the subject could do better than live up to his example, and that has been our aspiration here. Second, Jenny Broome has taken on the role of first reader of the book in typescript, and we thank her for astute counsel and unfailing support during writing and revision. Her invisible hand is to be found on the pages that follow. Beyond the help of individuals, the research for this book was supported by a faculty research grant from the University of California–Davis Academic Senate Committee on Research.

A previously published essay served as a working paper for this study: 'Apostasy, Apocalypse, and Religious Violence: An Exploratory Comparison of Peoples Temple, the Branch Davidians, and the Solar Temple,' by John R. Hall and Philip Schuyler, pp. 141–69 in *The Politics of Religious Apostasy*, edited by David G. Bromley. Copyright © 1998 by David G. Bromley. Portions of this text are reproduced in revised form with permission of Greenwood Publishing Group, Inc., Westport, Conn.

Beyond all the help from others – without which this book would not exist – as authors we thank one another for the enriching experience of sharing this project. In particular, John R. Hall thanks Philip D. Schuyler and Sylvaine Trinh for their contributions to the enterprise as a whole, beyond the specific chapters where they are credited as co-authors. Collectively, we take responsibility for the gap between this inevitably flawed book and our aspirations for observing an Apocalypse that resists any rational accounting.

John R. Hall
Philip D. Schuyler
Sylvaine Trinh

ABBREVIATIONS

The following sources are cited in the text by abbreviations:

CNN   Cable News Network
CT   *Chicago Tribune*
IHT   *International Herald Tribune*
JT   *Japan Times*
LAT   *Los Angeles Times*
NYT   *New York Times*
SFC   *San Francisco Chronicle*
USTD   United States Department of the Treasury
WP   *Washington Post*
WTH   *Waco (Texas) Tribune-Herald*

INTRODUCTION

The dawn of the modern era's third millennium has inspired a flood of news stories, about everything from celebrations at the end of 1999 (or 2000, depending on who's counting) to accounts of computers going haywire because they are programmed to give the year in only two digits. Our reckonings of time may impose only a social grid on the flow of cosmic time. Nevertheless, we widely recognize the passage from one millennium to another as momentous, and wonder what it portends. Are we witnessing the end of one era and the beginning of another? From what, and to what?

These are among the classic questions about the meaning of existence, and it is thus not surprising that religions have long concerned themselves with cosmic and historical time (Eliade 1954). Yet millennial time is itself subject to history. Sometime during the second millennium before the beginning of the modern era, in the region between Persia and the Mediterranean, religious ideas surfaced about a world historical struggle between good and evil (Cohn 1993). These ideas later crystallized in the Bible's New Testament book, the Revelation of St John the Divine, chapter 20:

> I *saw* the souls of them that were beheaded for the witness of Jesus, and for the word of God, and which had not worshipped the beast, neither his image, neither had received *his* mark upon their foreheads, or in their hands; and they lived with Christ a thousand years.

The cultural significance of the millennium in the West derives in large part from this passage.

Many readers of Revelation look for Christ to return to Earth to preside over a thousand-year era of peace, joy, and bliss: an earth become heaven. Some wonder whether passing from the end of the twentieth century to a new millennium might trigger the fulfillment of Revelation's prophecies. Newspapers and magazines report a number of unusual religious developments: increased sightings of the Virgin Mary, a surge of fascination with angels, and the emergence of small religious sects like the Taiwanese group that looked for Christ to come for the second time on 31 March 1998 at 3513 Ridgedale Drive, Garland, Texas 75041 (NYT 4 March 98, p. A10).

1

Most disconcerting among contemporary millenarian chronicles are the stories about little known and socially marginal religious sects that suddenly erupt in extreme violence: murder, terrorism, even mass suicide. The more biblically inclined may view such events as *signs* of the long prophesied Millennium. And even apart from personal religious belief, it is not difficult to imagine that the violence is happening *because* of the millennial shift.

The present book takes the new millennium as an occasion to discern portents of messianic revelation to be found in the denouements of five marginal religious sects that became involved in acts of extreme violence – "Jonestown," "Waco," the less widely known Solar Temple, Aum Shinrikyō, and Heaven's Gate.

- Jonestown is the American utopian settlement in Guyana, on the northeast coast of South America, founded in the 1970s by members of Jim Jones's Peoples Temple. When California congressman Leo Ryan conducted an investigatory visit to Jonestown in November of 1978, he and four other people were murdered by Jonestown sharpshooters as they prepared to depart from an airstrip near the community. Immediately afterwards Jim Jones led true believers and coerced other members at Jonestown into committing "mass suicide."

- Second, in February 1993, near Waco, Texas, the US Bureau of Alcohol, Tobacco, and Firearms (BATF) conducted a raid on the Branch Davidians, a sect led by David Koresh. The Branch Davidians resisted, and a shootout ensued. By the time a ceasefire was negotiated six Davidians and four BATF sharpshooters had died, and the Davidians continued to hold the compound. After a siege of more than a month, almost all Branch Davidians who remained in the compound died in a fire that started during an FBI assault.

- As for the Solar Temple, in October 1994, a New-Age homeopathic doctor named Luc Jouret and fifty-two of his associates died in Canada and Switzerland in an event that the deceased described in letters left behind as a "Transit" to the distant star of Sirius. Sixteen of their colleagues died in a similar incident in France fourteen months later, on the winter solstice of 1995, and five more committed ritual suicide at the time of the spring equinox in March 1997.

- Fourth, in March of 1995, a deadly gas released in the Tokyo subway system killed eleven people and injured thousands more. Other gas attacks, an assassination attempt, and a mail bombing were to follow, bringing Japan to a crisis of collective panic. Investigators eventually proved that the subway attack was part of a campaign of murder and terrorism conducted over several years by a sect called Aum Shinrikyō, led by the self-styled meditation guru Shōkō Asahara. The group never threatened collective suicide.

- Last, in March of 1997, police found a house in the affluent California community of Rancho Santa Fe filled with the similarly dressed bodies of thirty-nine men and women who had videotaped their farewells, taken a poison, and suffocated themselves. Led by Marshall Applewhite, a long-time denizen of the countercultural religion scene (who called himself "Do"), the assembled Higher Source web page designers presumed to reach Heaven's Gate by a space ship that awaited them behind the Hale–Bopp comet.

These five episodes are striking testaments to the power of marginal religions in our era. But they are hardly all of a piece. Certainly not all of them were "millennial" in any strict sense concerned with the second coming of Christ or the arrival of the year 2000. How then might they be understood? It is our thesis that, for all the understandable interest, focusing only on "the millennium" stands as an obstacle to recognizing *apocalyptic* tensions between the established social order and countercultural religious movements. In this introduction, we describe the approach that this book takes to exploring those tensions.

From millennium to Apocalypse

An advertisement placed by the Jewish Theological Seminary in the *New York Times* suggests that God's time is not the time of our calendar, and thus all the hype about the end of one millennium and the beginning of another is misplaced (NYT 7 October 1997, p. A9). The seminarians recount an old story. In it, God says, "Let us go to Earth and ask. . . . Whenever they say it's the Day of Judgment, I will appear in court." This story does not rule out the possibility that individuals and social groups might become instruments of "divine" forces that bring cataclysmic shifts, but it suggests that such events would not necessarily align with merely rationalized human measures of time.

There is an important implication for the relation of religion to time. Among certain Christian groups, belief in the second coming of Christ is strongly oriented to the calendar. For "premillennialists," the anticipation is that Christ will return *before* the thousand years. "Postmillennialists," on the other hand, expect His return only *after* the Millennium. But these millenarian anticipations are a subset of a broader category of religious ideas about the transition from one era to another that can be called, in the generic sense of the term, *apocalyptic*.

Anyone who reads the book of Revelation will understand that the anticipated golden era of the millennial utopia does not come easily; it is borne of a violent cataclysm of destruction, an "apocalypse" in which evil is finally vanquished from Earth. The last book of the New Testament is usually taken to "reveal" events of the last days. But a subtly different meaning can be teased out. In Greek, *apokalyptein* means "disclose." This suggests not only "revelation" in the prophetic sense, but more profoundly, God's disclosure of the powerful forces that envelop our earthly lives.

Both as prophecy and disclosure, the Apocalypse poses a potent contrast between ordinary existence and dramatic transformations of the world as we know it. For the most part, people live daily life, yearly cycles, and the succession of generations within a world that seems "normal." Even devastating events such as the death of a loved one are brought within the realm of the sacred through rituals that symbolically affirm social continuity (Berger 1967, p. 44). But the Apocalypse does not easily fit within taken-for-granted understandings of the world, even ritualized ones, and certainly not ones keyed to calendrical time as a marker. The sense of extraordinary time, not calendrical calculation, is the key element. It thus makes sense to look at apocalyptic episodes in their own times, whether they are millennial or not.

Even among the most marginal religious social movements, the murders and mass suicide at Jonestown, the conflagration in which the Branch Davidians died, the Solar Temple "transits," Aum Shinrikyō's terrorist war, and the attempt to reach Heaven's Gate through collective suicide stand out as extremely unusual episodes. Nevertheless, whatever we make of the violence and deaths, even if they are only the products of collective pathologies with no implications for broader cultural shifts, they all resulted in collective death somehow connected to religious belief, and this suggests powerful social forces at work. Their very occurrence thus calls for critical consideration. All the more so if "cult" episodes in the news are strongly connected to societal transformations, social conflicts, and cultural dilemmas in the world where they occur.

The Apocalypse as cultural disjuncture

Students of religion now acknowledge what casual observation attests: contrary to the expectations of twentieth-century social theorists such as David Martin (1978), the rise of modern society has failed to bring the thorough-going secularization that would undermine widespread religious belief. Instead, as in times past, people who need spiritual and social support continue to turn to religion in huge numbers. Beneath the superficially smooth facade of everyday life, many people still experience "tribulations." Others, not so personally traumatized, nevertheless search for salvation in, and for, a world that seems to have lost any shared transcendent meaning. Their quests for redemption often find expression in religious vocabularies.

Among the many possibilities, people entertain fugues of apocalyptic thought. How easily they can do so is suggested by interviews that psychoanalyst Charles Strozier conducted with fundamentalist Christians in the United States during the early 1990s. One woman, thirty-two-year-old Mary, envisioned Armageddon as a "showdown in the OK Corral in Israel." Another, Cynthia, connected the book of Revelation with the New World Order. "Right now in Brussels, Belgium," she asserted, "the huge computer system there that controls the Common Market and everything is called 'the Beast'." A man named Otto warned, "First you centralize the world, the technology and the government, and that's what allows the Antichrist." Yet despite these foreboding images, not all the fundamentalists whom Strozier interviewed were fearful of the end days. Some rejoiced in them. Wilma seemed ready for a purification beyond the reach of mere human ritual. "Burning," she explained, "will cleanse the earth" (Strozier 1994, pp. 57, 60, 69, 142, 150).

Apocalyptic images bring focus to anxieties and suspicions about a world undergoing dramatic change. But what is the appeal of their seemingly fantastic, almost legendary stories? The end of the doomsday struggle between the capitalist West and Stalinist Communism in the last decade of the twentieth century might finally seem to confirm "the end of history" announced by Francis Fukayama (1992). The collapse of the Cold War, however, has initiated an era radically different than Fukayama anticipated. Today, the old Soviet Union's "evil empire" as "Other" no longer defines what democratic capitalism stands against. The rapid transition beyond this stark geo-political reality mirrors a more diffuse and gradual cultural shift. Over the last four decades of the twentieth century, the sharp modern lines between fact and fiction, reality and the imaginary have blurred. Partly, what Daniel Boorstin (1962) earlier identified as "pseudoevents" – events staged for consumption via mass media – shifted the locus of "reality" to the mass media themselves. The result is a development that exceeded Boorstin's anticipation. At the end of ideology and history, incontrovertible "facts" can no longer be taken for granted. Those of us who live within the orb of mass media in the more "developed" regions of the world (which is to say, virtually everyone participating in this book) now partake of a "simulacrum," a mediated experience that no longer portrays a real world located elsewhere: it *produces* the real (Baudrillard 1988). In turn, with media differentiation, even the simulacrum has become fragmented.

Not everyone is equally affected by these slippages. Nevertheless, now that global capitalism has lost its opposition and the imaginary has gained new currency, life is no longer so easily channeled within normative boundaries of the established social order. Rather than yielding the end of history, the waning of high modernism has opened up new possibilities for people to construct their own meaningful understandings of reality. As sociologists of religion understand, these possibilities had their roots in the tendency of secularization to promote religious pluralism (Berger, Berger, and Kellner 1973). But the consequences eclipse mere pluralism.

In the United States, to take one example, the modern hierarchy of religion mapped across grids of class and ethnicity (Herberg 1983, pp. 211–30; Lenski 1961, p. 80) has become transformed by shifts in religious affiliations, outright disaffiliation, and personal spiritual quests (Roof and McKinney 1987; Wuthnow 1988). These changes, however, have neither increased secularization nor reduced belief to a private matter (Warner 1993). Rather, religion has remained social, but it has become even more variegated. Most notably, beginning in the 1960s and 1970s, there emerged a dazzling array of "new religions," from eclectic personal-identity and meditation movements to highly organized religious sects such as the Krishna Society, the Unification Church, and the Church of Scientology. These new religious movements met with great controversy when they first came to public awareness, and they spawned a countermovement of fundamentalist religious mobilization that began in the 1970s and continues today. During the same period, long-established religions have undergone their own internal upheavals over issues such as homosexuality and the role of women as religious practitioners. As a consequence of all these changes, there is a now more or less institutionalized climate in which individuals and groups take license to contest old religious meanings and create new ones.[1]

Cultural change and the Apocalyptic

The Revelation of Saint John the Divine "disclosed" a history that gained an apocalyptic coherence in the telling. But where is the coherence to be found today? It is not centered in the public *zeitgeist* of millennial anticipation or the personal beliefs of people like those Charles Strozier interviewed. Such developments are for the most part mere *reflections* of a more unsettling scene to be found toward the heart of the Apocalypse. As literary critic Harold Bloom learned when he sought to describe what he called "the American religion," beyond a certain point the Apocalypse and the established social order divide against each other. Jehovah's Witnesses, Bloom was disturbed to find, are animated by a resentment toward the rich, the powerful, and the successful, and they feel a deep revulsion toward contemporary society (Bloom 1992). Here, the Apocalypse becomes something more than a mobilizing motif of popular evangelism or a gnawing angst among everyday people. It marks a deep gulf between the existing temporal order and the most strongly alienated and antagonistic of its inhabitants.

Hunter S. Thompson, the gonzo journalist, once suggested, "when the going gets weird, the weird turn pro." Some of them, it seems, take up life in a parallel social universe. Instead of embracing one or another *subcultural* stance toward the world, they cognitively migrate to the *countercultural* side of a symbolic boundary marking fundamental differences over the meaning of existence, how people ought to act, and what values they should affirm. There, visions of the Apocalypse circulate widely, conjuring dire imminent events of turmoil that require extraordinary actions.

Unfortunately, there is seldom a shortage of current events to cite in support of the apocalyptic claims. Despite all the wonders of science, social organization, and economy wrought over the last thousand years, we have hardly reached the New Era. Today, the spread of democracy and human rights seem much more complicated than they did at the peak of triumphant modernity a half-century ago. Even at that time, the widespread and resolute faith in progress depended on ignoring a great deal, and it still would. Despite progress on many fronts, major historical debacles, immense moral tragedies, and an enormous toll in human lives haunt the twentieth century. The scale of calamities is suggested by even a short list: the First World War, the 1917 Soviet revolution, the Great Depression, the Holocaust, the Second World War, Hiroshima and Nagasaki, the wars and genocide in Indo-China, more recent episodes of "ethnic cleansing" in Africa and the Balkans, and the slow but undeniable ecological apocalypse (for an overview, see Hobsbawm 1994).

War, plague, pestilence, economic depression, famine, genocide, and nuclear war have "apocalyptic" significance for whole societies, continents, even the global community. The fate of the human race truly hangs in the balance. Yet short of some epochal disaster that would transform the fundamental conditions of civilization, even the most devastating occurrences under the flag of the Apocalypse affect people unevenly. As German sociologist Karl Mannheim noted in the 1920s, events do not always have the same significance for everyone. Meanings are formed in different generations, concrete social groups, and social strata; they are "socially located" (Mannheim 1952).

Today, in the most economically developed societies, there is an absence of dramatic social conflicts. Nevertheless, the decline of working-class occupations, the rise of service and tourism sectors, and the relentless spread of computer-based culture have created new cultural disjunctures. On the one hand are people whose lives were built around an agriculturally and industrially based, class-ordered society; on the other are new generations who participate with greater facility in a multi-cultural, gender-modified, globalized domain of information that has subsumed almost everything, even the older economic sectors.

Because people may experience social life during the same era in radically different ways, the Apocalyptic is uneven in its manifestations and open to diverse elaborations, not only within Christianity, but also in other religions, in revolutionary social movements, and in secular accounts of the meaning of history. Like beauty, its image arises in the eyes of its beholders. People may resent a world that has left them behind, or they may search for transcendence spawned of jaded alienation. They may envision the struggles of the last days, become convinced that government is the manifestation of Satan, or conclude that troubled times may call for escape to a better world. Extraordinary circumstances can be both threatening and liberating, sometimes simultaneously.

When fully manifest, whatever their contents, apocalyptic narratives work against the grain of existing social orders. They hold the power to reorganize cultural meanings, and sectarian groups that invoke them thus sometimes become intertwined with broad historical currents: poor people's movements of redemption, crusades against infidels, revolutionary movements against an established order. Messianic apocalyptic religion has played into rebellions and revolutions as diverse as the Protestant Reformation in Germany and the Tai Ping rebellion in mid-nineteenth-century China (Cohn 1970; Wilson 1973; Lewy 1974). But if in one direction the apocalyptic connects with rebellion, revolution, and cultural change, on a different front, its strongest manifestations of religious possession cannot easily be distinguished from madness, a point that the psychologist William James (1902) made about religion in general. Perhaps for this reason, Emile Durkheim once suggested that anyone who wanders too far from the warm solidarity of socially legitimated reality risks entering an uncharted landscape of the mind (Durkheim 1961, pp. 48–9). This point is especially important for people who separate themselves from an established order. Peter Berger (1967, p. 39) spelled out the risk that they face: "To deny reality as it has been socially defined is to risk falling into irreality, because it is well-nigh impossible in the long run to keep up alone and without social support one's own counter-definitions of the world."

True, individuals occasionally act out an apocalyptic imperative on their own, taking up a one-person holy war. Thus, during the 1892 Homestead Steel strike in Pittsburgh, Pennsylvania, the anarchist Alexander Berkman embraced "propaganda of the deed," and he made an unsuccessful attempt to assassinate wealthy industrialist Henry Clay Frick. And in the late twentieth century, Ted Kaczynski, the Unabomber, used mail bombs to terrorize scientists, engineers, and entrepreneurs associated with the long march toward a technologically organized society. Yet these examples are telling. Both men acted as individuals, but Berkman was strongly connected to a social network of anarchists, and both he and Kaczynski took inspiration from wider countercultural movements. Deviance, seeking to avoid mere madness, looks for collective utopian legitimation.

Karl Mannheim designated as "utopian" ideals that cannot be realized within a given established order without sweeping aside existing social arrangements. He emphasized, however, that just because such ideals would require radical change does not mean that they are inherently fanciful or intrinsically unworkable (Mannheim 1936). Dismissal of countercultural movements as bizarre, manipulative, irrational, and "utopian" thus sometimes only confirms their countercultural status, and underscores the point that organized deviance can be perceived as posing a threat to an existing order.

An important implication can be drawn from Mannheim's analysis. To understand the apocalyptic, we need to look to the (potentially contested) utopian and ideological narratives that come to frame it. People make meanings about their social circumstances through narrated self-understandings, stories, we can call them if we take the word in a non-pejorative sense. These stories borrow, rework, and improvise meanings that invoke historical memories, available cultural motifs, interpretations of the present situation, and collective aspirations (Somers 1992; Hall 1995; Hall 1999, chap. 3). The apocalyptic narratives that people embrace, however, are not purely individual inventions. Instead, meanings are socially formed and distributed.

Not all utopian narratives are apocalyptic, and some apocalyptic narratives create less tension with the established order than others. Moreover, as Perry Miller reminds us, the meanings of such endeavors for both their participants and the wider world can shift over time. Thus, the "errand into the wilderness" by the Pilgrims who journeyed from England to North America was originally construed as an effort to establish a Christian "city on a hill" that would inspire Europe. But the immigrants discovered that Europe was indifferent to their project, and they set about recasting their "errand" in ways that made sense for themselves, not others (Miller 1956).

The Apocalypse thus is not just a fixed and stable metaphor of the final battle between good and evil. Nor is Armageddon sitting predefined and prepackaged in some universal cultural storeroom, available for people to "use" in an instrumentalist fashion as the occasion warrants. Instead, historical processes of apocalyptic emergence are dialectical: through the invocation of specific narrative motifs – such as the Second Coming of Christ, the transformative potential of revolutionary struggle, or the dawning Age of Aquarius – people simultaneously interpret and enact the Apocalypse in relation to an established social order. Even if the end is an illusion, as Jean Baudrillard (1994) claims, the illusion is a social one, narrated in the time of a historical present.

As with utopian narratives more generally, the Apocalyptic is open as to content. But because apocalyptic narratives all manifest one or another story of how the last days relate to the new morning, they centrally organize understandings of *time*. Thus, two alternative ideal types of apocalyptic sects can be identified on the basis of where their narratives place them in temporal relation to the apocalypse. The *pre*-apocalyptic "warring sect" in effect enacts the Apocalypse by pursuing a struggle in strategic time against "the forces of evil." On the other hand, the *post*-apocalyptic "other-worldly" sect establishes the putatively timeless tableau of a "heaven-on-earth" *beyond* the Apocalypse deemed underway in the secular world they presume to have left behind (Hall 1978).[2]

Most apocalyptic narratives never approach anything like the cataclysms so obscurely yet vividly detailed in the book of Revelation. Some movements that invoke apocalyptic imagery forge their collective story in cognitive tension with the existing order, while managing to implement their missions in culturally conventional ways: they may form a non-profit organization dedicated to stemming global ecological disaster, or carry out a revival crusade to save people who would otherwise be damned to the flames of an eternal hell. Even the more compelling visions of the end times or the new Jerusalem can either fail to gain a following or, attracting one, develop along quiescent lines, retreating to a heaven-on-earth where life unfolds "beyond" this world, but in ways that don't arouse the suspicions of neighbors or the investigatory interest of the state. And sometimes the worldly success of an organization pulls it into accommodation with the wider world.

The iconic case of the latter possibility is the sect that formed around Mother Ann Lee beginning in the late eighteenth century. Convinced that the Second Coming was at hand, the Shakers (so-called for their rollicking sex-divided dancing) foreswore procreation. Still, Mother Ann's followers established substantial communities in New England, Kentucky, and elsewhere, and they were extremely hard-working and innovative at agriculture and crafts production. Even though Mother Ann anticipated the end of the world, her followers kept making room for more followers in a way of life appropriate to waiting for the end times, improving their lot in this world by inventing labor-saving devices and looking for better ways to market their seeds, tinwork, and other goods in the nascent capitalist marketplace (Andrews 1971; Foster 1991).

Occasionally, however, the Apocalypse no longer simply serves as the mobilizing image employed by a conventional social movement, no longer beckons people to live out their days in the timeless tableau of an isolated heaven-on-earth. Instead, the book of Revelation is read as a script. The trials of seeking a better world in the turmoil of the end days take on the form of an unfolding drama. For better or worse, the Apocalyptic comes alive.

Apocalyptic movements, their relationships to wider society, and the sometimes violent and recently suicidal episodes that grow out of them remain only dimly understood, despite widespread public attention and considerable scholarly research. It is easy to use the most tragic episodes to show the psychotic and manipulative evil manifested in some generalized category of "cults" as a way of warning people, especially children, about the dangers of experimentation beyond the boundaries of conventional religion. But this approach is facile. It simultaneously closes off understanding of incidents like Jonestown and Heaven's Gate and condemns wider countercultural religious movements by association. Violent confrontations and mass suicides become mere magnifications of the internal dynamics of "cults" more generally. Treated as stories of megalomania and collective psychosis, accounts of apocalyptic violence operate as cautionary tales. But whatever their effectiveness as narratives of social control that affirm established ways of life, they tell us very little about the phenomena they purport to describe.

If we are to move beyond merely ideological responses to the apocalyptic, we need to avoid the premature conclusion of the conventional wisdom: that apocalyptic disasters are wholly explained by features *internal* to the movements or their leaders. We should not accept uncritically, for example, assertions that the conflagration in which seventy-four Branch Davidians died was the sole responsibility of David Koresh. Instead, it is important to explore why and how such movements come into cultural tension and sometimes direct confrontation with wider society.

A sociohistorical model of apocalpytic religious conflict

The contemporary Apocalypse bears a more than passing resemblance to other cultural boundary conflicts over the centuries: the tensions between the Roman Empire and early Christians, the Inquisition against people defined as heretics in medieval Europe, the Protestant Reformation in Europe during the sixteenth and seventeenth centuries, the Old Believers' movement against czarist reforms of the Orthodox church in seventeenth-century Russia, and the skirmishes between the Mormons and their opponents in the nineteenth-century United States, to name but a few. Insofar as these and other religious conflicts manifest cultural struggles between a powerful predominant social order and an emergent heterodoxical movement, they may be considered broadly apocalyptic. Given these parallels, instead of just answering the question, "Who joins cults?" either by offering a psychological profile of the alienated individual or by dismissing people's attractions to deviant movements as the product of "brainwashing," it is more fruitful to ask how the Apocalypse unfolds.

The generic apocalyptic time that marks the end of history and the beginning of eternity is a mercurial cultural catalyst. For both the state and established religions, "cultural legitimacy" has a *spatial* basis in relation to territory and a *temporal* basis in relation to the social construction of history, memory, and the future. Some apocalyptic movements proclaim a time of struggle or survival. They may even claim territory "outside" the state, or elsewhere in the universe. Others announce an end to the time of the old cultural and political order and the onset of a "timeless" heaven-on-earth. Occasionally, they even succeed in promoting a novel ethic of salvation among a wider audience. For the most part, however, even the most extreme deviant constructions are ignored outside the group that formulates them, or treated as exotic novelties. And most such groups remain relatively peaceful. But sometimes a religious social movement becomes caught up in violence, including in the most extreme cases, murders, terrorist acts, or mass suicide. One way of explaining such extreme religious violence is by a sociohistorical model based on a thesis of apocalyptic religious conflict.

As Georg Simmel observed long ago, conflict is by its nature social, and it is taken up on the basis of factors that both join and separate two parties. "Conflict," he goes on, "is thus designed to resolve divergent dualisms; it is a way of achieving some kind of unity, even if it be through the annihilation of one of the conflicting parties" (Simmel 1955, p. 13). Thus, as we specify the model of apocalyptic religious conflict, it explains extreme collective religious violence as a product of the *interaction* between a broadly apocalyptic religious movement and opponents in the outside world who are contesting whether the movement has the cultural legitimacy to pursue its collective vision.

For this model, it is obviously important to define violence, and to do so, we follow sociologist Mary Jackman (forthcoming). *Violence*, she argues, encompasses "actions that inflict, threaten, or cause injury." Violent *actions*, she continues, may be "corporal, written, or verbal," and the *injuries* may be "corporal, psychological, material, or social." This definition undermines the conventional tendency to assume that violence is always deviant, and it emphasizes that violence takes many forms (ear-piercing, industrial accidents that could be avoided, individual harassment and group repression, as well as assault, murder, and suicide). Recognizing this diversity is important for tackling the puzzle of why certain religious movements erupt in extreme violence – terrorism, murder, and collective suicide – for Jackman's definition does not assume either that highly visible violence is the only kind of violence or that visible violence occurs in isolation. On the contrary, it is possible that people unleash extreme violence as acts of escalation in relation to other, less visible forms of violence. Not all social groups and individuals have access to the same tools of violence. Thus, less powerful parties sometimes use extreme violence against more powerful (or better positioned) opponents who are themselves engaged in violent acts, just not always ones that involve corporal injury. Put differently, in some cases, dramatic public violence may be an extreme variant of what James Scott (1985) calls "weapons of the weak."

Our model of apocalyptic religious conflict holds that extreme violence is especially likely to occur in relation to countercultural religious movements that are broadly apocalyptic in orientation. Such groups tend to occupy structural locations "outside" an existing social order, and their ideologies and practices are likely to yield high degrees of social solidarity (Hall 1988). However, the apocalyptic solidarity of a group, though important, does not in itself explain extreme violence. Rather, such violence grows out of escalating social confrontations between, on the one hand, an apocalyptic religious movement and, on the other, ideological proponents of an established social order who seek to control "cults" through emergent, loosely institutionalized oppositional alliances.[3] These anticult alliances are typically crystallized:

- in the first instance by *cultural opponents* of deviant groups, especially apostates and distraught relatives of members.[4]

Whether the social conflict has violent consequences depends on the degree to which cultural opponents succeed in mobilizing public institutional allies, namely,

- *news reporters* who frame cult stories in terms of moral deviance, and
- modern *governments* that have subsumed the "religious" interest in enforcing cultural legitimacy into a state interest in monopolizing political legitimacy.

In relation to an apocalyptic group with a high degree of solidarity, extreme religious violence is thus the product of interaction between a complex of factors typically set in motion by apostasy and antisubversion campaigns against it.

Because apocalyptic movements are both voluntary and deviant, they are likely to produce defectors who will take up the role of oppositional apostates and work to mobilize broader cultural opposition (Bromley 1998). If the opponents succeed in convincing agents of established social institutions (in our era, the mass media, politicians, and the state) to frame the movement as a threat to the established order, these agents may take actions intended to discredit the movement in the public eye, or subject it to actions and policies that undermine its capacity to exist as an autonomous collectivity. The principals of the apocalyptic group, in turn, may perceive these external challenges as threats to their legitimacy and the power of their prophecy.

In terms of Jackman's definition (forthcoming), the movement's opponents credibly threaten or inflict social injury and the religious movement responds with corporal violence toward opponents, followed by collective suicide. These acts offer a way for the group's true believers to attempt to salvage their own sense of their honor, albeit at the cost of their own survival, by refusing to submit either to state authority or to external definitions of their identity. The potential for extreme violence under these conditions is especially strong, Thomas Robbins (1986) has argued, when the deviant group aspires to a legitimacy of a state within its domain and its continued existence is threatened by a more powerful and legitimate surrounding state.

12

This explanatory model seems to have considerable plausibility. Case studies of Peoples Temple, the Branch Davidians, Aum Shinrikyō, and the Solar Temple – in chapters 1 through 4 – will show that the extreme violence unleashed by these groups did not arise solely on the basis of dynamics internal to the groups themselves. In all of these cases, an external dynamic of apocalyptic religious conflict came into play. Clearly, the four religious movements are quite different from one another. Both Peoples Temple and the Branch Davidians included relatively poor people, but they had diametrically opposed religious politics: Peoples Temple was a leftist political religious movement, whereas the Branch Davidians awaited the fulfillment of prophecies drawn from the book of Revelation. On the other hand, both the Solar Temple and Aum Shinrikyō were notable for the many educated and affluent people who joined their ranks, although the cultural differences between these two groups are also substantial. In Japan, Aum Shinrikyō centered on Shōkō Asahara, the self-styled Buddhist guru who taught levitation to young professionals; in francophone Europe and Québec, the Solar Temple attracted mostly wealthy, establishment, or new-middle-class former Catholics who embraced reinvocations of medieval European traditions, concerns about imminent ecological apocalypse, and New-Age notions of immortality.

Not only were these four groups diverse in circumstances and character; their trajectories of religious violence were variable and highly contingent. As we will see, the Jonestown deaths may properly be considered murders followed by mass suicide, whereas the deaths of the Branch Davidians at Mount Carmel occurred under direct assault by governmental forces, and in a much less ritualistic way. The Aum violence never turned toward self-destruction; it was directed at opponents and eventually took the form of a grandiose terrorism that marshalled germ and chemical warfare against governments, military forces, and the general public. The case of the Solar Temple is different again. Its core of believers murdered detractors and then took their own lives, but their rationale was only partly apocalyptic.

In other words, though apocalyptic violence surfaced in each of these episodes, it is not obvious that parallel sociohistorical dynamics were at work. These circumstances can be turned to the cause of analytic explanation. Even though the outcomes are sometimes superficially regarded as "the same," precisely the opposite is the case. The variety of the cases makes it possible to consider how specific conditions affect the play and outcome of extreme violence. According to the logic of comparison formulated by John Stuart Mill (1950), if commonalities are found among these otherwise diverse cases, these commonalities are likely to be implicated in any explanation of analogous aspects of their outcomes.[5] Thus, looking at Jonestown, Waco, the Solar Temple, and Aum Shinrikyō offers a basis on which to evaluate the validity and range of applicability of the general model that explains apocalyptic religious violence as the product of escalating conflict between a sect and its detractors.

In turn, certain anomalies point toward an alternative pathway of religious violence. Whatever power the thesis of apocalyptic conflict has, it does not seem particularly well suited to explaining various aspects of the Solar Temple affair, and it seems even less relevant to the collective suicide of Heaven's Gate, despite the "apocalyptic" way that both these events breach wider cultural strictures about the sanctity of life. As chapter 4 shows, the external opposition to the Solar Temple did not pose any imminent threat. Furthermore, on two occasions many months after the initial Solar Temple "Transit" of mass suicide, surviving believers followed suit, taking their own lives after their leaders were already dead. The obvious question is why. The case of Heaven's Gate, considered in chapter 5, seems even more remote from any explanation based on apocalyptic religious conflict, despite its being a clear case of collective suicide. In their efforts to reach a spaceship lurking behind the Hale-Bopp comet, Marshall Applewhite and his followers did not direct any violence outward, and their deaths lacked any obvious connection to external conflict. People seem to have taken their own lives because they shared a belief in something that most people would find absurd. Examining these episodes, where external conflict seems absent, clarifies a second broad apocalyptic script: the mystical apocalypse of deathly transcendence.

There has been much shock, outrage, and handwringing about so-called cults, but these reactions do little to help us understand religious violence. In the present book, we do not directly address the moral issue of whether the actions of religious social movements, their opponents, the mass media, or the state are justified. We are opposed to the violence associated with apocalyptic religious movements, but we concentrate on explaining it, not passing judgment. However, we do hold that all parties whose lives become connected to religious movements need to consider their own actions in light of the social processes in which they participate.

Social critic Walter Benjamin once suggested the importance of recognizing how the historical present is "shot through with Messianic time" (Benjamin 1940, p. 263). In this light, though potent episodes of apocalyptic violence seemingly transpire outside the linear flow of History, they cannot be separated from the established social orders in which they arise. Such episodes bring broader religious, cultural, and social shifts to the surface at the dawn of a New Age. Apocalyptic violence marks the faultlines of an Apocalypse wider in scope. Observing the one will help disclose the other.

1

THE APOCALYPSE AT
JONESTOWN

Two years to the day after the 19 April 1993 conflagration at the Branch Davidians' Mount Carmel compound near Waco, Texas, a bomb destroyed the federal building in Oklahoma City, Oklahoma, killing at least 167 people and injuring hundreds more. Two years after that, in April 1997, jury selection finally began in the trial of Timothy McVeigh, the man eventually convicted of the bombing. Anticipating the upcoming trial, *The New Yorker* magazine's "Talk of the Town" section led with a piece where Scott Malcomson (1997) recounted his visit to "Elohim City," a dirt-poor white-separatist Christian fundamentalist community in the Ozarks. Over supper after church on Sunday, the sect's founder, Robert G. Millar, mentioned to Malcomson that he had met a Pastor Jones in the 1950s, "a good pastor," he called him. Did the *New Yorker* writer remember Jones? "Oh yes, the man in Guyana," Malcomson replied, ending his piece, "Yes, I remembered him."

Thus readers encountered yet another allusion to the first mass suicide in modern times. Jonestown was the communal settlement founded by Peoples Temple in the small, poor, socialist country of Guyana, on the Caribbean coast of South America. On 17 November 1978, a congressman from California, Leo Ryan, arrived there on an investigative expedition, accompanied by journalists and some sect opponents who called themselves the "Concerned Relatives." The next day, Ryan and four other people – three newsmen and a young defector – were murdered at an airstrip several miles from Jonestown as they prepared to depart with more than a dozen defectors that the visitors had brought out of the jungle utopian community. While this carnage unfolded, back at Jonestown, the Temple's white charismatic leader, Jim Jones, orchestrated a "revolutionary suicide" where the members of the agricultural community – mostly black, some white – drank a deadly potion of Fla-Vor Aid laced with poison. Counting the murders at the airstrip, 918 people died.[1]

Well before Timothy McVeigh's trial, "Jonestown" had become so infamous as the ultimate "cult" nightmare that Malcomson could invoke the mere name of its leader as a chilling conclusion to his story about an isolated, radically anti-establishment religious community of true believers. In his short, sophisticated *New Yorker* report, Malcomson symbolically aligned Waco, the Oklahoma City

15

bombing, and Jonestown with the racist survivalist sect he had visited, all without saying much of substance about any of these episodes. He offered no reflection on even the most immediately intriguing question raised by Elohim leader Robert Millar's mention of Jim Jones: why was a right-wing racist fundamentalist praising the founder of Peoples Temple, a left-wing religious movement dedicated to racial integration?

The power of Malcomson's piece hinges on the mention of Jim Jones, but the rhetorical form of this mentioning depends on glossing any understanding of what happened at Jonestown. Instead, it plays to a generalized collective memory that has enshrined Jones in popular culture as the image incarnate of the Antichrist, and Peoples Temple as the paragon of the religious "cult." Fed by a flood of news articles, a film, a television docudrama, more than twenty books, and countless oblique allusions, this collective memory now floats free from what, in a simpler era, historians liked to think of as facts. But when we search for the sources of this memory, they trace back to the "Concerned Relatives," the organization that had opposed Peoples Temple in the first place, and to the representatives of the media whom the Temple opponents drew into the ill-fated journey to Jonestown. After the murders and mass suicide, the Concerned Relatives became the outsiders with the most knowledge about a group that had carried out an appalling act of mass suicide. Indeed, because the Concerned Relatives had consistently sought to raise the alarm against Peoples Temple before 18 November 1978, they could take the mass suicide as a sad validation of their concerns. But by the same token, popular accounts of Jonestown depended heavily on the accounts of the Concerned Relatives, and these accounts tended to suppress a crucial question. Did the actions of the Concerned Relatives and the media in any way contribute to the grisly outcome of events in which they were not only observers, but also participants?

Given the tragic deaths, the cultural opponents had a vital interest in denying that their actions had any consequences. This interest may help account for their consistent promotion of a doctrine of *cult essentialism*, whereby the dynamics of religious movements are treated as wholly internal, and unaffected by interaction with the wider social world. Such an analysis would free the cultural opponents and the media from any responsibility for incidents of religious-movement violence. But precisely because the proponents of cult essentialism themselves participated in the events, it is important to give their actions consideration along with other factors that may have contributed to the outcome of murder and mass suicide.

In the absence of this analysis, Jonestown becomes, as Roland Barthes wrote of myths more generally, "a story at once true and unreal" (Barthes 1972, p. 128). In this case, the story is one of a sick and fiendish man who plotted the deaths of those who would expose his sham community, capping the murder of opponents with the ritualized ceremonial murder of followers, many of them perhaps well-intentioned, but too naive or powerless to break the hold of Jim Jones, a man sufficiently obsessed with his orchestration of events to die of an apparently self-inflicted gunshot to the head.

Treatment of Peoples Temple as the *cultus classicus* headed by Jim Jones, psychotic megalomaniac *par excellence* drifts on a sea of memory, only loosely tied to any moorings of history. Still, like other myths that maintain their power, the one signified by "Jonestown" must be culturally powerful, and perhaps even necessary, for it remains evocative even today. In Barthes's terms, the power of Jonestown is the power of the unreal to offer a meaningful narrative of an event that is otherwise difficult to reconcile with the world as we understand it. The myth of Jonestown has a long half life because it serves vital needs *not* to understand the murders and mass suicide historically. In effect, the myth of Jonestown displaces history by suppressing alternative narratives that might debunk ideology. Only when this ideological lens is broken can we search for historical explanations.

Devil, psychopath, con artist, Antichrist, Jim Jones was also a discomforting critic of American society, embraced by followers as a prophet, redeemer, and friend. His strongest countercultural images borrowed old Protestant ideas about the Church of Rome as the whore of Babylon, ideas that themselves come from deeper apocalyptic wellsprings of Western thought. But Jones transmuted these ideas into a new religious dispensation: of the United States as Babylon, the Apocalypse as race and class warfare that would engulf a society trapped in its own hypocrisy. An unrelenting iconoclast, Jones sought to forge a militant movement of people committed to the vision of a utopian alternative to a racist, class-dominated, imperialist society. Peoples Temple thus carried a double onus: it was a countercultural communal group and a militant anti-American social movement.

Communalism *per se* has long been viewed as a way of life alien to mainstream America. Legitimate organizations such as religious orders and the military may rightly require submission to collective authority, but in public discourse, the collectivism of countercultural organizations flies in the face of the dominant American ideology that embraces capitalism, individualism, and the nuclear family, and it is thus vulnerable to becoming coded as antidemocratic and subversive (cf. Alexander and Smith 1993).

Like other religious social movements, Peoples Temple practiced a communal socialism. Yet unlike most countercultural hippie communes and utopian communal groups of the 1960s and early 1970s, Peoples Temple located its communalism in a leftist political vein of crude communism. Jones simultaneously evoked apocalyptic imagery that appealed to members of his audience steeped in the codes of religious rhetoric, and used the political language of class and race to amplify latent resentment among those drawn to his cause. By this dual strategy, he forged a religious radicalism that attracted true believers to a movement framed in militant opposition to American capitalist society. Because Jones so sharply opposed the predominant ideology, that ideology requires that his movement and its demise be misunderstood.

The Jonestown myth can be deconstructed if we ask a straightforward question: "why did the murders and mass suicide occur?" To answer this question without recourse to the lens of ideology brings into view a complex relationship between Peoples Temple and the established social order. As we will see, the carnage in Guyana was not simply the product of the politically-infused apocalyptic mentality that took hold within Peoples Temple. Nor can it be explained as wholly the result of Jim Jones's demented manipulations. Jones was more complex than the caricature of him, and Peoples Temple was both utopia and anti-utopia. "Jonestown" was the disastrous outcome of a protracted conflict between Peoples Temple and a loosely institutionalized but increasingly effective coalition of opponents. But the myth of Jonestown has had consequences of its own. It did not simply arise *after* apocalyptic history. It has contributed *to* apocalyptic history.

Jim Jones and the origins of Peoples Temple

Peoples Temple began, like many American religious groups, in the mind of a self-styled prophet. James Warren Jones was born in east central Indiana in the time of the Great Depression on 13 May 1931. The only child of poor white working parents (his mother was later rumored to have Indian ancestors), Jones grew up with a strong sense of resentment toward people of wealth, status, and privilege. Exposed as a child to a variety of Protestant churches – from the mainstream Methodists to the pacifist Quakers and the holiness-movement Nazarenes – Jones found himself especially impressed by the religious enthusiasm, revival-style worship, and speaking in tongues that he encountered in the fellowship of the then-marginal Pentecostalists, where he later described finding a "setting of freedom of emotion."

During his high school years Jim Jones preached on the streets in a factory neighborhood of Richmond, Indiana, to an audience of both whites and blacks. In the summer of 1949, he married Marceline Baldwin, a young nurse from a Richmond family of Methodists and Republicans. Marcie was shocked, Jim later recounted, when he revealed the views that he seems to have taken from his mother, namely his sympathies with political communism and his disdain for the "sky god."

In 1951 Jim and Marcie Jones moved to Indianapolis. Although Jim Jones was barely twenty years old at the time, he quickly became a preacher and created a volatile mix of theology and practice. Exposed variously to the Methodists' liberal social creed, communist ideology, and the broadly apocalyptic vision of the Pentecostalists, Jones would promote racial integration and a veiled communist philosophy within a Pentecostal framework that emphasized gifts of the spirit, especially faith healing and the "discerning" of spirits. He displayed a knack for preaching, and he learned some tricks already in use in the mid-South Pentecostal revival circuit: how to convince audiences of his abilities in matters of "discernment" and faith healing by sleights of hand,

18

spying, and fakery. Jones was hardly the first faith healer on the circuit to cause elderly ladies confined to wheel-chairs to rise up and walk again, though he may have been the first to come up with the idea of having a perfectly sound leg bone placed in a plaster cast so that it could be removed after a faith healing. Yet for all the deceit, some followers swore that the young minister had the gift of healing, and independent observers later acknowledged that hokum aside, Jones could produce results with a person whose condition "had no major physiological basis."

On the grounds of his religious chicanery alone, Jones would have been hard to distinguish from other self-styled Pentecostalist faith healers of his day. But the audiences attracted by Jones's gifts of the spirit encountered something far different from other tent-camp evangelists and small-time preachers who operated in the mid-South.

Organizationally, Jones started in Indianapolis with a small church called Community Unity. His first important break came when visitors from the Pentecostalist Laurel Street Tabernacle in Indianapolis took in his services following a successful revival appearance that he had made in Detroit, Michigan. In September 1954 some of the visitors invited Jones to preach at Laurel Street. Jones created a stir by bringing blacks to the service of the racially segregated church, but after his preaching and healing performance a substantial segment of the Tabernacle voted with their feet, leaving their congregation in order to walk with Jones. Together, on 4 April 1955, they established Wings of Deliverance, the corporate vehicle of what was later named Peoples Temple.

In his ministry, Jones extended the always-strong Pentecostalist ethic of a caring community toward racial integration, and he initiated urban ministry programs more typically associated with the social gospel of progressive middle-class Protestant denominations like the Methodists. Peoples Temple became a racially integrated self-help community of believers in practical service under the umbrella of a church. Out of this unlikely amalgamation of disparate ideas and practices, Jones gradually built the church into a communalistic social movement. Beginning as a somewhat unconventional preacher, he increasingly took on the mantle of a prophet who warned of an impending capitalist apocalypse and worked to establish a socialist promised land for those who heeded his message.

The movement grew up around the Jones family itself. Already by 1952 Jim and Marcie had adopted a ten-year-old girl. Then in 1955, they capitalized on Marcie's nursing experience, bringing an older follower to live in their own home, thereby establishing a nursing home under a formula whereby their ever-widening family could be supported in part by cash payments from outside. In the late 1950s the couple adopted children who had been orphaned by the Korean War, initiating what they would call their multi-ethnic "rainbow family." Two years after the birth of their natural son Stephan Gandhi Jones in 1959, the Joneses became the first white couple in Indianapolis, and perhaps in the state of Indiana, to adopt a black child. At the time, when the civil rights

movement was just gaining steam in the US, Jones remarked, "Integration is a more personal thing with me now. It's a question of my son's future."

For all the dynamism of Jones's early family-centered ministry, however, he was hardly original in developing strategies, practices, and organizational forms. Instead, Jones was something of a living syncretist sponge who could absorb ideas, people, and their energies from the most diverse sources into the development of his organization.

Most importantly, Jones connected to the legacy of blacks' search for redemption in the United States. Several times in the late 1950s, he visited the Philadelphia Peace Mission of the American black preacher Father M. J. Divine, who, in the 1920s and 1930s, had established himself at the center of a racially integrated religious and economic community. Father Divine himself stood in a long tradition of "black messiahs" who promoted migration from the Old South Black Belt after the American Civil War. The cultural sources are even deeper, going back to the time of slavery, and from it, to cultural memories drawn from the Bible. "The rhetoric of this migration" from the South, as James Diggs has noted, "was often reminiscent of antebellum Black nationalism, with its talk of escape from the land of bondage and quest for a promised land" (quoted in Moses 1982, p. 135). Like the biblical Jews under Moses, nineteenth-century black ministers had sometimes portrayed the collective suffering of their people and their quest for redemption as part of a higher religious purpose to history. Collective migration could serve as a vehicle to this purpose, for example, in the departure of "exodusters" from the South to settle in Oklahoma and Kansas during the latter part of the nineteenth century. In the early twentieth century, Marcus Garvey took up the theme anew with his back-to-Africa movement (which never repatriated a single US black to Africa while Garvey operated in the US). And then there was Father Divine. During the 1930s, he dabbled with the Communist Party but, more centrally, he relocated the destination of back-to-Africa dreams by setting up his peace missions in major Eastern US cities and establishing "The Promised Land" – rural, interracial cooperative communities – in upstate New York (Weisbrot 1983).

Jim Jones borrowed much from the Peace Mission model (and stole some of its members). Like Father Divine, he took to a patriarchal style of organization, with himself at the center, surrounded by a staff that included a heavy concentration of attractive, white women. Like Divine, Jones took to being called "Father," or sometimes, "Dad." Over the years, he would vacillate between operating an urban human-service ministry akin to Divine's peace missions and establishing an exurban settlement in California not unlike the black messiah's upstate New York communities. But Jones's mission eventually took a more radical direction: emigration to escape the degradation of racism and class inequality in the United States. Again borrowing from Divine, the community that Peoples Temple founded in Guyana – Jonestown – would sometimes be called the Promised Land.

In the 1950s and 1960s, Jones shaped Peoples Temple in Indianapolis as an

extended family that offered the shelter of communal fellowship from an uncertain world beyond. Like Divine, Jones worked to develop Peoples Temple as an agent of social action, establishing care homes for the elderly, running a free restaurant to feed the hungary, and maintaining a social service center to help people get their lives back together. In time, the unconventional congregation attracted the notice of the Christian Church (Disciples of Christ), which had long been committed to a social ministry. By 1960, Peoples Temple had affiliated with the Disciples, and in 1964 Jones was officially ordained a minister.

Peoples Temple thrived in Indianapolis, but it also gained a certain notoriety. Jones was more political than Father Divine, and he seemed to go out of his way to precipitate public controversies, seizing on opportunities to dramatize how racial segregation in Indianapolis extended even to its hospitals and its cemeteries. Indianapolis was not a progressive place and bitter resistance to integration surfaced in some quarters. By publicly challenging segregationist policies from the 1950s onwards, Jones enhanced his own status as a civil-rights leader. Seeing the benefit of having reactionary opponents, he also sometimes staged incidents which made him, his family, and his church look like the targets of racist hate crimes. Nonetheless, some of the harassment was real, and Jones does not seem to have held up well under the pressure. In the face of the public tensions, his doctor hospitalized him for an ulcer during the fall of 1961. After his release, Jones began to seek a way out of Indianapolis. Leaving his congregation in the care of associate pastors, he and his family visited British Guiana (Guyana before independence from colonial rule), and then lived for two years in Brazil.

California heyday

Even as Jones returned to Indianapolis in 1964, he already was laying the groundwork for a collective migration by his most committed followers. Tired of racial intolerance in Indiana and citing fears of nuclear holocaust, in the summer of 1965 they moved to the hamlet of Redwood Valley, near the quiet northern California town of Ukiah, in the Russian River valley. About seventy families, half white, half black, made the journey.

The congregation established itself slowly, comprising only 168 adult members by 1968. In 1969 the Temple completed its own church building, enclosing a swimming pool they had previously built on the Joneses' land just south of Redwood Valley. But Jim Jones failed to make much headway in drawing converts from the various apostolic fundamentalist congregations in the Ukiah area, and he became increasingly matter-of-fact in discussing secular socialism with his own congregation. He also pointedly criticized black ministers still promoting spiritualistic theologies of heavenly compensation for suffering during life, proposing to replace it with an alternative model: the activist church as social movement. On this platform Peoples Temple gradually attracted a wide range of people: working and middle-class blacks, hippies, socially concerned progressive professionals, fundamentalist Christians, former tenant farmers from

the South, political activists and militants, street people, delinquents, and the elderly. These diverse sources fed an organization that began to grow rapidly. In the early 1970s, the Temple established a "human services" ministry of "care" homes for juveniles and the elderly, set up churches in San Francisco and Los Angeles, and began operating a fleet of buses to carry followers to church functions attended by thousands of people.

The corporation of people

The care homes, like many other Temple enterprises, worked to the benefit of the organization in multiple ways. Like private-sector operators, the Temple was able to use care-payment income to leverage real estate investments that expanded the care-home operations and increased the property holdings of the organization. It could also use the care homes to employ Temple members. In turn, because people were willing to work so hard for "the Cause," the homes produced substantial profits. The Temple treated these profits as organizational income rather than the income of individual operators, but it neglected to pay taxes, even though the money would have been considered "unrelated business income" falling outside the "nonprofit religious organization" tax-exempt category of the Internal Revenue Service. Beyond the strictly financial benefits, the care-home operations became the nucleus for promoting a collective life and communal orientation more widely among followers. The people served by the care homes were more than clients; they participated as active members of the movement itself.

By its heyday in the mid-1970s, the Temple had established multiple streams of income, from petty church fundraisers and offerings at services, to a radio ministry, the care homes, and the salaries, social security checks, and real estate donated by members who "went communal." The money added up. After the mass suicide in 1978, a court-appointed receiver was able to consolidate $10 million of Temple assets, even though he couldn't recover all the defunct organization's holdings. Before the disastrous end, Jones had once said, "I have made the poor rich." But this isn't quite right. If the value of the receiver's Temple assets were allocated among the 913 members who died in Guyana, it would have come to around $12,000 per person, less if allocated among the total number of Temple members. The Temple thrived on the basis of expanding real-estate investments, a care-home business largely supported by state welfare payments, economies of scale of communal consumption, the labor of committed members supported by the group, and a whole host of evangelical fundraising techniques. But no one got rich. Effectively, Jones forged a collective organization that was wealthier than the sum of its individual parts.

Peoples Temple was devoted to some distinctly anti-establishment ends, but the success of the operation largely depended on disarmingly conventional means, from the petty fundraisers to corporate entrepreneurship, rationalized methods of administration that served a large membership, and active coordination

Figure 1.1 Jim Jones at a Peoples Temple service during the early 1970s in a publicity
photograph that emphasizes the preacher's charismatic attraction to his followers.

Source: Peoples Temple

with external organizations such as welfare agencies and the Social Security
Administration. On the whole, the Temple avoided the sorts of shady practices
that sometimes have plagued both evangelical religious organizations and the
care-home industry. Just as clearly, the group sometimes operated outside the
law, certainly in failing to report care-home income, and perhaps in its transfers
of assets to off-shore bank accounts. Yet at least the quest for profits through tax
avoidance and off-shore banking share an understandable rationale with more
legitimate organizations that engage in similar practices.

The collectivist reformation

Where Peoples Temple deviated much more dramatically from conventional
social practice was in its members' high rates of tithing, unsalaried labor, and
donation of real and personal assets. In turn, these differences were part of a
more profound difference: replacing individualism and the family unit with the
communal equation of an organization that pooled the economic resources of its
most highly committed members, and in return, offered them economic security,
an extended collectivist "family," and the opportunity to participate in a politically meaningful social cause larger than themselves. Balancing that equation,
the Temple demanded commitment, discipline, and individual submission to
collective authority.

Social control and the social monitoring required to prevent "freeriders" who
fail to do their share are issues faced by all organizations of any significant size,

from corporations, stores, schools, and monasteries, to mental hospitals, prisons, and armies (Hechter 1987). But in most organizations, procedures of monitoring and control tend to be legitimated by legal authority, contract, or long-established convention. By contrast, countercultural communal organizations face more formidable issues of control, because they are quasi-familial yet voluntary groups with much weaker capacities to claim authority over their members.

Historically, the most successful communal groups have promoted solidarity and commitment through practices such as wearing uniforms, sharing a communal table, regulating sexual relationships, and monitoring members' behavior through techniques such as confession (Kanter 1972). Among the wide variety of communal groups, ones with apocalyptic orientations have a particularly strong basis to legitimate their demands for members' commitment, for they frame their existence in relation to a society at large construed as the embodiment of evil (Hall 1988). In such sects, the "end of the world" is taken as a central tenet. But the content of collective demands on members depends on how the apocalyptic group construes its position in relation to the end times. As we saw in the introduction, a key issue concerns whether the group locates itself *before* or *after* the end of the current epoch. Before the dawn of the new era, a pre-apocalyptic "warring sect" will exhibit a high degree of solidarity in pursuing the battle of Armageddon, that last and decisive struggle between the forces of good and evil. On the other hand, a post-apocalyptic "other-worldly sect" detaches itself from the evil society held to be in its last days, retreating to an isolated heaven-on-earth where the time of this world is treated as part of the past (Hall 1978).

In these terms, Jim Jones sometimes invoked other-worldly images of Peoples Temple as an ark of survival, but during its California years the Temple had higher stakes of commitment than the typical other-worldly sect. This was, first, because it operated in urban and small-town settings where control was not enhanced by physical isolation, and second, because religious rhetoric masked a supposedly secret political antagonism toward the established order signaled by the Temple's posture of alignment with political communism. Thus, an odd juxtaposition emerged: Peoples Temple developed its regime of social control within the framework of an organization that had the external appearance of a conventional church. Internally, however, control increasingly operated in ways more often found in militant political movements and clandestine warring sects.

Authority ultimately derived from the careful legitimation of Jim Jones's proclaimed charismatic mission as a socialist prophet. In practical terms, he enhanced his position by staging demonstrations of his paranormal powers and cultivating a network of personal relationships that was sometimes tinged with sexual domination of both women and men. Jim Jones was bisexual, and sex became something like a currency that he used, supposedly, "for the cause." With it, Jones gave some people intimacy and controlled or humiliated others. The first offspring of his sexual unions was Stephan, the child born in Indiana in 1959 to his legal wife Marcie. In California, Jones fathered Carolyn Layton's son

Kimo Prokes, and he was widely believed to be the father of John Victor Stoen, born in 1972 to Grace Stoen, wife of Temple attorney Tim Stoen.

Beyond social control based on personal relationships and charismatic projection, the Temple adopted practices derived from wider cultural sources: first, pseudo-Pentecostalist practices of "discernment" that Jones transformed into a vehicle of intelligence gathering used by Temple staff to monitor members; second, a military-drill security unit like those found more widely in black American culture of the day; third, techniques derived from the 1970s social-work and counselling-psychology culture of California, and, fourth, a fundamentalist Christian ethic of punishment for wrongdoing. These practices helped sustain collective authority that was legitimated in an even more fundamental way by the widespread distribution of relatively equal benefits of group life. In turn, by giving the broad base of participants a stake in the organization, Peoples Temple created a broad interest in maintaining social control (cf. Hall 1988). The leadership was able to consolidate a pervasive apparatus of monitoring in which rank-and-file participants provided information on their own and others' personal problems, sexual conduct, social relationships, degree of commitment to the Temple, and deviant or criminal activities. In turn, Temple staff used this information for collective intervention in individuals' lives and their social relationships. They conducted individual and group counselling sessions, and they held public meetings for "catharsis," where Jim Jones sometimes publicly humiliated backsliders and asked the assembled populace to determine punishments that included paddlings and boxing matches for wrongdoers. The assembled collective itself participated in the practices that sustained organizational authority.

Many of the Temple techniques of monitoring, counselling, and social control were borrowed from the wider society. But there was a critical difference: however pervasive the webs of social control in society at large, they do not become consolidated in a single apparatus. Peoples Temple, on the other hand, amalgamated control in the hierarchy of a total institution that enveloped its participants in a single web of surveillance, even though many Temple members freely participated in the wider world through school and jobs. As in any social order, the burden of this regime fell more heavily on the less committed than on loyal members who followed the rules. From inside the Temple, monitoring, catharsis sessions, and physical punishment seemed necessary to maintain standards of acceptable conduct and prevent internal dissension from taking hold. But from outside, all this came to be viewed as manipulation, physical abuse, and brainwashing.

Politics and public relations

Social control in the Temple gained a special edge through its connection to the group's disciplined struggle against injustice in the wider society. Compared with both conventional churches and retreatist communal groups of its day, Peoples Temple was an anomaly, a highly organized radical religious collective that pursued activist politics within the society at large. Perversely, the Temple used textbook public-relations (or PR) techniques to protect an apocalyptic socialist movement opposed to the capitalist society where practices of public relations had originated.

In the political climate of California during the 1970s, shaped by the counterculture and the anti-Vietnam war movement, the Temple used PR strategies within a broad political coalition committed to racial integration, social and economic justice, peace, and other progressive and radical causes. Because of its discipline, the Temple could turn out the troops. Members demonstrated against the *Bakke* decision by the California Supreme Court when it outlawed a University of California affirmative-action procedure. They joined a coalition denouncing apartheid in South Africa. Temple staff met with the Jewish Community Relations Council about combating the increase in Nazi propaganda in the Bay area. And the Temple supported gay rights, depicting the anti-gay stances of advertising celebrity Anita Bryant as "giving birth to a new wave of fascism . . . spreading its poison in attacking anything that's not straight, white and conservative."

More concretely, the Temple provided a ready supply of political workers to the Democratic Party. By 1975 Peoples Temple was sufficiently adept at conventional party politics to become a formidable force in the left-liberal political surge that propelled democrat George Moscone into office as mayor of San Francisco. A year later the Temple reaped the political rewards. Temple attorney Tim Stoen was called from his position as assistant district attorney in Mendocino Country to prosecute voter fraud for the San Francisco district attorney, and Mayor Moscone appointed Jim Jones to the San Francisco Housing Authority Commission. At the end of the year, the San Francisco *Chronicle* quoted Jones as favoring "some kind of democratic socialism."

The attractions of the Temple

By any standard, Peoples Temple was a deviant organization in American society. Its spartan regimen of social control depended on practices of humiliation and emotional and physical abuse abhorrent to norms of mainstream American culture. Yet the dubious practices of Peoples Temple do not seem sufficient to explain the solidarity of its members and cannot in themselves explain how the organization was able to thrive and grow. What was it about Peoples Temple that attracted tens of thousands to its services and led to the active participation of over one thousand people?

In part, the group's success was the consequence of the ways it exploited conventional pathways of action in the wider society. The Temple operated as a church, and drew on the legitimacy of churches. Its staff became accomplished at organizational coordination, public relations and political stratagems that largely mimicked conventional practices. And as in other organizations, public and private, they channelled resources from the state welfare system into the material benefits that the Temple offered.

26

Yet these conventional features and benefits came in an alien utopian package that presumably would have put people off, had they not been willing to embrace a radical alternative to their previous life circumstances. Peoples Temple differed dramatically from conventional organizations in the wider society, including the vast majority of its religious organizations. It was first and foremost a highly unusual testament to an alternative mode of ethnic relations, a racially integrated community of people who lived daily life together. In a striking way, the Temple also reconfigured the various available missions of the local church as a social institution (cf. Becker 1999) by radicalizing the social gospel through a congregational communal formula of "apostolic socialism" and direct social ministry, combined with a leftist political agenda in the wider society. This model attracted people from many stations in society, even secular political leftists who might have been expected to take the view of Karl Marx and Frederick Engels in the *Communist Manifesto* that "social Utopias" amount to "castles in the air."

However, if Peoples Temple was atypical as a religious congregation, it was hardly the typical social utopia either. Most communitarian groups that developed "worldly utopian" alternative models of society – New Harmony in Indiana during the nineteenth century, the Farm in Tennessee during the American countercultural wave of the 1960s and 1970s – did so at some remove from the society-at-large (Hall 1978). On the other hand, during its California heyday, Peoples Temple became an unusual hybrid: an urban-based, relatively autonomous communalistic organization that was nevertheless complexly connected to the wider society, and to the state, corporate, political, and media institutions of that society. By contrast with worldly utopian communal groups, Peoples Temple developed what may be called a "collectivist bureaucracy." Through their joint efforts, Temple staff organized the lives of everyday members in a way fully articulated with the complex governmental and capitalist order around them. Yet by this collective enterprise, the Temple increased the autonomy of its individual members from that external order, giving them time and direction to channel their energies in politically activist ways.

No one should gainsay the reprehensible features of Peoples Temple public relations, politics, and social control. Yet rejection of the reprehensible should be accompanied by recognition that the Temple's practices – both those widely regarded as legitimate and other more questionable ones – are hardly foreign to the wider world. Nor should we deny the organization's appeal during its California years. Peoples Temple was distinctive in its capacity to chart a pathway of expansion within the wider society under the auspices of a utopian vision and innovative form of social organization that harnessed the energies of many people of good will. From multiple walks of life, its members came together in a community that transcended the operative institutions, cultural boundaries, and social divisions of the existing social order.

Gone to the promised land

The organizational and political successes of Peoples Temple by the mid-1970s give cause to wonder why Jim Jones did not move directly into the realm of politics, as other activist leaders of religious social movements have done. But the question is moot because the Temple became embroiled in controversy and migrated en masse to Guyana. Indeed, these developments reveal the precarious nature of Peoples Temple's political successes, for those successes depended on the public-relations facade that hid the Temple's more radical and dubious aspects from the wider society.

Within the shell of a church, Jones called his followers to what Max Weber called an "ethic of ultimate ends." He sought to recruit highly committed individuals, and he insisted that followers pursue the cause of Peoples Temple selflessly, tirelessly, and without compromise. It is a measure of the total commitment Jones demanded that he invoked a doctrine originally developed by Black Panther Party member Huey Newton, namely, that the slow suicide of life in the ghetto ought to be displaced by "revolutionary suicide." The life of the committed revolutionary would end only in victory against economic, social, and racial injustice, or in death. In keeping with this thesis, the Temple expected Jones's followers to give up their previous lives and became born again to a collective struggle that had no limits. This radical ethos both deepened the gulf between Peoples Temple and the wider society, and served as the ideological point of departure for the uncompromising posture that the Temple developed during its protracted conflict with increasingly organized apostates and their allies, who became equally committed to their own cause of opposition.

Forging a regime of militant activism, Jones attracted the very "persecution" that he both feared and prophesied. Eventually, the Temple leadership uncovered information which, they thought, confirmed Jones's dire prophecies that the group would not be able to survive in the United States. Jones and over a thousand followers thereupon undertook a collective emigration to Guyana, leaving the path of militant political struggle within the United States behind.

While Peoples Temple remained in the United States, it operated *in* the world. Yet Jones never expected acceptance *from* the world. In Indianapolis, he promised followers that the Temple would protect them from a hostile society, yet he also projected the belief that his racially integrated congregation would have to leave their present surroundings. Like Moses and the ancient Jews searching for a land of "milk and honey" or the Puritans who fled to North America from religious persecution in England to found a "city on a hill," Jones sought redemption for his followers in collective religious migration to a promised land by leading his congregation to California. But there, Jones's promised land soon took a new form: the creation of a sanctuary outside the United States itself. Beginning in 1972 and 1973, Jones used internal defections and small incidents of external "persecution" in California as the warrant to establish Peoples Temple's "promised land" – an "agricultural mission" eventually called Jonestown – in a remote corner of Guyana, an ethnically diverse country with a socialist government on the northern, Caribbean, coast of South American.

At its inception, Jonestown was just a pioneer camp. But even before the site was established in early 1974, a memo by Temple attorney Tim Stoen suggested that the Temple should methodically prepare for collective migration from the US by consolidating its finances and other affairs. The plan was to remain in California "until first signs of outright persecution from press or government," then "start moving all members to mission post." In practice, the Temple followed the basic thrust of this plan. The initial party of settlers devoted most of their efforts toward construction of enough housing and other facilities to accommodate a large influx of newcomers, while Temple operatives in Guyana's capital of Georgetown used their public relations and political skills (and sexual allure) to establish secure political alliances with members of the patrimonial socialist regime of the country's black prime minister, Forbes Burnham.

Jonestown remained a small outpost until Peoples Temple undertook the collective migration of some 1,000 people during the summer of 1977. Unlike the mid-1960s migration to California to escape Hoosier racism, Jones did not justify this migration solely on the basis of his personal perceptions about a hostile environment. The migration unfolded as a move in an escalating conflict between Peoples Temple and an emerging coalition of external opponents.

Over the years, members had occasionally left Peoples Temple, but they had never actively turned against the organization. A handful of outside critics of the Temple, who questioned Jones's faith healing and other unusual practices, remained relatively isolated. But this all changed toward the end of 1975, when Deanna and "Mert" Mertle, two high-ranking members of the Temple leadership, departed, leaving a series of unresolved conflicts in their wake, including a dispute over an unrecorded deed to a property that the couple had signed over to the Temple. In February 1976, the Mertles changed their names to Al and Jeannie Mills, symbolizing that they were new people now that they had left the Temple. Eventually, the Mertles/Millses made contact with others who were leaving the Temple. Among them was Grace Stoen, who in July 1976 drove from Redwood Valley to Lake Tahoe with a Temple bus mechanic, Walter "Smitty" Jones, leaving behind her husband, Temple attorney Tim Stoen, and her son, four-year-old John Victor Stoen.

By the autumn of 1976 a handful of these apostates coalesced into a small group, and the Mills's teenage daughter Linda decided to follow the rest of her family out of the Temple. Linda's exit reduced the issues of contention between the Millses and the Temple and strengthened the family's separation from the group. At the time, there was a wider tide of public concern about "cults" like Sun Myung Moon's Unification Church and the Hare Krishnas (Shupe, Bromley, and Oliver 1984). In this climate the reunited Mills family began to see Peoples Temple as a cult. They followed the public controversies about families seeking court-ordered conservatorships for custody over relatives lost to strange messiahs, and they gravitated toward the centerpiece of anticult movement activism: the "coercive persuasion" explanation of conversion and commitment. As one Mills daughter explained to her sister, "We were all brainwashed in there, Linda. The one thing we have learned is not to blame ourselves for the things Jim made us do."

The apostates did not simply reinterpret their own experiences and actions. They sought to bring the Temple to a public accounting. David Conn, a long-time critic of the Temple and a confidant of the opponents who had come together around the Mertles/Millses and Grace Stoen, brokered the crucial contact. In early 1977, Conn put the apostates in touch with his daughter's boyfriend, George Kleinman, a reporter for the Santa Rosa *Press-Democrat*. In turn, George Kleinman put the opponents in touch with a Customs Service agent in the US Treasury Department. The agent met with thirteen Temple opponents and assured them that a full-scale investigatory effort would be directed at Peoples Temple, involving all levels of government.

Around the same time, journalists for conservative media magnate Rupert Murdoch's *New West* magazine decided to write a story on Peoples Temple because of political efforts to unseat a political patron of Jones and the Temple: liberal San Francisco mayor George Moscone. Initially, the *New West* reporters didn't know about the apostates and didn't have any viable source of information about life inside Peoples Temple. Lacking sources, in June 1977 they got the San Francisco *Chronicle* to publish a story about how the Temple was trying to suppress the story they were working on. By this "ploy," as one of the reporters called it, they managed to hook up with the defectors. After gaining inside information in this way, *New West* published an exposé series which generated a flood of negative newspaper accounts, beginning in July 1977, just weeks before the election vote over whether to recall Mayor Moscone. The opponents appeared in these stories as apostates and relatives courageous enough to expose the group, despite their fear of reprisals. The narratives overwhelmingly depicted Peoples Temple through an anticult lens that raised questions about supposed financial ripoffs, extravagant living and hair-raising practices of psychological catharsis, physical punishment, and brainwashing.

At the time of the exposés, Peoples Temple had already initiated the collective migration to Guyana, and it was widely believed that they had done so in anticipation of the *New West* story. But the exodus had a more complex genesis in Temple concerns during early 1976 about an alignment that they perceived emerging among former members, reporters, and the federal government.

In the years of preparing for a migration to Guyana, the Temple had gone to considerable lengths to keep "black people's money" out of the hands of the US Internal Revenue Service (IRS). By the standards of poor people, they had created substantial collective wealth. Beyond maintaining Peoples Temple in California, the Temple used the resources to finance Jonestown and to prepare for a possible migration. To pursue these activities they shifted millions of dollars into overseas bank accounts beyond the reach of authorities in the United

States. In 1976, the Temple leadership took steps to resolve its tax situation with the IRS by applying for tax-exempt status as a religious communal group. However, as the year wore on, they became increasingly worried that their application had inadvertently triggered an IRS investigation into their care-home financial practices, political involvements, and what the government might deem "private benefits" that the group provided to its communal members. Then in early March 1977, the IRS notified the Temple that their application for tax-exempt status had been turned down.

Soon thereafter, and well before the inside sources met with *New West* reporters, David Conn, the confidant of the Temple opponents, did something that had the unintentional consequence of heightening the Temple's longstanding concerns about its tax status. In late March, he met with American Indian Movement (AIM) leader Dennis Banks, whom Conn hoped to warn about the hidden side of Peoples Temple. But unbeknownst to Conn, Jim Jones had loaned Banks $19,000 to bail his wife out of prison, and Banks was a close and indebted Temple ally. At the meeting with Banks, Conn revealed a great deal about what he knew of the Temple: the defectors' stories of faked healings, beatings, property extortion, threats and intimidations, the fact that he was working with a reporter, and the existence of the US Treasury investigation (initiated through the contact between opponents and the Customs Service agent that reporter George Kleinman had brokered). When Dennis Banks passed on what David Conn had told him to the Temple leadership, they mistakenly supposed their opponents' "treasury agent" (that is, the Customs Service agent) to be connected with the Temple's tax situation. Faced with what they regarded as a serious governmental threat to their organization, Temple leaders launched urgent final preparations for mass departure to Guyana. In the glare of the media spotlight, the collective migration began in earnest in July of 1977. By September, the population of Jonestown had mushroomed to around a thousand people, around 70 per cent blacks, 30 per cent whites. A steady trickle of immigrants continued to arrive through October of 1978.

The Concerned Relatives and the "concentration camp"

There is no way of knowing how Jonestown would have developed as a communal settlement in the absence of the increasingly polarized conflict with its opponents. The migration to Guyana did not cut the Temple off from controversy; it simply shifted the dynamics of the struggle. The opponents continued to offer reporters revelations about the Temple and they fed information about "nefarious acts" to a wide range of government authorities, including the San Francisco Police Department, the Customs Bureau, and the Federal Communications Commission. Their central concern was the fate of Jonestown's residents.

The flood of negative press stories that accompanied the collective migration to Jonestown during the summer of 1977 heightened the anxieties of Jones's opponents and stirred concerns among relatives who might otherwise have been less involved. The strangest and most notorious case concerned the "child god": John Victor Stoen. Legally he was the son of defector Grace Stoen and her husband, Temple attorney Tim Stoen. But Jim Jones claimed that he was the biological father of John Stoen, and the boy was indeed raised socially within Peoples Temple as the son of Jim Jones. Three months after Grace had set off with Smitty Jones in July 1976, Tim Stoen, John's legal father, signed a notarized power of attorney for his son, appointing Jim Jones and others "to take all steps, exercise all powers and rights, that I might do in connection with said minor." The four-and-a-half-year-old was trundled off to Guyana, to live at the agricultural community. Grace Stoen came to recognize that her abandonment of John Victor Stoen to an identity within a collective organization contradicted basic social mores in the wider society that she had rejoined, and in February 1977 she began to assert her interest in getting the child to come back and live in San Francisco. In response, the Temple declared that the legal father, Tim Stoen, would go to Guyana to live with John. If Grace decided to press the issue, the Guyanese courts would surely side with the resident parent. Soon thereafter, Grace went to court to file for divorce and custody.

The resulting struggle became the most celebrated among a series of contestations that eventually raised the question of whether adults at Jonestown lived there of their own free will. The conflict intensified in the summer of 1977 when Tim Stoen went over to the camp of Temple opponents. After a California court granted custody to Grace Stoen on August 26, her lawyer travelled to Guyana. When people at Jonestown refused to hand over John Stoen, the lawyer went to the Guyanese courts and obtained an arrest order for the child and a court summons for Jim Jones. Jones learned of these court actions on 10 September, and he responded with a highly dramatized state of siege in Jonestown. Reaffirming his biological paternity of John Stoen, he threatened death: "I related to Grace, and out of that came a son. That's part of the deal. The way to get to Jim Jones is through his son. They think that will suck me back or cause me to die before I'll give him up. And that's what we'll do, we'll die." Jones's staging of the crisis was by all accounts intense, but it quickly abated; through intensive political and legal maneuvering, Temple staff managed to vacate the Guyanese court order by successfully arguing that Grace Stoen had never revoked a standing grant of custody to a Temple member living at Jonestown.

The Stoen custody battle was a particularly complex case that brought to the fore basic legal and social issues surrounding communal versus conventional societal definitions of parenthood and family. But this was not the only such case, nor were custody struggles the only frontiers of conflict engulfing Peoples Temple. The increasingly organized network of opponents grew in numbers and activities. Participants initiated court proceedings in both the US and Guyana to seek legal custody of other Jonestown children, and they made "welfare and whereabouts" requests for the US State Department to have its embassy in Guyana check on their relatives in Jonestown. One distraught father embarked on a desperate and ineffective scheme to kidnap his adult daughter from

Jonestown. Once Tim Stoen came over to their side, the opponents began to use political pressure and public relations, the same methods that Peoples Temple had employed so effectively in the United States. Calling themselves the "Concerned Relatives," they launched a highly visible campaign against Peoples Temple: they wrote to members of Congress, met with State Department officials, and organized human rights demonstrations.

Despite the intensity of the Concerned Relatives' manifold efforts, they were largely unsuccessful. The Stoen custody case became bogged down in legal issues in the Guyana courts, and the US State Department insisted on due process, refusing to take sides in a matter still proceeding through the courts of a foreign country. On other fronts, multiple governmental investigations in the US failed to come up with significant prosecutable offenses. And when US embassy officials in Guyana checked up on the "welfare and whereabouts" of Jonestown residents for their relatives, they found people living an austere third-world lifestyle who nevertheless "expressed satisfaction with their lives," as one embassy consul reported after a visit to the jungle community. In the absence of evidence that supported the opponents' charges of mass starvation and people living in bondage, the consul later observed, "The Concerned Relatives had a credibility problem, since so many of their claims were untrue" (Hall 1987, pp. 217, 234).

Overall, the campaign against Peoples Temple backfired. But the meager results on legal and governmental fronts did have an important consequence: the frustrated opponents sought other avenues of remedy. Increasingly, they amplified and generalized their public charges against Peoples Temple.

In turn, even though the opponents failed in their direct goals, the Jonestown leadership took the campaign of opposition as inspiration for an increasingly apocalyptic posture, reinforcing the siege mentality that had started to take hold of the community during the September 1977 custody crisis over John Stoen. Most ominously, they began to elaborate the concept of "revolutionary suicide" that Jones had borrowed years earlier from Black Panther leader Huey Newton. The writer of a March 1978 Temple letter to members of Congress warned, "I can say without hesitation that we are devoted to a decision that it is better even to die than to be constantly harassed from one continent to the next. I hope that you can protect the right of over 1,000 people from the US to live in peace." A woman who defected from Jonestown in May of the same year, Debbie Blakey, told an embassy official and the Concerned Relatives that Jonestown was developing plans to carry out a mass suicide, murdering any resisters. In turn, the Concerned Relatives repeatedly publicized the Temple's diehard threats of death and suicide as a way of raising the alarm against Jonestown. "When you say you are 'devoted' to this decision," they asked rhetorically, "does that mean it is irreversible?" (Hall 1987, p. 229).

In a public petition, the Concerned Relatives also portrayed Peoples Temple as "employing physical intimidation and psychological coercion as part of a mind-programming campaign" in violation of the United Nations human-rights declaration of 1948 (Hall 1987, p. 229). This petition effectively raised new issues about Jonestown. Legally, adults at the jungle community had the right to avoid contact with their relatives if they so chose. However, if their mail was censored, if they were intimidated, if they couldn't travel, then it could be argued that they had neither free will nor free access to the outside world. In the words of one of the Concerned Relatives, the residents of Jonestown had become "mind-programmed." By small steps, the struggles by the Concerned Relatives to gain custody over particular children and access to particular relatives became refocused into an effort to "dismantle" what they eventually portrayed as a "concentration camp" (Hall 1987, pp. 232–3). The Concerned Relatives demanded nothing less than that Jonestown cease to exist as a bounded communal society. In effect, they gambled that they could bring Jonestown to a public reckoning without precipitating the extreme acts of violent resistance that the community had threatened. On the other side, the leadership of Peoples Temple would want to know what were the prospects for people who had staked their lives on emigration to a foreign country thousands of miles from California, only to find their opponents hell-bent on shutting down the community they had sacrificed so much to build. Contradictory fears and postures fed the conflict over whether Jonestown was to survive.

Frustrated in both their legal efforts and their attempts to get the US State Department and its embassy to take their side in the tangle of disputes, yet propelled by the belief that Jim Jones had to be stopped, the Concerned Relatives increasingly pinned their hopes on political intervention. In Washington D.C., they had already attracted the support of Leo Ryan, a US congressman from San Mateo, California, known to be sympathetic to the US anticult movement. In December 1977, Congressman Ryan wrote US Secretary of State Cyrus Vance, asking him "to investigate what action might be taken in connection with Mr. Jones." The State Department responded by describing the situation as a legal controversy that did not warrant any "political action without justification." Ryan rejected this view. In May of 1978, as the Concerned Relatives became increasingly frustrated with their lack of success in the courts and with the State Department, Ryan wrote to Peoples Temple, "Please be advised that Tim Stoen does have my support in the effort to return his son from Guyana." Then he began to work with members of the Concerned Relatives to organize a visit to Jonestown.

Mission to Jonestown

The expedition that Leo Ryan led to Jonestown was publicly billed as the "fact-finding effort" of a congressional delegation, but this public facade obscured a working alliance between Ryan and the Concerned Relatives. As preparations unfolded, no other congressman would join Ryan on the trip, and for this reason the expedition failed to meet congressional criteria as an official congressional delegation. Another California congressman, Don Edwards, advised that taking the trip under such conditions "was not the right thing to do." Edwards later recalled, "I said congressmen are ill-advised to take such matters into their own hands." But Ryan pressed ahead anyway, accompanied unofficially by a number of Concerned Relatives and some journalists.

Diverse motives shaped the planned trip. At least two opponents, Tim Stoen and Steve Katsaris, wanted to retrieve their relatives "by force if necessary," as Stoen put it. A less clandestine strategy hinged on the view of some opponents that conditions at Jonestown were desperate. In this scenario, the presence of visiting relatives together with outside authorities would break Jones's discipline and precipitate a mass exodus. The press had agendas too. A freelance journalist, Don Harris, organized an NBC crew to cover a story about a congressman and ordinary citizens travelling to Guyana to investigate the plight of their relatives trapped in a jungle commune.

Given the participation of a congressman and the newsmen, the expedition promised to confront Jones with the choice of either submitting to external scrutiny and possible intervention, or precipitating a flood of bad press and governmental inquiry. When Peoples Temple staff first learned of Ryan's plans, they sought to negotiate conditions about press coverage and the composition of the congressional delegation. Ryan considered the negotiations a delaying tactic, and on 14 November 1978, accompanied by the group of Concerned Relatives and the news reporters, he boarded the Pan American Airlines flight from New York to Guyana's capital, Georgetown. The group would try to gain access to Jonestown once they arrived. But in Georgetown, Ryan met further resistance. With time running out before he would have to return to the US, on 17 November he flew with the reporters and a subgroup of the Concerned Relatives to Port Kaituma, a small settlement near Jonestown. From there, a dump truck brought Ryan, the US ambassador to Guyana, and Temple lawyers Charles Garry and Mark Lane up the muddy road to Jonestown, where they conferred with Jim Jones. Faced with the prospects of news reports about a congressman and relatives barred from entering a jungle compound that had been called a concentration camp, Jones acquiesced to the visit of the Concerned Relatives and most of the journalists.

At Jonestown, Jim Jones already had coached his community for days about how to respond to the visitors. On the evening that Ryan and the others arrived, Jonestown gave them an orchestrated welcome at the main pavilion, serving up a good dinner and musical entertainment from "The Jonestown Express." But during the festivities, a message was passed to NBC reporter Don Harris: "Help us get out of Jonestown." The note was signed "Vern Gosney." On the reverse side was the name "Monica Bagby." The next day, Jonestown staff tried to occupy the visitors with public-relations activities, but Ryan and embassy staff began to make arrangements for Gosney and Bagby to leave. NBC reporter Don Harris then tipped off Leo Ryan's assistant, Jackie Speier, about members of the Parks family, who also might want to leave. Jones pleaded with the Parks family not to depart with his enemies; he offered them $5,000 to cover transportation back to the US if they would wait several days and go on their own. But they decided to leave with Ryan. "I have failed," Jones muttered to his lawyer, Charles Garry. "I live for my people because they need me. But whenever they leave, they tell lies about the place."

Figure 1.2 Flanked by members of the musical group, the Jonestown Express, California
Congressman Leo Ryan makes remarks in the Jonestown pavilion after dinner
on 17 November 1978. During the evening a NBC reporter received a note
from two Jonestown residents who wanted help leaving the community.

Source: San Francisco Examiner

As the dump truck was loaded for departure, Ryan told Jones that he would
give a basically positive report: "If two hundred people wanted to leave, I would
still say you have a beautiful place here." Ryan talked about the need for more
interchange with the outside world. Suddenly he was assaulted by a man bran-
dishing a knife. Blood spurted across Ryan's white shirt. Within seconds, Temple
attorneys Charles Garry and Mark Lane grabbed the assailant, a man named
Don Sly, the former husband of a Concerned Relative. Jones stood impassively
by. Ryan was dishevelled but unhurt: Sly had accidentally cut himself, not the
congressman.

"Does this change everything?" Jones asked Ryan. "It doesn't change everything, but it changes things," Ryan replied. "You get that man arrested." Then the
US embassy deputy chief of mission, Richard Dwyer, led Ryan to the departing
truck and they piled in with the reporters, the four Concerned Relatives and the
Jonestown people who had decided to leave with the entourage. The truck lurched
into low gear and down the muddy road toward the nearby Port Kaituma airstrip.

Gone from the promised land

All told, sixteen defectors, mostly whites, departed under the auspices of a US
congressman whom the Jonestown leadership regarded as allied with their

opponents. One of the apostates parted saying that the community was nothing but "a Communist prison camp." From Jones's viewpoint, the episode was certain to be used by the Temple's opponents to fuel further accusations, more media scrutiny, and increased intervention in the affairs of Jonestown by external legal authorities. These were the circumstances in which the Jonestown leadership translated revolutionary suicide into a final decisive act against their opponents, sending sharpshooters to the airstrip in pursuit of the dumptruck.

When the truck reached the Port Kaituma airstrip and Ryan's group started boarding two planes, a Jonestown man posing as a defector suddenly pulled out a loaded pistol in the smaller plane and fired it. Simultaneously, a tractor came up pulling a flatbed trailer carrying men from Jonestown. When the trailer had pulled to about thirty feet from the larger plane, the men picked up rifles as if by signal and started shooting at the people still clustered outside the plane. After a seeming eternity of gunfire, the tractor pulled away, leaving behind ten people wounded, and five dead bodies: Congressman Leo Ryan, Don Harris and two other newsmen, and defector Patricia Parks.

By directing the airstrip attack on Leo Ryan and his entourage, Jones and his followers constructed a situation of such overriding stigma that their enemies would surely prevail in their plan to "dismantle" Jonestown. The Jonestown leadership chose to finesse this outcome. Back at the pavilion, Jim Jones told the assembled residents of Jonestown that they would no longer be able to survive as a community. With a tape recorder running, Jones argued, "If we can't live in peace, then let's die in peace." Medical staff set up cauldrons of Fla-Vor Aid laced with cyanide and tranquilizers.

A total of 913 members of the community became caught up in the orchestrated ritual of mass suicide that ensued. How many people willingly participated? The question will always be open to debate. Certainly young children could not have understood the consequences of drinking the poison, and during the suicide council a woman named Christine Miller pleaded against Jones's proposal. But many people supported the plan: mothers willing to have their infants killed, elderly people telling Jones they were ready to go, the sharpshooters who had killed the congressman. Amidst low wails, sobbing and the shrieks of children, they all came up to take the "potion," then moved out of the pavilion to huddle with their families and die. Whatever their individual sentiments, the people of Jonestown departed their own promised land through an improvised ritual of collective death. As people lined up to die, Jones preached to the believers and the doubters assembled in the Jonestown pavilion. Invoking Huey Newton's words, he assured them, "This is a revolutionary suicide. This is not a self-destructive suicide." In the confusion, two black men slipped past the guards. At the very end, Jim Jones and a close aide, Annie Moore, died by gunshots to the head, wounds consistent with suicide. Annie had scribbled a last sentence to the note she left: "We died because you would not let us live in peace." During the mass suicide, the community's two American lawyers, Charles Garry and Mark Lane, had been sequestered at a perimeter house, and after their guards left to join the suicide ritual, Garry and Lane plunged into the jungle. One elderly woman slept through the event. Everyone else died.

After Jonestown

What is the cultural significance of Jonestown? The answer to this question hinges on highly contested questions about why the mass suicide occurred. With a basic narrative of the group's history at hand, we can consider these questions. A general list of *necessary preconditions* – without which the murderous attack and mass self-destruction would not have occurred – might reasonably focus on the *internal features* of a group that could undertake such acts, specifically:

- a charismatic religious social movement
- an apocalyptic ideology
- a form of social organization adequate to maintain solidarity
- legitimacy enough among followers to exercise collective social control over the affairs of the community
- sufficient economic and political viability
- life within strong social boundaries in cognitive isolation from society at large.

Without these circumstances, minor incidents of violence might occur within a countercultural communal movement or in a conflict between it and external adversaries, but it is difficult to imagine that they would trigger violence on a large scale.

These preconditions well describe Peoples Temple. Yet if the preconditions are particularly conducive to violence, they are hardly sufficient. Numerous apocalyptic and quasi-apocalyptic religious communities – from Mother Ann Lee's Shakers to contemporary "heavens on earth" like Seattle's Love Family and the Krishna farm in West Virginia (Hall 1978) – have all these *internal* characteristics without experiencing anything remotely like murder of enemies followed by collective suicide. Thus, strongly bounded apocalyptic religious movements may be especially prone to external violence and mass suicide, but that outcome is extremely rare compared to the number of groups adequately described by the list of preconditions. There must be specific additional *precipitating factors* that would result in murders and mass suicide.

In contemporary circumstances, the necessary precipitating factors would seem to be the ones described in the model of apocalyptic religious conflict described in the introduction:

- the mobilization of a group of cultural opponents who possess a high degree of solidarity
- the shaping of news media coverage through the cultural opponents' frame of interpretation about "cults"
- the exercise of state authority.

If through the operation of these factors, the apocalyptic group's very capacity to persist comes into question, it would be under these conditions (and in a strong explanation, these conditions alone) that group leaders might unleash aggression toward detractors and use the device of mass suicide to cut off any external exercise of authority over the group.

How well does this general causal explanation capture the circumstances that led up to the murders and mass suicide at Jonestown? Clearly, the proximate cause of murder and mass suicide was the refusal of Jim Jones, his staff, and the loyalists among his followers to brook compromise with opponents whom they believed (with some reason) were out to bring Jonestown as a community to an end. Rather than submit to external powers that they regarded as illegitimate, they chose to stage the airstrip murders as revenge and shut out their opponents by ending their own lives.

After the fact, the narrative structure of myth carved the stigma of this massive carnage into infamy. Jones became a megalomaniacal Antichrist; Peoples Temple, a cult of brainwashed robots; the Concerned Relatives, tragic heroes who valiantly tried but failed to save their loved ones. However, the mythic structure of this narrative depends on a particular analytic claim: that the avoidable carnage was solely a consequence of the acts of Jones and his accomplices. It is by lifting the mantle on this claim that we come to the heart of the apocalypse at Jonestown.

Without the airstrip attack on Ryan and the others, the mass suicide would have lacked a credible rationale, whereas in the context of the airstrip murders Jones presented collective death as the only honorable collective choice in the face of certain subjugation to external authority. In other words, the Jonestown leadership constructed the murders and mass suicide as a unity, but that unity was predicated upon the airstrip attack. The attack itself was not an act of random violence: other than the perhaps accidental killing of a young girl who defected, the gunfire seems to have been carefully targeted toward individuals whom Jonestown principals regarded as their opponents in the ongoing struggle. It was a preemptive strike that snatched victory from opponents, albeit by fulfilling their most nightmarish prophecies.

Given the targets, the attack itself has to be understood as an extreme escalation of an intense conflict between the Concerned Relatives and Peoples Temple. This conflict had already unfolded for more than a year in the press, the courts, the US State Department, in the conduct of espionage on both sides, and in strategic actions that had previously come close to direct confrontation. Under these circumstances, it seems incontrovertible that the expedition of Congressman Ryan, the Concerned Relatives and journalists, and especially their departure with sixteen Jonestown residents, was the precipitating factor in the murderous attack. As a specific event, the mass suicide must be seen as a consequence of the expedition.

It is not easy to answer the question of what would have happened had the expedition not taken place at all, or not turned out as it did, since there are so many alternative scenarios. Conducting "mental experiments" to consider "what would happen if . . ." is a delicate matter. Yet as Geoffrey Hawthorne (1991) has argued, the consideration of alternative scenarios can deepen an analysis if the counterfactual hypotheses are neither so distant from the course of events as to be irrelevant nor so unstable in their dynamics as to make prediction unreliable. With these guidelines in mind, it is possible to push toward a deeper – though necessarily tentative – understanding of the murders and mass suicide.

On the one hand, had the Concerned Relatives not formed an organized group, and had they not achieved some success in their substantial efforts to bring a critical mass of journalistic coverage and a US congressman to their side, it seems unlikely that the mass suicide would have occurred. Indeed, when they first formed, the Concerned Relatives understood their own powerlessness and sought out sympathetic news reporters precisely as patrons who would help them. After Jones and his followers migrated to Jonestown, the opponents took concerted actions through legal and administrative channels, but these actions failed to advance their cause, and it was because they became frustrated with their prospects within institutional channels of conflict resolution that they turned to publicity campaigns in the media and the political intervention of a congressman's "fact-finding" expedition.

Clearly then, the actions of the apostates and relatives were crucial to catalyzing the dynamic of conflict between Peoples Temple and the outside, and this conflict is a necessary component of any explanation of the mass suicide that actually occurred. It is impossible, however, to say with certainty whether a mass suicide would have occurred without the Ryan expedition. Certainly there are plausible scenarios in which a mass suicide would *not* have taken place. For example, the opponents might have won some legal battles, gained better access to visitation with relatives, and won other concessions without confronting the Temple with complete subordination to external authority. Even more likely, given time, the entire enterprise at Jonestown might have collapsed from internal dissension, as the vast majority of communal groups do (cf. Kanter 1972). In light of these possibilities, the murders and mass suicide were in no way inevitable.

On the other hand, it is also apparent that even without the Ryan trip, the conflict between the Concerned Relatives and the Temple was extremely intense, and the Concerned Relatives were willing to pursue it even in the face of threatened violent responses. They might have gained other victories to which the leadership at Jonestown would likely have responded with violence. For example, had Grace and Timothy Stoen won legal custody over John Victor Stoen, a different violent confrontation – and mass suicide – might have ensued. In other words, within the broad channels of contestation between Peoples Temple and the Concerned Relatives, the potential for violence could have been unleashed in more than one scenario.

The question of John Victor Stoen's biological paternity is the remaining major mystery of the tragedy. Much anecdotal evidence suggests that Jim Jones was his biological father: his paternity was affirmed in an affidavit by Tim Stoen in 1972 only days after the boy's birth (Hall 1987, pp. 127-8), and taken as fact both within the Temple and by certain people outside the group well before the issue became folded into the conflict between the Temple and its opponents. Tim Stoen only denied Jones's claim publicly much later, when he took the side of Grace Stoen in the custody battle. To date, the evidence is not conclusive, but the weight of it leans to the paternity of Jim Jones.

If Jones was indeed the biological father, then a central atrocity claimed by the Concerned Relatives during their campaign against the Temple that Jones amounted to the kidnapper of a child would lose much of its moral (though not legal) force. Thus one significant element of the opponents' brief against Peoples Temple would turn out to have been based on a public construction of reality that differed from privately held knowledge. Resolving this question might sharpen our opinions about the moral high ground held by the two sides. At the time, however, it would have resolved neither the cultural conflict between communalism and familial individualism nor the struggle over whether the adult people of Jonestown had the right to live in isolation from the direct intervention of opponents who sought to dismantle their community. And it probably would not have altered the commitments of the true believers at Jonestown to extreme violence, should their opponents prevail in subordinating them to external social and legal authority.

A second controversy – about government agencies – is even murkier. The Concerned Relatives triggered some governmental investigations of Peoples Temple. But other government initiatives *preceded* the emergence of the Concerned Relatives as an organized group, and the inquiries of various government agencies fed on one another. In particular, the US government had diplomatic and strategic concerns about the socialist government of Guyana, and its embassy in Georgetown sent operatives on monitoring visits to the Jonestown settlement. Because the United States government might have been able to prevent the tragedy, and also because government officials and representatives may have acted in ways that propelled it, there has been considerable speculation about the government's role. One book weaves some well established facts together with highly questionable inferences to raise the question of whether Jonestown was a "CIA medical experiment" (Meiers 1988). Whatever the truth of the matter, such accounts cannot be easily assessed because the US government has suppressed information about its dealings with Peoples Temple, partly on the basis of the sensitivity of its geopolitical interests.[2] If remaining government files on Peoples Temple can be examined, they may well yield significant reassessments of its history (the same holds for the NBC video "outakes" from its Jonestown coverage, which the network has refused to make public).

Whatever comes of the search for more information, causal analysis of available evidence substantially revises the popular myth of Jonestown. Without question, the apocalypse at Jonestown was an immense tragedy. The Concerned

Relatives, Leo Ryan, and the press will no doubt continue to be portrayed as tragic heroes in the affair. Yet there is a deeper tragedy. It is now evident that the opponents' own actions helped to precipitate a course of events that presumably led to the fulfillment of their own worst fears. The murders and mass suicide cannot be adequately explained except as the outcome of an escalating conflict between two diametrically opposed groups: Peoples Temple and the Concerned Relatives.

Other religious groups important to American religious history – the Pilgrims and the Mormons, for example – previously met with pitched opposition from relatives and public detractors, yet they managed to persist and to succeed in ways important for the culture of American religion. By contrast, Peoples Temple was a dramatic failure. Yet even so, the history of the movement reflects many of the tensions and contradictions of American culture. Its members sought to participate in an integrated community that transcended persistent racism in the United States. In a society where the practice of religion is largely segregated from everyday socioeconomic organization and practice, the group infused its members' working lives and social relationships with new "religious" meaning. These aspects neither justify nor compensate for the tragic conflict that Jones long cultivated. But the seldom-acknowledged accomplishments of Peoples Temple stand as stark reminders that the US has failed to achieve anything like a societal community based on racial integration, equal opportunity, and economic justice. Jonestown, we now know, came at the time when the liberal and left social movements that had been active in American politics during the 1960s and 1970s were losing their influence. Ronald Reagan soon followed, proclaiming a pride-filled "morning in America."

There is considerable irony in all this. Much of the criticism of Peoples Temple focused on the group's practices: faked healings, money-making schemes, glorification of a prophet, intimidation and punishment, public relations, and political manipulations. This *auto-da-fé* could only proceed by placing on Jim Jones and Peoples Temple the stigma of bearing evils that are widespread and sometimes institutionalized in the wider society. Unfortunately Jones was hardly a creative man. On the contrary, however crudely, he mimicked and sometimes intensified practices that he drew from the wider culture. Jones established an organization with alien *ends*, to be sure, but that organization owed its success in no small part to the fact that its cultural inventory of *means* mostly came from the wider world. Thus the Temple's realm of opposition to the world at large was often enough but a mirror of it, and sometimes a grotesque reflection of its seamier side. After the mass suicide, those who loaded the moral burden of evil onto Jonestown symbolically cleansed the wider society, but this ritual exorcism left behind elements of Jonestown culture still alive in our world – in techniques of social control, religious practices, politics and public relations. The "negative cult" of Jonestown thus stands as an ominous monument to an arsenal of manipulations that persist in wider institutional practices. To isolate this arsenal, its boundaries must be drawn more widely than the jungle commune.

A different irony was reflected in the future of memory. Jonestown fulfilled the most dire warnings of its opponents. After the murders and mass suicide, Peoples Temple became the quintessence of the "cult," stereotypically portrayed as an organization that drains both property and free will from its members and "brainwashes" them into a "group mind." Yet these issues have nothing specific to do with Peoples Temple's sustained and increasingly violent interpretation of revolutionary suicide as a doctrine of struggle against an established social order. Instead, they stem from a more general cultural reflection of communalism as a form of life alien to capitalist democratic society. The tragedy of Jonestown thus became an opportunity for scapegoating a broader form of social organization that is not inherently associated with mass suicide. Here, the conflict that produced Jonestown was recapitulated at the core of its mythical reconstruction, for the demonization of communalism as "other" reinforces the ideology of individualism, thus providing the grounds for further antagonism between communalists and their cultural opponents. As we will see, the image of Jonestown resonated in the life of the Branch Davidians in subtle yet consequential ways.

2

FROM JONESTOWN TO WACO

The basic events of "Waco" are strongly etched in many people's minds. On the morning of Sunday, 28 February 1993, about eighty heavily armed agents of the US Bureau of Alcohol, Tobacco, and Firearms (BATF) engaged in a shootout with members of the Branch Davidians, a Seventh-Day Adventist splinter sect led by a young charismatic who called himself David Koresh. Six or more sect members and four BATF agents died in the firefight. After an uneasy truce was finally established that Sunday, a new phase of confrontation began: the Federal Bureau of Investigation (FBI) initiated a siege of the compound. In the weeks of the standoff that followed, however, FBI attempts to unnerve the Davidians with floodlights, sound blasts of Tibetan chants, and an old Nancy Sinatra record seem to have pushed the Davidians only to more intense Bible study. The FBI concluded that their negotiations with the Davidians were unlikely to bring the besieged Davidians out anytime soon. Then, in the early morning hours of 19 April, the FBI, frustrated at the lack of progress at negotiating a surrender, rolled tanks up to the front of the woodframe compound, started injecting tear gas, and in the course of the morning began destroying walls of the building itself. Shortly before noon a fire broke out, quickly engulfing the structure. Seventy-four Branch Davidians died in the inferno, either in presumed "mercy killings" by gunshot or from the smoke and flames of the blaze itself.

This sad saga, which unfolded in slow motion under intense media scrutiny, rapidly became the subject of right-wing conspiracy theories about the US government, and these theories fed into the largest single act of terrorism in US history – the bombing of the US federal building in Oklahoma City on 19 April 1995 – two years to the day after the FBI tank attack on Mount Carmel. Quite apart from the role that "Waco" came to play in collective memory of militia groups, it also has been the subject of numerous governmental, journalistic and

This chapter is a revised version of "Public narratives and the apocalyptic sect," by John R. Hall, pp. 205–35 in Stuart A. Wright, ed., *Armageddon in Waco*. Chicago: University of Chicago Press, 1995. © 1995 The University of Chicago. All rights reserved. Reprinted with permission.

scholarly inquiries. There is wide agreement that BATF mishandled their initial investigation of the Branch Davidians and their raid, ostensibly conducted to serve a warrant. The performance of the FBI during the siege and its decision to roll the tanks against the compound have been more hotly debated, in part because some government officials – including the Attorney General, Janet Reno, and President Bill Clinton – initially defended the FBI's performance and held that ultimate responsibility must rest with David Koresh. These claims fit well with a rhetoric of cult essentialism, but they are contradicted both by the report of the US Treasury Department about the BATF raid and by any careful effort at sociological explanation. As with Jonestown, the legacy of Waco is tightly bound up both with the cultural tensions that led to the debacle and, subsequently, with the contentious questions about its significance that drive public cultural denial and popular mythology alike.

Long before the Bureau of Alcohol, Tobacco, and Firearms set out on their ill-fated raid against Mount Carmel, David Koresh's apocalyptic sect was becoming another Jonestown. So said former Branch Davidians more than a year before the February 1993 shootout (Breault and King 1993, pp. 11–12). It might seem that the apostates were prophetic: in the minds of the public, "Waco" quickly became a new – albeit more ambiguous – Jonestown. But was the former Branch Davidians' prophecy in part self-fulfilling? We can probe this question by tracing how the central public meaning of Jonestown – mass suicide – came into play at Mount Carmel.

This analysis can proceed by examining "intrinsic narratives": the diverse stories that various social actors tell within emergent situations to which they are oriented mutually but in different ways. Looking at intrinsic narratives can help show how cultural meanings become nuanced, shaded, interpreted, challenged, and otherwise reworked through the agency of participants, and how such shifts of meaning affect the course of unfolding events (Somers 1992; Sewell 1992; Hall and Neitz 1993, pp. 12–13; Kane 1997; Hall 1999, chapter 3). Tracing narratives of mass suicide reveals how meanings about Jonestown became changed into meanings about the Branch Davidians.

There is deep irony in the early prophetic warnings by former members against Mount Carmel as another Jonestown, a "cult." The term "cult" has a variety of meanings. But whatever the possible dictionary definitions, in the late-twentieth-century United States, the term became almost universally recognized as a stigmatic label for countercultural religious groups. The term thus takes on its current cultural significance through meanings promulgated by the anticult movement. In this cultural sense, it is easy to understand Mount Carmel as the second Jonestown, the prison-fortress that Jim Jones was said to have created in Jonestown, Guyana, where "brainwashed" and powerless individuals, broken of their will, were subjected to the whims of a megalomaniac who orchestrated their deaths in a "mass suicide" that was really an elaborate murder.

As chapter 1 showed, this comparison is superficial and misleading, because the people who put the most effort into labeling Jonestown as a cult were not

passive bystanders or critics after the fact. They were the active opponents organized as the Concerned Relatives. In the case of Jonestown, the organized
campaign of the Concerned Relatives, mobilizing journalists and a congressman
to their side, was a necessary causal factor without which it is extremely unlikely
that the murders and mass suicide would have occurred. The mass suicide could
not be properly analyzed solely through the "frame" (Snow et al. 1986) of the
anticult movement because that frame itself contributed to the accelerating
dynamic of conflict. If Mount Carmel is really to be understood as another
Jonestown, then like Jonestown, it cannot be adequately understood as a "cult";
instead, we must ask whether anticult labeling played a part in the conflict. The
thesis to be considered here is a sobering one: because of a culturally programmed
failure to learn from Jonestown, cultural opponents of David Koresh could
invoke and rework narratives about mass suicide from Jonestown and bring them
to bear on the Branch Davidians in ways that proved central to how the tragedy
at Mount Carmel unfolded.

Like Peoples Temple, the Branch Davidians approximated the "apocalyptic
sect" as an ideal type. But as we saw with Peoples Temple, two contradictory ten-
dencies – the warring sect's battle against the construed forces of evil and the
other-worldly sect's retreat to a heaven-on-earth – can remain in volatile play
within the same group. Because apocalyptic sects both construct and respond to
the Apocalypse as they construe it, no conclusions can be drawn in advance
about their trajectories. For a group that has not stabilized a heaven-on-earth in
low tension with its environment, the play of events is especially contingent
upon the interaction of the group with the wider social world. Like Jim Jones,
David Koresh never established a stable heaven-on-earth, and thus we cannot
understand the Branch Davidians, any more than Peoples Temple, as a group
with its own autonomous fate. Instead, we need to recognize that, like
Jonestown, the conflagration at Mount Carmel was the product of religious conflict between a militant sect and opponents who, wittingly or unwittingly, helped
shape and fulfill the sect's emergent apocalyptic vision.

The apocalyptic visions of Jim Jones and David Koresh were quite different,
of course. Jones blended Pentecostal and liberal Christianity with political sympathies toward the world-historical Communist movement, and he consolidated
a politically engaged movement built on the apocalyptic premise that Peoples
Temple would offer an ark of refuge in the face of a prophesied US drift toward
race and class warfare. By contrast, David Koresh did not forge a new apocalyptic vision; he appropriated a long-standing one. The Seventh Day Adventists,
from whence the Branch Davidian sect had emerged, was founded during the
nineteenth century in response to the "Great Disappointment" in the wake of
William Miller's failed numerological prophecy that the world would come to an
end in 1844 (Boyer 1992). From this millennialist beginning, some Adventist
groups have tried in the twentieth century to suppress their most florid apocalyptic visions, hoping to attain a legitimate denominational status within US
religion, undertaking the sect-to-denomination trajectory that Weber, Troeltsch,

and Niebuhr described. However, in doing so, in the eyes of truly apocalyptic seekers, the more mainstream Adventist groups have compromised their claim as the authentic bearers of radically transcendent revelation; thus, they have become vulnerable to the emergence of Adventist splinter sects that reclaim the "true faith" and revitalize anticipation of the imminent advent.

The Davidian movement was founded by Victor Houteff in 1929, in an attempt to provide Seventh Day Adventists with the new revelations teachings that could bring the faithful to their deliverance and prepare the way for the final denouement of earthly history. The Davidians moved from Los Angeles to the Mount Carmel site in 1935, and in the main building there Houteff installed a clock with its hands set to around 11:00, precipitously close to the end of historical time. After Houteff died in 1955, his widow Florence predicted God's day of judgment would come on the Jewish passover of 1959. When neither the Second Coming nor any other discernible event materialized, the Davidian movement succumbed to sectarian splintering. One group, the Branch Davidians led by Ben Roden, eventually managed to gain control of Mount Carmel. Roden emphasized the importance of the restored state of Israel and launched what religious historian William Pitts (1995, p. 34) has described as "a virulent strand of anti-Catholic attacks, peppered with epithets aimed at papal authority and accusing Rome of subversion and conspiracy." Upon Roden's death in 1978, his widow Lois won charismatic succession to the leadership of the group in a power struggle with her son, George. During Lois's reign, Vernon Howell came on the scene, and it seems that she sought to pass the Branch Davidian mantle to this handsome young man who showed such promise in Biblical thinking and teaching. After Lois's death in 1986 came another struggle for succession. Howell – who eventually changed his name to David Koresh – prevailed over George Roden after an exchange of gunfire that resulted in George Roden being sentenced to six months in jail. The day after Roden went to jail, Howell and his followers took over the property. One of them commented, "it has all been worked out by the will of God" (Pitts 1995, p. 38).

Overall, a deep lineage of fervent expectationism typical of Seventh Day Adventist sects rooted Koresh's Branch Davidian movement. Compared to Jones's left-wing political apocalyptic vision, Koresh's prophecies about the end times were thus much more directly keyed to the New Testament's Book of Revelation. Indeed, the apocalyptic rhetoric of David Koresh is little different from the language of other offshoot groups opposed to the Advent establishment, groups whose rhetoric is equally filled with references to the seven seals, plagues (AIDS), visions of glory, enemies of the faith, apostates, and the day of testing that is "just before us." Koresh could well have borrowed the warning of a contemporaneous Oregon group: "The members of the church will individually be tested and proved. They will be placed in circumstances where they will be forced to bear witness for the truth."[1]

Jones's apocalyptic vision was a Marxist-Christian amalgamation tied to the social issues of the day, whereas Koresh continued the longstanding Adventist

Figure 2.1 Vernon Howell, who later changed his name to David Koresh, soon after he arrived at the Branch Davidians' Mount Carmel settlement in 1981.

Source: AP/WORLDWIDE PHOTOS

tradition of mapping detailed interpretations of the Book of Revelation in relation to specific signs of the final days. Yet Jones's Temple and Koresh's Branch Davidians had much in common. Both Jones and Koresh took up the project of founding expansionary religious social movements. Like early Mormon polygamists, both Jones and Koresh fathered children with multiple sexual partners, in Koresh's case, some of them under the legal age of sexual consent (Ellison and

Bartkowski 1995, pp. 126–31). In addition, Koresh seems to have established a quasi-military "men's house" (Weber 1978, p. 357) separated from the women. Such communally organized sexual and gender patterns are culturally taboo within modern Western societies, even though (indeed, perhaps because) they are tested, durable forms of social organization. Polygamy and the men's house can be used to create a militant, proto-ethnic religious movement bound together by the patri-monialist cadre of a prophet's followers and hereditary succession of prophecy. By bridging and blurring familial relationships in a larger communal organization, Koresh effectively transformed a patronal sectarian clan into a prophetic movement centered on his charismatic leadership (Bromley and Silver 1995).[2]

Following much the same proto-ethnic formula, Jones had established what amounted to a state within a state, close to Guyana's disputed border with Venezuela. By contrast, Koresh remained in the United States, and Mount Carmel became a tiny principality on a back Texas road. Through interaction with real (and in Jones's case, sometimes imagined) opponents, both Jones and Koresh prepared for militant armed struggle, something to which Koresh was no stranger because of his violent confrontation in 1987 with George Roden. In the face of increasing exter-nal opposition, Koresh, like Jones, steeled his followers to "metanoia" (revolutionary rebirth). For his followers, like those of Jones, the meanings of life – and death – became bound up with unfolding events. In different ways, the dominant groups at both Jonestown and Mount Carmel came to affirm their refusal to submit to an external authority they believed to be intent on destroying them.

Such parallels show that the Branch Davidians, like Peoples Temple, shared a propensity toward conflict with outside opponents and authorities, but they do not account for the tragedy at Mount Carmel any more than they explain the apocalypse at Jonestown. Given that other standoffs between authorities and religious sects have been resolved peacefully, the outcome at Mount Carmel, as at Jonestown, could have been different.

How the initial standoff at Mount Carmel was precipitated by the BATF raid has been the subject of minute analysis. The US Treasury Department report on the subject defended the BATF pursuit of Koresh for weapons violations as legal and legitimate (USTD 1993, p. 120), and it strongly denied that the BATF acted against Koresh because of his deviant religious beliefs (ibid., p. 121). However, the latter claim is open to question, since Mount Carmel was cast as a "cult" in the affidavit in support of application for the warrants (US District Court 1993). Indeed, the Treasury review is self-refuting on the supposed irrelevance of Koresh's religion, since it presents Koresh's apocalyptic theology as evidence of the threat that he posed. These incongruities suggest a need to understand how cultural rather than official lenses shaped the vision of BATF in the conflict.

Because cultural narratives about "cults" are distinctive in comparison to, say, the rhetoric of law enforcement, it is possible to trace the interplay between cul-tural constructions and legal ones. Anticult usage identifies "cults" as subversive both of families and individuals and of the core values of society as a whole. After Jonestown, one cultural signification – mass suicide – became a term of general cultural currency that offered a ready touchstone for describing the stark danger posed by "cults." Opponents of the Branch Davidians invoked this ambiguous but compelling motif frequently, beginning more than a year before the BATF raid. Because diverse documents mention these and other invocations, it is pos-sible to trace in detail the emergence of mass suicide as a cultural meaning about Mount Carmel well before the final fiery debacle. Thus, by examining a rela-tively circumscribed set of events we can track the emergent play of cultural meanings that surrounded an increasingly public religious conflict.

The shifts in the significance of mass suicide can be traced by examining the "intrinsic" narratives that were offered as events unfolded. People use narratives (which we can call "stories," if we refrain from judgments about truth status) in a variety of ways. They can "construct" reality by enveloping people in accounts of events beyond their own personal knowledge. People also individually and jointly compose narratives ("scripts" and "scenarios") in order to make sense of projects that they are undertaking. In a different way, narratives can be used to "reconstruct" events after the fact in collective memory, and they can "deconstruct" competing narratives in advance, as events unfold, and after the fact. Narratives in each of these forms may draw upon "cultural meanings" that help render them coherent and accessible. Thus, analyzing narratives – in relation to the social identities, locations, and power of the narrators – can bring to light the specific connections between cul-tural constructs and situational public discourses about religious conflicts. As will become apparent, narratives are particularly important when the meaningful content shifts, when the narrative moves from one source to another, when affini-ties develop between the narratives of two individuals or groups, and when the incorporation of a received narrative rearranges other meanings for an individual or group. When such narratives are freighted with cultural meanings, they may exercise influence on a course of events in ways that exceed, or do not depend upon, merely factual, legal or professional considerations.

How, then, did cultural meanings about mass suicide figure in the interwoven narratives of Waco? What accounts did Koresh and his followers at Mount Carmel, the former sect members, authorities, and the media offer to themselves and to others? How did various individuals assess other people's stories? To what extent were stories "cultural scripts," that is, "formulaic" or liturgical narratives that bear significance independently of the actual circumstances? Charting the narratives about mass suicide for the Waco affair up through the BATF raid on 28 February 1993 shows more than parallels; it establishes a genetic connection between Jonestown and Waco. Public discourse of citizens, media and governmental author-ities was built up through the reformulation of cultural meanings in successive historical events in ways that had disastrous consequences (cf. Gamson *et al.* 1992).

The narrative of apocalyptic militancy

The central narratives of Waco are, of course, those of David Koresh and his committed followers. Unfortunately, not only are these the ones about which we know the least, but most of what we know is filtered through their protagonists, both former cult members and governmental authorities. Yet available information suggests a pattern that parallels the emergence of the "mass suicide" motif at Jonestown. Jones appropriated Huey Newton's Black Panther party ideology of revolutionary suicide. At Jonestown, the Panther ideology of revolutionary struggle ultimately became mass suicide. But this outcome was not foreordained; it emerged during Peoples Temple's struggles with its opponents (see chapter 1).

The Branch Davidians did not invoke the Black Panthers. If Koresh's political sentiments ran in any direction, it was to the anti-state populism of right-wing Christian survivalist movements. But the attachments of Koresh and his followers to apocalyptic theology were, if anything, stronger than those of the Black Panthers and Peoples Temple. From its origins in the 1920s, the Branch Davidian movement was centered on the classic Seventh Day Adventist questions about how exactly to interpret the Book of Revelation's clues about the last days. Koresh did not have to create an apocalyptic theology from the ground up; he did not even have to shift it from a pacifistic to a militant dispensation, for Adventist discourse already had developed themes about militancy, sacrifices required of the faithful, their subjection to trials from the outside. It invoked the strongest motifs drawn from a long tradition of Christian martyrdom that centuries earlier had led Christians to fight for their faith, even to seek to die for their faith, in ways that probably precipitated Augustine's injunction against suicide (Hall 1987, pp. 296–8).

Yet there is considerable evidence that Koresh was an existentialist, not a pre-destinationist: he anticipated the apocalypse, but its form was open-ended and only to be understood through prophetic interpretation of events as they unfolded. During the long standoff with the FBI, Koresh kept waiting for "signs" that would reveal the godly course of action. Before the BATF raid, he negotiated with governmental officials, including a sheriff and deputy who served an arrest warrant over the Roden shoot-out in 1987. After the BATF raid, the prosecuting district attorney involved in the 1987 arrest, Vic Feazell, recounted, "We treated them like human beings, rather than storm-trooping the place. They were extremely polite people" (Bragg 1993, p. 7A). In this situation, when treated with relative civility, Koresh did not leap to a siege posture. He acted with courtesy and a degree of compliance. Koresh struck a similar chord during the BATF raid, in a recorded telephone conversation with the BATF: "It would have been better if you just called me up or talked to me. Then you all could have come in and done your work" (in Wood 1993, p. 2). This claim might be dismissed as self-serving but for the fact that it describes how Koresh had dealt with authorities in previous situations.

Still, the question of how Koresh might have responded if the BATF had approached him in a different way can only be the subject of conjecture, for tensions heightened considerably early in 1992. To note the existential civility of the Branch Davidians is not to deny that Koresh was willing to resort to violence, as the incident with George Roden established in 1987. However, neither is it evident that Koresh was preparing to attack, and it is at least plausible, as even the Treasury Department review acknowledges, that he "might simply have been preparing to defend himself against an apocalyptic onslaught" (USTD 1993, p. 127). In the final analysis, these considerations about what directions the apocalyptic struggle *might* have taken are moot, because Koresh came upon direct signs that he could interpret by way of ancient Biblical prophecies about the last days.

The narrative of mass suicide in the opponents' cries for help

Given the long standoff before the final FBI assault and the subsequent fire, it is clear that David Koresh had no single apocalyptic scenario in mind. Although there was a generalized apocalyptic narrative within Mount Carmel before the BATF raid, the first known specific invocation of mass suicide came from *outside* the Branch Davidians, from former sect members who had become opponents. What was this narrative, and how and where did it become more widely diffused? The pattern was complex, but as with Jonestown, relatively small and converging clusters of opponents, informed by the discourse of the anticult movement, raised the alarm with the media and multiple government agencies. Like Temple opponents, the cultural opponents of Koresh invoked the threat that Koresh posed to his followers and the wider society by citing key incidents and "proof texts" taken from Koresh's preachings. In turn, government agency scenarios for dealing with Koresh gradually became infused with the opponents' narrative motifs of mass suicide, and in ways that shaped the logic of the BATF raid. How did these developments come to pass?

Certain details about how the discourse of mass suicide spread into the public and governmental domains have not yet (and may never) become public knowledge. But the major channels are clear. Mostly they trace from Marc Breault, a Roman Catholic from Hawaii who joined the Branch Davidians in 1986. Breault left the group after becoming increasingly dismayed about Koresh's practice of engaging in sexual relationships and siring children with young teenage girls whom the leader initiated into the "House of David." As Breault recounted, he was disgusted to witness thirteen-year-old Aisha Gyarfas pass by his desk after spending the night with David Koresh sometime in July 1989. On 5 August 1989, Breault heard what he called Koresh's "New Light" doctrine justifying the sexual economy of the Branch Davidians, a doctrine connected to the role Koresh assumed as the "sinful messiah" (Tabor and Arnold 1995, pp. 205, 211). In September, Breault flew to Australia and became a self-described "cultbuster," working tirelessly to bring Koresh down. In early 1990, he used theological arguments to turn Australian followers against Koresh. Together, the band of apostates began a clandestine struggle, even meeting in the middle of the night to avoid what they feared were stakeouts by Koresh loyalists (Breault and King 1993, pp. 151, 213; WTH 27 February 1993, p. 10A; 1 March 1993, pp. 8A, 9A).

Step by step, a story about possible violent retribution for their opposition emerged among the gathering apostates, as they worked to help other people break away from the Branch Davidians and raised the alarm to government agencies. Two families were central to their efforts: the Bunds and the Jewells. Koresh had banished David and Debbie Bunds. They later claimed that they received a threatening phone call after Breault got in touch with them, and they decided to move from Waco to California. There, they linked up with David Bunds's sister, Robyn, a Koresh "wife" who broke with Koresh over a period of months beginning in the summer of 1990. In Breault's description of Robyn's defection, he suggested a theme that went beyond vengeance against enemies: child sacrifice. Robyn Bunds had given birth to a child who remained with the Branch Davidians, and she became distraught: "I've heard that he's talking about sacrificing children! My God, what if he tries to kill Wisdom?" Concerned, Robyn retrieved her son Shaun ("Wisdom"), apparently through the intervention of Sgt John Hackworth of the LaVerne, California, police (WP 25 April 1993; Linedecker 1993, pp. 145–6).

As Breault later explained, "We were worried that Koresh might be thinking about human sacrifices. We didn't know for sure, but Koresh was unstable enough to make even our darkest nightmares seem possible" (Breault and King 1993, p. 220). This sort of atrocity tale was repeated, elaborated and amplified over time. Breault later recounted that while he was a member, Koresh warned about outsiders coming in and killing the children. After Breault left, "we started hearing rumors that he was planning it himself" (WP 25 April 1993). Similarly, Breault began to fear for his own life: "Koresh wanted to lure me back to Mount Carmel and kill me" (Breault and King 1993, pp. 226, 233).

Taken together, these stories weave a vision of sadistic violence and unrestrained retribution. To date, however, we have no way of tracing them back from Breault's accounts. But perhaps there is a good reason: for the most part the narratives do not claim to be about actual events: they are about rumors, nightmares, and anticipated agendas. In an odd and disturbing way, Breault's narrative takes a rhetorical form similar to some of the prophecies of Jim Jones (Hall 1987, pp. 22, 33–6).

Nightmares are not cause for government intervention, but other matters were. Robyn Bunds informed the US Immigration and Naturalization Service that she had been a party to one of several sham marriages arranged between foreigners and US citizens (Breault and King 1993, pp. 245–6). Bunds' complaint was one of a barrage that Breault's group launched towards government officials in September 1990. The previous March, the defectors had hired an Australian private investigator, Geoffrey Hossack, to help in their struggle against Koresh, and they had begun collecting affidavits.

In August, Breault called his band of defectors to a meeting in Australia and offered a "Bible study on human sacrifices." He told them a story that he said he had been told by Koresh's close associate, Steve Schneider: "God was going to demand that Koresh do with his son Cyrus what Abraham of old was commanded to do with Isaac" (Breault and King 1993, p. 229). (According to the book of Genesis, God instructed Abraham to sacrifice his son, and stopped him only at the last moment.) Breault's wording here is intriguing: he does not say that God actually made any such demand of Koresh, and although he asserts that he is in possession of damaging tape recordings of Koresh's preaching, he does not quote Koresh directly on the matter. Yet the story of child sacrifice, in various versions, became a key element in Breault's account of the dangers at Mount Carmel.

Borrowing a page from the tactics of so-called cults themselves (Hall 1987), Breault used the story at the Australia meeting to "shock" his audience, and "weeded out those [he] couldn't trust" (Breault and King 1993, p. 230). Those whom Breault could trust drew up affidavits about statutory rape, immigration violations, food and water deprivation, and concerns about child sacrifices. Hossack flew to the United States with the affidavits, and in September 1990 he met with officers from the LaVerne, California, police department, and, in Waco, with a Texas Department of Public Safety investigator, Lt Gene Barber of the McClennan County sheriff's department, the McClennan County district attorney, and the assistant US attorney. Hossack also talked with the US Internal Revenue Service and Immigration and Naturalization Service. Soon after these meetings, the FBI and the assistant US district attorney, Bill Johnston, determined that no federal violations had occurred, and closed their case (Breault and King 1993, pp. 228–30, Linedecker 1993, pp. 148–9, USTD 1993, p. D3).

Like the opponents of Peoples Temple, Breault and his allies were frustrated at the lack of official response, and they pursued some of the same avenues of the Jonestown opponents, namely the media and their own court actions. In late 1991 and early 1992, Koresh's adversaries worked through two connected efforts: a television exposé and a custody battle. Like certain Temple opponents, Breault hoped media attention would protect him: "If Vernon [Koresh] knew that Breault had gone public, he'd think twice about trying to kill him again" (Breault and King 1993, p. 256; cf. Hall 1987, p. 268). Breault tried to interest the American media, but he got nowhere. In October of 1991, however, he attracted the interest of the Australian television program, A Current Affair, known for its "in-your-face" investigative journalism. Like one reporter who accompanied Congressman Leo Ryan on his ill-fated to Jonestown (Hall 1987, pp. 257–8), the Australian television reporters projected an objective and impartial facade for most of their visit, and then confronted Koresh at the end with opponents' accusations. The crew of A Current Affair undertook what they believed to be a dangerous mission, exposing Koresh "as a cruel, maniacal, child-molesting, pistol-packing religious zealot who brainwashed his devotees." When the television crew visited Mount Carmel in January 1992, they recalled Jonestown, where the reporters had been killed first. Already, they had been warned by "former cult members" that Mount Carmel might become "another Jonestown" (Breault and King 1993, pp. 256–7, 189, 11–13).

The Australian television report portrayed the Branch Davidians as a "dangerous cult" (Wright 1995b, p. 87). But the program that offered this warning did not yield much in the way of direct results, other than the footage of Koresh preaching that became so familiar to television viewers after the BATF raid. However, the other initiative, the custody battle, was critical to consolidating the movement against Koresh in the US. The effort began in June 1991, well before the television program planning. Marc Breault had returned to the US from Australia, having decided to target Kiri Jewell, who was the pre-teenaged daughter of Branch Davidian member Sherri Jewell and her former husband David, a disc jockey who was never a Davidian. Breault was concerned that the young Kiri was "destined for" the "House of David", but he did not know how to reach David Jewell. Instead Breault approached Sherri Jewell's mother, Ruth Mosher, with what he said was Robyn Bunds's first-hand account of Koresh's statements about his plan to take Kiri as a sexual partner. He confronted Sherri in front of her mother with accusations about Koresh having sex with teenagers, and he got her to admit that a fourteen-year-old girl named Michele had become pregnant at Mount Carmel. He transcribed the conversation and provided it to the LaVerne, California police. (Police sergeant John Hackworth later recounted that the charges were "unsubstantiated, and some of what was alleged occurred in Texas.") Breault also telephoned Gene Barber, of the McClennan County, Texas sheriff's department, and found that an investigation of Koresh in Texas (probably the September 1990, investigation of sham marriages) had been closed for lack of probable cause. On 4 July 1991, Breault wrote Barber a letter detailing his allegations of tax evasion and Koresh's sexual relations with children; he also claimed that a woman had been "raped by Vernon . . . and had a loaded gun pointed at her head." Enclosed with the letter was a "tape of Vernon's [Koresh's] 'Bible study' in which he blatantly and clearly threatens to kill." These efforts did not result in any specific law enforcement actions (Breault and King 1993, pp. 233–45; WP 25 April 1993; USTD 1993, p. D5).

Marc Breault does not seem to have been very sophisticated about the legal process in the US, and he clearly became frustrated when his careful efforts to compile information did not produce action by the authorities. The custody struggle over Kiri Jewell, however, involved a specific grievance on the part of someone with legal standing. On 31 October 1991, in a telephone call from Australia to Michigan, Breault was able to warn Kiri's father, David Jewell, about the fate that awaited Kiri in the "House of David." David Jewell promptly engaged an attorney, coordinated with Breault by email on CompuServe, and worked to obtain a Michigan court order for temporary custody of Kiri when her mother sent the child to Michigan for the Christmas holidays of 1991. Breault and the staff of A Current Affair had planned the January 1992 visit by the Australian television crew partly to distract Koresh's attention from Kiri Jewell. As these events unfolded, the opponents received information that reinforced their vision of cultic destruction and they, in turn, used the information to further spread alarm. In a letter of 1 January 1992 to Breault, David Bunds reported that his sister had told him what his mother, Jeannine Bunds, had reported sometime the previous summer. In this third-hand account, Koresh was said to be telling people that his goals would be accomplished in half a year. "My mother also got the impression of mass suicide or homicide, she was not really sure." Breault also claimed to have learned from former members (the likely source is Jeannine Bunds) that he was at the top of a "hit list" prepared by Koresh.

In the case of Peoples Temple, the struggle between Jim Jones and Grace and Tim Stoen over the custody of John Victor Stoen – the "child-god" whom Jim Jones claimed as his son – had been a cause célèbre of the movement against the group. As at Jonestown, the Davidian custody battle became the focal point. Koresh sent Steve Schneider to help Sherri Jewell in the February court case, and Breault and his allies decided to contact the Schneider family. On 22 February 1992, during preparations for the Jewell custody case, Sue Schneider, Steve's older sister, gave Breault chilling news.

> She said that Steve had called them to say goodbye. He said that he would probably have to do something which would cause him to die, but that he would be resurrected shortly thereafter and fulfill Isaiah 13 and Joel 2. . . . He sounded suicidal. The something which would cause him to die was termed "the end." This was not something limited entirely to Steve himself, but concerned the whole group.
>
> (Breault and King 1993, p. 268)

Breault could not sleep one night, "thinking of my best friend blowing his brains out, or taking cyanide [part of the Jonestown Fla-Vor Aid mass suicide potion], or getting shot in a gun-fight with the authorities" (Breault and King 1993, p. 276; USTD 1993, p. 28).

Despite the fears of Koresh's opponents, however, the custody battle involving the Davidians was strikingly different from Jonestown in its resolution. On 28 February 1992, before the court case was concluded, David and Sherri Jewell reached an agreement for joint custody of Kiri. The case was over. But as in the case of the apostates and relatives who opposed Jim Jones, the experience had given David Jewell, Marc Breault and others a vision that transcended their own individual interests in the custody of particular children. They collectively worked to stop someone they regarded as morally abhorrent. When David Jewell learned of "two thirteen-year-old friends [of Kiri] also targeted to become brides in the House of David, he telephoned the Texas Department of Human Services" (Breault and King 1993, p. 279; Linedecker 1993, p. 144 [quotation]; WP 25 April 1993; WTH 1 March 1993, p. 9A). On the basis of a complaint on 26 February 1992, from "outside the state of Texas," as the affidavit supporting a search warrant put it, Joyce Sparks, of Texas Child Protective Services (CPS), visited Mount Carmel with two sheriff's deputies the next day. In early March, Koresh came to see Joyce Sparks at the Waco CPS office, and Sparks visited the compound twice more, on 6 and 30 April 1992. Davidian children and adults denied any abuse, and examinations of children produced no evidence of current or previous injuries. Over the objections of Sparks, her agency closed the nine-week investigation. Sparks then became a key informant for other government agencies, subsequently talking with the FBI in May 1992, maintaining contact by telephone with Koresh through June 1992, and providing the BATF with floor plans of the Mount Carmel compound in early December 1992 (USTD 1993, pp. D3–4; WP 25 April 1993; ABC *Primetime* 13 January 1994).

Whether or not Koresh's opponents were directly in contact with the anticult movement's Cult Awareness Network (CAN), they increasingly followed the playbook of that organization, operating on multiple fronts to inform authorities and the media, and trying to turn individual Branch Davidian members to their cause, using affidavits, media clips, and evidence gathered from defecting members to build documentation that could in turn be used with subsequent initiatives. In at least one case, in July 1992, a former Davidian named David Block was supposedly "deprogrammed" by someone associated with CAN, Rick Ross.[3] It seems odd that Block could have developed such strong Davidian beliefs as to require deprogramming after living at Mount Carmel for only around two months, from March or soon thereafter until he left in June 1992 (CNN, transcript #260–1, 2 March 93; cf. WP 25 April 1993; USTD 1993, p. D9; Bailey and Darden 1993, p. 156; US District Court 1993, p. 13). There is thus room to wonder whether Block was a *bona fide* convert in the first place or a "plant" sent in from the outside, either by opponents or by an investigating law enforcement agency (both Texas CPS and FBI investigations were active at the time of Block's presence at Mount Carmel).

Soon after the custody court case, in March 1992, Marc Breault, David Jewell, and their allies began to spread the word that the Branch Davidians might commit "mass suicide." All the substantive evidence that Breault and King offer on this key question comes from the ambiguous second- and third-hand statements of Jeannine Bunds and Sue Schneider. Apparently, the statement from Sue about her younger brother Steve Schneider and the account of an unnamed young female apostate carried particular weight (Linedecker 1993, pp. 152–3).

The cited evidence is ambiguous at best, but like Peoples Temple dissidents (Hall 1987, p. 234), Koresh's opponents embellished their accounts in order to magnify the dangers of the organization that they sought to expose. In March 1992, both Jewell and Breault wrote specific statements to David Jewell's congressman in Michigan, Fred Upton, about the possibility that the Branch Davidians would end their lives during Passover. In Breault's words,

> the cult leader, one Vernon Wayne Howell, is planning a mass suicide somewhere around April 18th of this year. . . . Time is fast running out and I *need* to talk to the FBI or someone who can do something. If this does not happen, I believe that over 200 persons will be massacred next month. . . . Every day brings us closer to another Jonestown.
> (Breault and King 1993, pp. 290–1)

Upton forwarded the letter to Chet Edwards, the congressman from Waco, and Edwards passed it to the FBI. In April of 1992, the FBI opened an investigation of Koresh for "involuntary servitude." In May they interviewed Joyce Sparks of Texas CPS. But in June, the FBI closed the investigation, apparently for lack of evidence (Breault and King 1993, pp. 289–92; Linedecker 1993, p. 152; USTD 1993, p. D4 [quotation]).

The account of mass suicide began to percolate through other channels. An April 1992 statement by Australian Bruce Gent argued that government authorities would only take notice "when there's a pile of bodies . . . and then they're going to go in and find them and then it's all over. It'll be another Jonestown" (Breault and King 1993, p. 249). Also in April, the US consulate in Australia sent a cable to Washington, citing "local informants" to the effect that the Branch Davidians were gathering at Mount Carmel, "where they expected to die as part of a mass suicide." The cable went on,

> The informants also told us that they believe that [Koresh] has armed himself with guns and ammunition in order to effect a shootout with authorities if they attempt to enter the cult's Waco property to take away any of the children now living there, or investigate living conditions.

The same month, after hearing reports from the Australian press about a possible mass suicide over the Davidian Passover, a reporter from the *Waco Tribune-Herald* began investigating the Branch Davidians (USTD 1993, p. D4; Bailey and Darden 1993, p. 152; WP 25 April 1993).

Whether there was ever any plan for mass suicide in April 1992, we have no direct evidence. Koresh's opponents spread the report, and although the event failed to materialize, the only public explanation came a full year later with a cryptic statement made in the *Washington Post*: "The suicide plan was called off" (25 April 1993, p. 1). Breault's book with Martin King is silent on why the suicide prediction was not fulfilled. The first record of David Koresh making any statement about mass suicide was his response to *Waco Tribune-Herald* reporter Mark England at the time. Koresh questioned why, if the stories were true, the Branch Davidians would be improving the facilities at Mount Carmel: "I've got the water-well man coming in. I mean, two weeks in a row we're supposed to be committing suicide. I wish they'd get their story straight" (quoted in Bailey and Darden 1993, p. 152).

What was going on here? One likelihood is that the opponents of David Koresh engaged in a long-standing fundamentalist practice – citing "proof texts" – to build a particular theological interpretation out of the deeply apocalyptic discourse that Koresh shared with other renegade Adventist sects. However, it is also evident that Koresh would have perceived increasing external signs of opposition during the first half of 1992. In January, he was the target of the Australian television story centered on his opponents' claims against him. Throughout January and February there was the custody struggle over Kiri Jewell. At the end of February Mount Carmel was visited by Joyce Sparks of the Texas CPS. In early

March, during the same days that Koresh met in Waco with caseworker Sparks, a SWAT (Strategic Weapons and Tactics) law enforcement team undertook practice exercises near the "Mag Bag," a building some miles from Mount Carmel owned by the Branch Davidians.

It was in these circumstances, beginning on 1 February 1992 and accelerating on and after 9 March 1992, that Koresh made his great leap forward towards a siege mentality. He began arming his followers at Mount Carmel with assault rifles and other paramilitary equipment, and he called upon some forty Branch Davidians to come to Mount Carmel from California and England (USTD 1993, pp. B168ff., D3–4). The timing in relation to the custody dispute and subsequent Texas CPS investigation suggests a not unreasonable inference: Koresh probably believed that authorities might try to remove Branch Davidian children by force from the compound (as has happened at other religious communities both before and since).[4] He may have decided to resist any such possible move. No CPS raid ever occurred. However, the efforts of Koresh's opponents precipitated a distinctively heightened siege posture at Mount Carmel. In addition, the narratives of plans for mass suicide and Koresh's decision to further arm his followers contributed directly to the events that led to the ill-fated BATF raid and the subsequent standoff with the FBI. As with Peoples Temple, the stories about the group told by their cultural opponents shaped the dynamic of religious conflict between the sect and the wider world. In form, content, and audience, the narratives of Koresh's opponents invoke the formulaic narratives told within the anticult movement about "cults" (e.g., Zilliox and Kahaner n.d.).

Mass suicide as a narrative of strategic law enforcement

To this point, we have seen how the cultural opponents of David Koresh gleaned a narrative of "mass suicide" from Koresh's preachings and the hearsay accounts of defectors, and concretized and spread that narrative to government agencies and politicians at the state, federal, and local levels, and to the media in Australia and the United States. The question to consider in turn is how narratives about mass suicide became infused into the scenarios that government authorities constructed in relation to the Branch Davidians. To be sure, much other information came into the hands of officials, but by focusing on the question of mass suicide it is possible to trace the influence of a central cultural motif.

The BATF investigation was initiated in May 1992, after a United Parcel Service driver discovered inert grenades in a package to the Branch Davidians and reported his discovery to the McClennan County, Texas, sheriff's department, which passed the information to the BATF office in Austin. BATF agent Davy Aguilera was assigned to investigate, and he met on 4 June 1992 with Waco Assistant US Attorney Bill Johnston and Gene Barber of the sheriff's office (both of whom had been at the 1990 meeting with the Breault faction's private investigator, Geoffrey Hossack). Gene Barber briefed Aguilera on the Branch Davidians. The

Treasury Department reviewers may be technically correct to deny finding evidence of any BATF motivation that "targeted Koresh because of his religious beliefs and life-style." And, clearly, the BATF had its own interests in demonstrating its effectiveness as a law enforcement agency in relation to an armed "cult." As we will see, however the BATF investigation was immersed from the outset in webs of discourse that had been spun by Koresh's opponents (USTD 1993, pp. D4, 121, 125; Breault and King 1993, pp. 228, 240; Bailey and Darden 1993, p. 153).

The BATF investigation was slow getting started. On 23 July 1992, Aguilera sent a report to BATF headquarters listing shipments to the Mag Bag and requesting analysis of whether the Davidians were "possibly converting or manufacturing Title II weapons [unlawful machine guns]." In October 1992, around the time a *Waco Tribune-Herald* reporter asked Bill Johnston about whether the Davidians' firearms were legal, Aguilera was told to begin preparing an affidavit for search and arrest warrants (he was also authorized to set up an undercover house near the Mount Carmel compound). On 2 November 1992, BATF headquarters reported that there was not sufficient evidence to justify a search warrant based on the firearms listed in the 23 July report (USTD 1993, pp. B190, 193–4, D5; US District Court 1993).[5] It was only – and immediately – after the disappointing news about lack of probable cause for a search warrant that the BATF began to contact former members and relatives of Branch Davidians directly.

The contacts were extremely sensitive because the BATF did not want to compromise their secret investigation; for this reason, it would seem, they limited themselves to interviewing committed opponents of Koresh. The contacts were substantial. On 3 November, Davy Aguilera flew to California and met both with LaVerne police and with Isabel and Guillermo Andrade, who had two daughters living at Mount Carmel; one of them, they said, had given birth to a child fathered by Koresh. Aguilera arranged for the Andrades to fly to Waco to visit their daughters from 5 to 7 November, and then he "debriefed" them (what information he obtained is not clear). In addition, on the basis of sexual allegations raised by the defectors, the BATF contacted Joyce Sparks, the Texas CPS caseworker. She reported that she had never been able to confirm any abuse because of staged tours, but she had seen a target range and heard a child talk about (and seen herself) "long guns." She also quoted Koresh as having told her: "My time is coming. When I reveal myself as the messenger and my time comes, what happens will make the riots in L.A. pale in comparison." Defectors and relatives related similarly apocalyptic visions. From LaVerne police sergeant Hackworth on 12 December, Aguilera learned about Marc Breault and the Bunds family. Jeannine Bunds told Aguilera about a "hit list" that she said Koresh once mentioned to her, and David Bunds recounted a conversation in which his father, Donald, had said that he was armed and prepared to die for Koresh. When Aguilera telephoned Breault on 15 December, Breault reinforced these accounts by providing the BATF with the affidavit he had prepared in Australia and offering new information about the posting of armed guards around the compound with instructions to "shoot to kill," and a story of how, in the Treasury Department's words, "a cult member had taken a shot at a newspaper delivery person" (USTD 1993, pp. 27–30, 211, B24, D5–7; Breault and King 1993, p. 294ff.).[6]

The BATF operatives drew no clear and hard line between the gathering of evidence to establish probable cause for the search warrant and obtaining intelligence for tactical planning, which they initiated even while agents continued to gather information for probable cause. Moreover, the BATF tended to treat opponents' accounts as facts without considering whether the former members had "individual biases, or if they had an ax to grind", as two outside reviewers later pointed out (USTD 1993, pp. B19, 129–30).[7] Thus, both the warrant and the BATF's tactical plan for responding to Koresh used information supplied by Koresh's opponents.

Tactical planners adopted the view that the BATF had to take action to deal with the Mount Carmel case. They did so partly because Koresh's documented 1987 attack on George Roden established his propensity toward violence, and partly because of reports to the BATF about "alleged threats against former cult members." The BATF "simply did not want to risk the added possibility that cult members would turn their weapons against members of the community," although they did not specify what evidence led them to this concern. With the decision to take action made, at various points the BATF envisioned three alternative scenarios:

1   attempting to serve warrants peaceably and, if they met resistance, laying a siege against Mount Carmel with negotiations for surrender
2   staging a "dynamic entry," in which agents would storm the compound and secure it for the search and any arrests, and
3   luring Koresh away from the compound in order to facilitate an execution of the search warrant.

Planners tended to discount the third option, partly because Joyce Sparks (incorrectly) told BATF that Koresh rarely, if ever, left Mount Carmel.[8]

The BATF's initial plan, laid out at a meeting in Houston on 18 December 1992, was to pursue the serve-and-siege option. But a 24 December briefing at BATF headquarters in Washington led to demands to slow down tactical-operations planning and requests for further documentation of probable cause. At the request of tactical planners, Davy Aguilera subsequently made arrangements to interview Breault and others jointly with William Buford, a BATF agent who had participated in the 1985 FBI and BATF siege against the Arkansas communal settlement of armed white supremacists who called themselves the Covenant, the Sword, and the Arm of the Lord (CSA). Buford was a member of the Special Response Team (SRT) that would be conducting any tactical operation at Mount Carmel (USTD 1993, pp. B47, 44, D7–8, 43).

Aguilera and Buford went to California, where the two agents interviewed Marc Breault, the Bunds, and the Andrades from 7 to 9 January 1993. After Breault was interviewed, he also helped the BATF locate David Block, the man who had spent several months at Mount Carmel. Breault knew that Block had submitted to deprogramming, and he contacted both *Waco Tribune-Herald* reporter Mark England and Steve Schneider's sister, Sue Schneider, who kept "detailed information on cult awareness groups and cultbusters." From the reporter, Breault managed to get the name of David Block's deprogrammer, Rick Ross, who, it turned out, was trying to persuade Sue Schneider to hire him to deprogram her brother. Breault passed on Ross's name to Aguilera. Apparently Aguilera reached David Block through Ross, and on 25 January 1993 Aguilera and Buford interviewed Block (USTD 1993, pp. 38, 53, 151, D7–8; Breault and King 1993, pp. 303–9).

The BATF agents' interviews with former Davidians and other opponents of Koresh contributed to the tactical thinking of the BATF about how to approach enforcement of weapons laws at Mount Carmel. Aguilera and Buford asked Breault what Koresh would do if he were issued a summons. Breault told them that Koresh would not answer a firearms summons, but he thought Koresh would respond to a Texas CPS summons because he "feels he has beaten that rap." What would Koresh do if authorities surrounded the compound: would he let the women and children go free? "No way," Breault replied, "He would use them as hostages" (USTD 1993, pp. 46, 53; Breault and King 1993, pp. 305–6).

> Several former cult members, most forcefully Breault, noted the distinct possibility that Koresh might respond to a siege by leading his followers in a mass suicide; Breault expressed a particular fear for the children at the Compound. One child who had lived at the Compound told a California police officer, who in turn informed Aguilera, that she had been trained by Koresh and his "Mighty Men" – Koresh's closest and most trusted advisers – to commit suicide in several different ways, including placing the barrel of a handgun in her mouth and pulling the trigger.[9]
>
> (USTD 1993, p. 46)

The BATF agents knew that Block had been "deprogrammed" by Rick Ross. Professional intelligence procedures would have suggested that the validity of both his and other opponents' accounts should remain an open question. Instead, the BATF inserted meanings from the reports of opponents into the scenario that they began to work up about the situation they faced at Mount Carmel. David Block claimed that Koresh controlled the distribution of weapons. It may be that this account was out of date, but it aligned closely with Breault's anticult portrayal of Koresh as a despot who possessed "absolute control" over his followers (Breault and King 1993, p. 309). Overinterpreting information of questionable accuracy, the BATF made serious strategic errors in developing its final tactical plan. More generally, the opponents' narratives concerning Koresh's stance of forcible resistance to authority and the threat of mass suicide shaped the development of the tactical plan. The BATF largely discounted the possibility that Koresh would willingly submit to a peacefully served warrant, so serving a warrant became strongly linked to the siege option.

In late December 1992, the tactical planners saw logistical difficulties in a siege because of the open terrain around the compound and the possibility of injuries, but as late as 21 January, they were still developing this option. However, after considering the 25 January interview with David Block combined with information provided by other opponents and other analysis, the planners shifted strategy toward the dynamic-entry option (USTD 1993, pp. 143–4, 45, D–9). Agent Buford's experience with the CSA standoff made him concerned that a siege would give the Davidians an opportunity to destroy evidence. Tacticians also were concerned about the prospect that a siege might end in mass suicide. For these reasons, "the concept of surrounding the compound and announcing their intention to enforce a warrant was discarded by BATF agents" at tactical meetings in Houston from 27 to 29 January.

Having already concluded that the luring-away option was unlikely to materialize, and having rejected the siege option, the tactical planners put too much weight on the (probably inaccurate) information provided by David Block, that Koresh controlled the weapons. Given the timing of the BATF shift in strategy relative to the times of interviews with opponents, it is likely that bad analysis of intelligence from David Block tipped the balance toward "increasing optimism" about the strategy of dynamic entry. If the assault could be carried out quickly under conditions in which Koresh's followers could not get to the weapons, the element of surprise would minimize the threat of mass suicide, a point that the tactical planners emphasized when they briefed BATF leadership in Washington about their plan on 11 and 12 February. Subsequently, on 26 February, two days before the raid, Treasury Department officials wanted to call it off. However, BATF director Stephen Higgins explained that the use of scores of heavily armed agents to execute the warrant by force was necessary "because BATF feared that Koresh and his followers might destroy evidence or commit mass suicide if given the opportunity" (USTD 1993, pp. 53, B126 [quotation], 142, B49, 65, 179 [quotation]; Breault and King 1993, pp. 303–9 [quotation]).

No doubt sensing that a dynamic-entry raid was a risky undertaking, BATF strategists continued during February 1993 to think about luring Koresh away from the compound. They decided to try to request that Koresh come to Waco, apparently following the scenario envisioned by Marc Breault when he had told investigators that Koresh might respond to a summons concerning child abuse. However, Texas Child Protective Services caseworker Joyce Sparks had already closed her investigation without taking any action, and her supervisor refused to allow the scheduling of such a meeting, so the BATF tried another avenue to the same end. On 12 February 1993, a BATF agent met with the Waco district attorney, Elizabeth Tobin, to discuss the possibilities. Kiri Jewell, the child at the center of the custody battle a year earlier, came to Austin, Texas, with her father on 18 February. She is probably the "female minor" who was taken by BATF agent Aguilera to District Attorney Tobin's office three days later. Whoever the child was, she "decline[d] to testify against Koresh," and the effort to lure Koresh away from Mount Carmel came to an end five days before the BATF raid on the compound (USTD 1993, p. 64, D11–12 [quotation]; see also Breault and King 1993, p. 306; Bailey and Darden 1993, pp. 157–8).

The final scenario for the BATF raid was dynamic indeed. "Ideally, if all went according to the script, all SRT teams would be able to 'exit the transportation vehicles in eight seconds, get into position and make entry at the front door in approximately 33 seconds.'" This rapid execution of the raid was deemed essential to the BATF's ability to keep sect members separated from the weapons supposed to be under Koresh's control (USTD 1993, p. B128).

Paradoxically, the accounts of mass suicide that shaped this scenario of dynamic entry may also have contributed to the failure of the BATF coordinators and commanders to call the raid off, once the element of surprise was known to have been lost. The strategy of dynamic entry invested a great deal in the narrative of surprise. According to BATF reviewers, any dynamic raid gathers "momentum" from the participants' bravado and will to succeed, and from the specters of failure, loss of tactical advantage, criticism by higher officials, and bad public relations. At Mount Carmel these pressures were exacerbated by the lack of any tactical alternative in the form of a fallback or contingency strategy (USTD 1993, pp. 173–5).

Why was there no fallback strategy? It must be recognized that a latent narrative of mass suicide would resurface if the scenario of dynamic entry were abandoned. There is no way to pinpoint the exact magnitude of this influence on command decisions during the attempted raid but certain evidence is suggestive. The BATF had come to the scenario of dynamic entry by a contorted process that eliminated an alternative scenario of serving a warrant and falling back to a siege position if resistance were encountered. Both in the discussions of tactical planners and in briefings up to the highest levels in the chain of command, the surprise raid strategy was justified because the alternative scenario of siege might lead to mass suicide. Perhaps because any scenario of failed surprise would be a scenario of siege, there was an "absence of any meaningful contingency planning for the raid" (USTD p. 175). On the day of the raid, then, to lose the element of surprise was to reopen the scenario of siege and, by extension, mass suicide. The lack of contingency planning, articulated in latent ways with the narrative of mass suicide, amplified the momentum of the raid. Taking mass suicide seriously did not lead to circumspection; instead the BATF forged ahead, working to prevent mass suicide through tactical planning, by designing a scenario in which it would not take place.

In turn, the repressed narrative of mass suicide may have also more directly influenced the actions of BATF commanders on the day of the raid, Sunday, 28 February 1993. On Sunday morning Robert Rodriguez, the BATF undercover agent who was visiting the compound, heard Koresh announce: "Neither the ATF nor the National Guard will ever get me. They got me once and they'll never get me again. They are coming for me but they can't kill me." Rodriguez knew that he had been "burned" (i.e., that his "cover" had been lost), and he knew that Koresh was making specific reference to the raid that had been planned for an hour later. Rodriguez left the compound, returned to the undercover house across the road and reported on his conversation with Koresh. On hearing the news, one BATF "forward observer" at the undercover house was so convinced that the raid would be called off that he started to pack up his gear. But the response of the raid commanders at the command post some miles away was exactly the opposite. BATF agent Chuck Sarabyn, who took the call from Rodriguez, learned that the element of surprise had been lost. In turn, Sarabyn asked Rodriguez whether he had seen any weapons, a call to arms, or preparations. Rodriguez replied that when he had left the compound, people had been praying. After confirming with another agent, who was watching the compound, that there was no sign of activity there, Sarabyn offered the opinion that the raid could still go forward if the agents moved quickly. He briefly conferred with other raid commanders. They broke from their huddle and moved to various tasks, using language like "Let's go," "Get ready to go, they know we're coming," "We better do this ASAP," and "They know ATF and the National Guard are coming. We're going to hit them now." Despite the effort to hurry, the agents conducting the raid did not arrive at the compound until forty minutes after the first report from Rodriguez (USTD 1993, pp. 89 [quotation], 195 [quotations], 166–7, 197, B43).

The Treasury Department review argues that the decision to hurry up "made no sense." Either Koresh was not going to prepare for the raid, in which case accelerating the schedule was unnecessary, or he was going to prepare, in which case – given the time required to get the raid under way – acceleration was useless (USTD 1993, pp. 171–2). In short, hurrying does not salvage lost surprise. Was there then some other available meaningful definition of the situation? One alternative motive that offers at least some rationale for hurrying is concerned with "prevention of an imminent event." If something is about to happen, quick action may prevent it. But what was about to happen? The imminent event could not have been "lost surprise" because at the time of the decision to "hurry up," the lost surprise was an event of the past, not the future. However, a clear concern that shaped the development of tactical strategies in the months before the raid was that Koresh and his followers might commit mass suicide. With the loss of surprise, might the raid commanders ask whether such an action was imminent? The three BATF raid commanders had all been present at the meetings in Houston from 27 to 29 January where concerns about mass suicide were discussed. With this concern already established in all their minds, once the element of surprise was lost, it would have been reasonable for the raid commanders to consider the possibility of mass suicide. At the compound were deeply apocalyptic religious people, reading the Bible after having been informed that the authorities were coming after them. In his conversation with Robert Rodriguez, Koresh referred to "the Kingdom of God," and stated that "the time has come" (USTD 1993, p. 89). Whether the raid commanders received this information from Rodriguez and explicitly interpreted it within the framework of mass suicide, I have no way of knowing. But the motive for accelerating the raid makes a good deal more sense within such a framework than it does within the context of lost surprise.

Moreover, even if preventing the imminent event of mass suicide was not a conscious motive for "hurrying up," the narrative of mass suicide was embedded in the *de facto* fallback position. On the day of the raid, with the media looking on, if the scenario of dynamic entry failed, then a siege – with its latent element of mass suicide – would be the consequence. Presciently, one tactical planner had already understood that with a siege, as the Treasury Department review put it, "ATF probably would have to assault the Compound anyway, once public pressure on ATF to resolve the situation grew and the government's patience wore thin" (USTD 1993, p. 53).[10] The only way to avoid a siege was to "hurry up." On the day of the raid, BATF raid commanders discounted the importance of lost surprise because accepting it would have required cancelling the raid, and cancelling the raid would precipitate a siege. Because of the specter of mass suicide, a siege was not a fallback option; it was an imminent event to be avoided.

Against all reason that the US Treasury Department report can summon, an ill-conceived raid went forward, even though it was deeply compromised immediately before it began. As we have seen, the liturgical narratives of danger told by cultural opponents strongly influenced the rationale and the planning for this raid. But the narratives of the opponents did not fall on deaf ears. Government authorities in the United States have a long tradition of using the state's monopoly on the legitimate deployment of violence to control utopian social movements. During the last quarter-century, the most violent examples that come to mind are the 1974 law-enforcement shootout with the Symbionese Liberation Army at their Los Angeles safehouse and the 1985 Philadelphia police use of fire to destroy the row house of the radical sect MOVE – a fire that killed people and destroyed many other homes in the process (Wagner-Pacifici 1994). These were not police enforcement actions, but annihilations. Such cases suggest an implicit state policy to fulfill purposes of state that go beyond any narrowly conceived issues of law enforcement. In the Treasury Department review of the BATF raid, Frederick S. Calhoun, a historian at the Federal Law Enforcement Training Center, explains that

> the raid fit within an historic, well-established and well-defended government interest in prohibiting and breaking up all organized groups that sought to arm or fortify themselves. . . . From its earliest formation, the federal government has actively suppressed any effort by disgruntled or rebellious citizens to coalesce into an armed group, however small the group, petty its complaint, or grandiose its ambition.
>
> (USTD 1993, p. G7)

I think that this is a true account. It underlines a concern about armed groups independently of whether the arms are legal or not. Both historically and currently, the BATF and its antecedents have been especially concerned when groups obtain weapons, and when they do so in a way that claims legitimate authority over land on the basis of some ideology that justifies their cause. The BATF thus may have been predisposed, more than other agencies, to read the narratives about an apocalyptic group in ways that went to the core of their own historic mission.

What the statement fails to mention is government antipathy toward groups which, although not armed, advance social visions that are alien to established social mores. It would be a mistake to think that antipathy toward utopian sectarian groups is universally shared by government officials. But it would be equally mistaken to ignore an ideology of state social control of radical sects that binds together officials from a variety of agencies at the federal, state, and local levels of government. Governmental agencies other than the BATF investigated the Branch Davidians, but they lacked the hard evidence necessary to intervene in the affairs of the sect. Yet broader concerns of the state about the Branch Davidians – especially concerning sexual and physical abuse of children – were strongly raised in BATF agent Aguilera's application for a search warrant for Mount Carmel (US District Court 1993). In effect, the BATF became the lead agency because it was the agency of the state with the strongest claim of jurisdiction, even though the evidence of weapons violations was circumstantial and inferential, and the basis for the arrest warrant for Koresh (who was to be detained without bond) is unclear (see US District Court 1993). As a BATF spokesperson later noted, a successful BATF operation would have opened Mount Carmel to the intervention of other government agencies (WP 25 April 1993). In part by using the icon of mass suicide, the cultural opponents of the Branch Davidians gained considerable influence in the development of a rationale and strategy for the raid because of an elective affinity between their concerns and the historic mandate of the BATF as a first line of state defense against subversion.

The standoff, the tank assault, and the fire

The BATF raid was a monumental failure. The next day, 1 March, under intense national media coverage, the federal government designated the FBI as the lead agency in dealing with the situation. The FBI moved to replace BATF personnel and control the perimeter around the Mount Carmel Compound, and they began negotiations to try to convince the Branch Davidians to release children and end the standoff. In telephone conversations, David Koresh denied that the group was planning to commit mass suicide, and he seemed amenable to coming out in return for the nationwide broadcast of a taped message that he would provide. However, all did not go as planned. The Christian Broadcast Network duly played the tape the next day but, late in the afternoon, Koresh was still preaching to his followers in the compound, and around 6 p.m. Steve Schneider informed the FBI that God had spoken to Koresh and told him to wait. Later,

Figure 2.2 A US government helicopter makes a low pass over the Mount Carmel compound during the standoff in early April 1993. Cut off from ordinary
communication with the outside world, Davidian members have unfurled a ban-
ner that reads "1st seal, Rev 6:12, Ps 45, Rev 19, Ps 2, Ps 18, Ps 35, KJV," referring
to chapters and verses of the King James version of the Bible.

Source: AP/WORLDWIDE PHOTOS

the FBI reported that the group had planned a mass suicide under the ruse of a
surrender, but that Koresh had called it off (Scruggs *et al.* 1993, pp. 35–6).

Thus began a long series of three-cornered negotiations between the FBI, the
Branch Davidians, and God. The FBI pursued negotiations with the Branch
Davidians, but they also brought an arsenal of strategic tactics to bear against the
group. Negotiators sought to build rapport with the Davidians, establishing a
relationship on small and large matters, from obtaining the release of puppies and
transmitting messages from relatives, to negotiating the terms of surrender. On
their side, the Davidians left any decision about surrender to Koresh, who in
general claimed to await instruction from God and the end of Passover, and in
particular became increasingly caught up in writing a new interpretation of the
Bible's book of Revelation, "unlocking" the Seven Seals that would finally reveal
God's intentions for the end times. Koresh also kept asking to speak with the
BATF undercover agent, Robert Rodriguez, who had visited the Davidians for
Bible study and espionage, but the FBI refused. Negotiators spent hours on the
phone trying to negotiate a resolution to the impasse, but often ended up
listening to Koresh expound on "the kingdoms of this world" becoming "the
kingdoms of our Lord and of his Christ."

While negotiations dragged on over days that became weeks, the FBI "Hostage Rescue Team" (HRT) tightened its control of the space around the compound. Sometimes negotiations were coordinated with other acts, such as the planting of surveillance bugs in milk cartons sent in to the group. But negotiators chafed at certain other actions, such as the decision to cut off electricity from time to time. The HRT circled ever tighter, removing diesel and gasoline storage tanks and vehicles, and using bulldozers to clear away trees, fences, and other obstructions from around the building. Bright floodlights began to light the scene at night, and the FBI played loud music, including Tibetan chants. Other than generating complaints from Koresh and Schneider, these tactics seem to have had little effect. As negotiators and psychological experts became ever more convinced that the members of the sect would not come out peacefully, they began to consider the use of "stress escalation" procedures such as introducing tear gas into the building. On 9 April, discussions of this possibility were initiated at FBI headquarters and with the Attorney General, Janet Reno. On 17 April, after reviewing an analysis of the situation at the compound, Reno approved the proposed tear-gas plan. President Bill Clinton approved it the next day, and FBI armored vehicles removed more cars, including David Koresh's personal pride, his Chevy Camaro. As the vehicles were being towed away, an FBI sniper saw a cardboard sign placed in a compound window. It read, "Flames await" (Scruggs *et al.* 1993, pp. 36–109; quote, p. 109).

The CS gas assault on the compound on 19 April, and the ensuing fire (whatever its cause) fulfilled only one state objective, that of suppressing an armed group. An enormous national audience watched the inferno on real-time national newscasts. Later Reno, and subsequently Clinton, defended the decision to move ahead with the assault as necessary to prevent further child abuse. Reno maintained, "We had information that babies were being beaten." But it turned out that there was "no contemporaneous information" about any child abuse that posed an imminent threat. Janet Reno had been misled. The children who were to be saved from abuse died. Was this the mass suicide that Marc Breault and the other opponents had predicted? The government disclaimed any direct responsibility for the fire, and hence for the deaths (Scruggs *et al.* 1993). But this was a narrow analysis concerned only with immediate causes. It seems incontrovertible that the fire that occurred would not have happened in the absence of the FBI assault. Even if the FBI assault was not the sole cause of the fire, the assault was an antecedent condition causally necessary to any explanation of the subsequent fire, the deaths that ensued, and the obliteration of Mount Carmel.

If the Branch Davidians actually started the fire on purpose, as evidence presented by the FBI suggested, their act certainly could be understood as an act of mass suicide. Because such an act would snatch victory away from their opponents at the cost of their own lives, it would directly parallel the deaths of over nine hundred people in the 1978 mass suicide and murder at Jonestown. In both cases the actions emerged in the process of extended and pitched conflict with opponents. At Jonestown, the threat to the destruction of the community was more emblematic than immediate, but at Mount Carmel on 19 April the FBI was engaged in the rapid and systematic physical destruction of the Branch Davidians' home. In the face of the continuing assaults, people at Mount Carmel died in different parts of the building, some from the fire, others from gunshot wounds, either self-inflicted or "mercy killings" at the hands of others. The deaths in the conflagration at Mount Carmel thus lacked the ritualistic and collective character of the mass suicide at Jonestown.[11]

The play of narratives about mass suicide in the FBI standoff with the Branch Davidians up to 19 April would be a subject in its own right. However, even a cursory examination of the FBI construct of mass suicide suggests that they viewed it as an inherent and static predisposition, rather than a sect's possible response to a dynamic and shifting situation. After the standoff had begun, and before the CS attack, FBI negotiators quizzed David Koresh and Steve Schneider repeatedly on whether the group intended to commit mass suicide, and the answer was always no (Scruggs et al. 1993, pp. 30, 33, 60, 65). However, Koresh did acknowledge that he had been preparing to fight authorities for years, and he warned negotiators that the Davidians might "blow the tanks to pieces." On several occasions Steve Schneider claimed that the FBI wanted to burn the compound down in order to hide evidence supportive of the Davidians' interpretation of events, and he also suggested that the FBI ought to use fire to force people to come out, nevertheless reaffirming that people did not want to leave (Scruggs et al. 1993, pp. 68, 87, 88).

After the conflagration, the FBI justified the tactical view they had taken in planning the assault – that mass suicide would not be a likely outcome – by citing David Koresh's future-oriented statements *in the absence of the assault*, such as his interest in auctioning his book rights (NYT 22 April 1993, p. A1). This static view of Koresh's predisposition was based on a tendency that governmental authorities at the time shared with the anticult movement, a tendency to see the dynamics of "cults" as *internal* to such groups, rather than examine *external* social interaction in conflict between a sectarian group and its opponents and the authorities themselves. Clearly the Davidians in the compound were a solidary group during the standoff, and they held off from self-destruction so long as conditions remained relatively stable. But, on present evidence, the destruction of their compound by tanks seems to have changed their calculus dramatically, toward a choice they were prepared to take: self-immolation over surrender.

The blurred meanings of narratives

Unfortunately, both authorities and opponents (and sometimes the media) have compelling vested interests in depicting the dynamics of "cults" as internal rather than external, and they are thus systematically biased toward misunderstanding the very social processes in which they assert the legitimacy of their interests. Despite the clear significance of the actions taken by cultural opponents, they have never seriously weighed their own roles in negative outcomes of pitched conflicts with alternative religious movements. This avoidance of critical review does not sit well with the legitimacy routinely extended by some government authorities and the media to operatives of the anticult movement.

The *modus operandi* of anticult groups is to target "cults" with increasing pressure on a number of fronts (Zilliox and Kahaner n.d.). At both Jonestown and Mount Carmel, the cultural opponents succeeded in bringing authorities and the media to their side. In turn, the opponents could point to the tragic outcomes to validate their initial alarm. There is no reason to doubt that Koresh's opponents pursued their mission according to the dictates of their consciences, and it is unthinkable that any opponent of alternative religions would want to precipitate violence in order to prove a point. Nevertheless, in effect, the anticult movement has benefitted from "cult" tragedy.

It is worth noting that in cases where the anticult movement did not play an active role in precipitating conflict, governmental authorities have sometimes been able to bring a standoff to a peaceful resolution – as with the armed Arkansas communal white supremacists called the Covenant, the Sword, and the Arm of the Lord (CSA). On the other hand, by 1993 there had been truly devastating and disastrous results in two cases where the anticult movement played a strong role: Jonestown and Mount Carmel. An obvious conclusion can be drawn from these facts: insofar as participants in the anticult movement fail to acknowledge that their strategies can lead to the escalation of apocalyptic conflict, both the media and government authorities should treat the movement as lacking portfolio in matters concerning deviant religious sects. More generally, governmental authorities would do well to bring certain anticult movement practices – especially kidnapping and forced deprogramming – under strict law enforcement.

The media bring a cultural perspective to their reportage on events (Gans 1979; Gamson and Modigliani 1989). As the cases of Jonestown and Mount Carmel both demonstrate, they are particularly vulnerable to influence exerted by cultural opponents of unusual religious groups. With freedom of the press, limitations on the media are largely ethical. However, the ethical response of journalism as a profession to media coverage of the Waco affair (Society of Professional Journalists 1993) sometimes seems shallow and self-justifying.[12] Until journalists take more seriously the social dynamics of religious conflict between opponents and groups that they label as cults, stories of "cult-busting" will continue to follow the genre of the heroic exposé.

The first amendment to the US Constitution legally forbids the state, in contrast to the media, from taking sides in matters of religion. Defenders of state action will no doubt emphasize the obligation of the state to enforce its laws.[13] They already claim (for example in the Treasury Department review) that enforcement was the objective at Mount Carmel. But such a defense of state action is flawed. It would be one thing if cultural opponents and governmental authorities acted independently of one another, even if they shared an affinity of goals due to different interests. But the emergence of narratives about mass suicide shows something quite different. The degree to which certain governmental authorities consciously took up the cause of the cultural opponents remains an open question. Whatever the answer to that question, the connection of governmental action to cultural opposition runs much deeper.

Mount Carmel does not merely bear comparison to Jonestown as a similar but independent event. Rather, there was a *genetic* bridge between Jonestown and Mount Carmel. David Koresh himself did not originate the invocation of "mass suicide," even though the image came to figure significantly in how the Waco affair developed. The connection came not through the apocalyptic groups themselves, but via a bridge created by the capacity of the Davidians' opponents to affect the exercise of state authority by raising the specter of mass suicide. The construction of this bridge was facilitated in part by national operatives of what has come to be called the "anticult movement" (ACM) (Wright 1995b, pp. 88–90; Lewis 1995). Drawing on wider anticult strategies, the opponents of Koresh took cultural meanings about mass suicide derived from the apocalypse at Jonestown, reworked them, and inserted them into accounts that they offered about the Branch Davidians. In turn, the opponents' reports about mass suicide directly structured the development of tactical scenarios for the BATF raid, and they may well have figured in the motive structures of BATF commanders on the day of the raid. In these direct yet presumably unselfconscious ways, BATF operations became subordinated to the narratives of cultural opposition.

Like the Jonestown drama, these events were complex. However, it seems uncontrovertible that the efforts of Davidian apostates against David Koresh were the animating process and the *sine qua non*, without which the BATF raid would not have taken place in the way that it did, and perhaps not at all. This process and outcome differ substantially from Jonestown, but adequate explanation of Waco involves exactly the same factors, namely, a group of cultural opponents who were able to focus mass media attention on the Branch Davidians and, more importantly, to mobilize overwhelming state power affected by their frame of interpretation.

Meanings in the realm of public life are formed in part by the stories that people tell, and the ways that other people hear these stories. On the basis of the stories that they hear, along with their own personal and cultural structures of meaning, and in relation to their own readings of their resources and situations, people make new meanings in both their accounts of past events and their scenarios of projected actions (cf. Sewell 1992, pp. 16–17). Understanding public meanings, then, depends upon excavating narratives embedded in social activities that feed into the domain of public life. Sociologists Jeffrey Alexander and Philip Smith (1993) have suggested that such processes of public meaning formation depend on the operation of binary codes, and they have analyzed a number of situations where people have invoked "Democratic" and "Counter-democratic" codes in public controversies in the United States.

In these terms, the anticult movement's stereotype of "cults" portrays cultists and their cultural structures of social organization as counterdemocratic. The anticult narrative of mass suicide is a virtual Triptik along the route of the Counter-democratic code's description of "passive," "hysterical," "unrealistic," and fundamentally "mad" people engaged in "secret" and "suspicious" activities that depend on "arbitrary" exercise of "power" at the whim of a "personality" (Alexander and Smith 1993, pp. 162–3). But in unfolding daily life, the play of narratives – even ones that fit a code – does not necessarily, or even typically, work in binary ways. Instead, examination of public meanings about the Branch Davidians suggests that in unfolding situations where different people tell their own "intrinsic" narratives – stories about issues and events to which they are mutually oriented – there is a historicity of emergent meanings. People do not frame their own narrative constructions simply by invoking two sides of a binary set of codes. Instead, cultural meanings become reworked and revised through the shading that occurs in the shift of narrative from one meaningful circumstance to another. Koresh's opponents certainly invoked a counterdemocratic code, but they did so through narratives drawing on cultural meanings about mass suicide that were historically formed and specifically tied to the apocalypse at Jonestown. For Koresh's opponents and the BATF, those narratives became revised through improvisation, resulting in novel, non-binary shifts in nuance and contexts of significance that altered meanings. Such narratives are not contained within any single frame of social reality, such as the public sphere. Instead, public narratives may be shaped by the most private experiences. Personal narratives of salvation from the evil of a "cult" can shape cultural cries for help, and in turn become elements of official state discourse.

Apocalyptic religious violence at Jonestown and Waco

There are substantial differences between Waco and Jonestown. True, both cases involve a refusal on the part of leaders of apocalyptic religious movements to submit to the power of external authority, and in each case, sect members killed external "opponents." But the final deaths of the Branch Davidians were not the highly organized mass suicide that Jones and his leadership group orchestrated. In Jonestown, the leaders launched their well prepared plan immediately after the murders of Congressman Ryan and the others, whereas the Branch Davidians did not choose death over submission to external authority until fifty days after the BATF raid, and then only in response to the FBI tank and teargas assault. Certain details about what happened on 19 April remain in dispute but, no matter how the fire started, few of the Davidians made any attempt to leave the burning building. Compared to Jonestown, the external threat was far more immediate, and the refusal to yield to teargas-injecting tanks can be plausibly viewed as an affirmation of martyrdom. Whether this martyrdom amounted to "mass suicide" is more ambiguous, but the incidents at Jonestown and Waco share two central sequential features: the killing of outsiders by members of the sect, followed by the group's own collective death as a community. The sociological question then is whether the outcome at Waco is best explained by factors parallel to those that we have shown at work at Jonestown, components of what we have termed apocalyptic religious conflict.

Clearly, other factors played into the events that led up to the final debacle. For one thing, the BATF itself was not simply driven by the anticultism of the cultural opponents. It had its own institutionalized tradition as something of a wild-west outfit, defending the state's monopoly over the legitimate means of violence, historically directed especially toward *groups* that take up arms and establish a "state within a state," engaging in or threatening non-legitimate violence within their own domain. In addition, the desire to justify the BATF federal budget allocation may have enhanced the bureaucratic interest in staging a "big bust," and BATF contacts with journalists before the raid may indirectly have destroyed the element of surprise on the day of the raid. Moreover, the dynamics of policy and action within the FBI during the siege (defined as a "hostage situation") were not only influenced by an anticult mentality (Wright 1995b; Lewis 1995); they were also affected by the media spotlight (Richardson 1995; Shupe and Hadden 1995) and by the issue of child abuse pitched to Janet Reno, itself a recurrent (and sometimes dubious) accusation raised by the anticult movement toward "cults" (Ellison and Bartkowski 1995).

Yet these factors add nothing of necessity or sufficiency to the explanation of Waco. If anything, the implementation of state and media agendas at Waco was simply a more extreme reenactment of events leading up to the Jonestown tragedy, perversely induced to a significant degree precisely by the cultural opponents' invocation of "another Jonestown." That is, sociological explanation of the genesis of the Waco debacle must consider the complex interaction of the same factors at work at Jonestown: cultural opponents, including apostates and relatives, who mobilize mass media coverage in an anticult frame, and draw in sympathetic or institutionally concerned segments of the state. In the case of Waco, these were state agencies that regarded the group as challenging state legitimacy (and in the case of the FBI, their own authority).

We can evaluate this explanation of Waco by considering the plausibility of hypothetical scenarios. The siege mentality and weapons acquisition at Mount Carmel began in earnest in early 1992, when *A Current Affair*'s television exposé, the custody court case, and the CPS inquiry were initiated, all through efforts of Breault and his allies. Without the increased weapons acquisition, it is not clear that evidence would have been produced that would have led the BATF to pursue an investigation. But even assuming that the BATF would have come to the point of investigating the Davidians without the concerted actions of the cultural opponents, the dense web of multiple agency concern in which the BATF acted was clearly the product of the opponents' efforts, and it was only with information provided by the opponents that the BATF was able to obtain a warrant. Most important, without the cultural opponents and the CPS investigator whom they rallied to their cause, the BATF strategy of dynamic entry would have been evaluated very differently, and alternative strategies – either placing the compound under siege or serving a warrant on Koresh away from the compound – would have received more favorable attention. Finally, to take a far-fetched hypothesis, without the efforts of the cultural opponents, the element of surprise would probably not have been lost on the day of the BATF raid, because news reporters probably would not have known about the Branch Davidians, since the group did not seek mass publicity but recruited among social networks of Seventh Day Adventists. True, the BATF might have wanted to stage a big raid for its own publicity purposes but, as we have already seen, the choice of a strategy of dynamic entry that made the raid a big operation was itself an outgrowth of cultural opponents' input into BATF strategy, not an action autonomously generated within the BATF. At Jonestown, the overall conflict could have followed alternative routes to disaster, but for the Davidians the fire was highly contingent on the botched BATF raid, subsequent siege, and tank attack. In the absence of the cultbusters' successful efforts to mobilize journalists, state officials, and politicians, it is thus difficult to generate a plausible scenario in which the deaths would have occurred.

This is not to say that cultural opponents are inherently powerful, or that they conspire to produce cult disasters. Instead, it seems that apostates and their allies in contemporary religious conflicts, following a general *modus operandi* developed within the anticult movement, take actions on multiple fronts. These may be intense enough to spark consequences that involve the dynamic interaction of an apocalyptic group with the opposition of legitimate authority under the spotlight of media coverage. These are conditions conducive to apocalyptic religious violence. Though cultural opposition has little power on its own, it seems *necessary* though *not sufficient* – in the strictly explanatory sense of those terms – as a *catalyst*. In effect, the actions of cultural opponents arrange previously disconnected elements into more coherent opposition that becomes greater than the sum of its parts. In confrontation with strongly apocalyptic movements, at Jonestown and Mount Carmel, the consequences were open conflict and, in different ways, collective death in the face of anticipated and increasing subjection to external authority. The interactions among apostates, other cultural opponents, the media, and the state were highly contingent, and precarious in relation to other contingencies. The consequences were hardly necessary, and we cannot rule out other dynamics that might have similar outcomes. Still, the parallels between two substantially different groups suggest a certain robustness to the process of religious conflict that results in apocalyptic violence. One way of determining whether that process has wider relevance is to consider the problem in an entirely different society: Japan.

3

THE VIOLENT PATH OF AUM SHINRIKYŌ

Sylvaine Trinh with John R. Hall

The Japanese sect Aum Shinrikyō, founded by self-appointed guru Asahara Shōkō in the 1980s, differs markedly from Peoples Temple and the Branch Davidians. The two American groups killed protagonists and then died themselves. Aum Shinrikyō went much further; it perpetrated an unprecedented act of indiscriminate murder. How and why, on 20 March 1995, did this religious movement launch its deadly sarin gas attack in the Tokyo subway system, killing twelve people and injuring thousands?

After the subway attack, two main hypotheses emerged in Japan. In the "ideological" scenario, Aum Shinrikyō was trying to destabilize the state by eliminating as many officials as possible. In this view, releasing sarin gas in the subway amounted to a purely political act of terrorism, prosecutable under Japan's antisubversive law of 1952. The second hypothesis – "brainwashing" – was based on the analysis of psychiatrists who studied several ex-disciples treated in hospitals. They concluded that a pathology of collective madness had prevented individuals from controlling their own actions.

Analytically, the two hypotheses seem diametrically opposed. The first

Sylvaine Trinh provided an English text based on a research she conducted in Japan from March to September 1996. She analyzed various publications, the daily newspapers (mainly *Japan Times* and *Asahi Shinbun*), the weekly Japanese press (in particular, *Bungei shunju, Chūō kōron, Aera, Shokun, Takarajima*) and public court reports, and conducted in-depth interviews with some twenty individuals, including ex-*shukkesha* (believer monks), religious and political figures, attorneys, and members of victims' associations. She has benefitted from support and discussions with her colleagues and friends at the Centre d'Analyse et d'Intervention Sociologiques (CADIS) in Paris. She thanks them. An earlier publication, Trinh 1997, draws on the same research. John R. Hall edited the text that Sylvaine Trinh provided, and added additional analysis. Dave Brewington contributed research in the United States. Rika Sato gathered research materials in Japan; she also provided invaluable insights that have been incorporated into the analysis. Shizuko Oyama checked Japanese spellings in English. We thank them all for their assistance. Japanese names are given in Japanese style, with the surname first. "Aum Shinrikyō" is sometimes shortened to "Aum" for simplicity.

centers on the violent acts of a politically oriented religious organization committed to violence against the state. The second is psycho-social, centered on a thesis that deeply alienated individuals would express their distress by directing violence outward. Of these two hypotheses, the first condemns the responsible persons without appeal, whereas the second suggests that those concerned did not act of their own volition.

It is worth revising and supplanting these with a third hypothesis, namely, that the trajectory of Aum Shinrikyō can be explained by the model of apocalyptic religious violence we already have explored in relation to Jonestown and Waco. In this hypothesis, violence came to serve as a catalyst to determine who would survive the day of the Last Judgment. Aum Shinrikyō initially was supposed to save all humanity. Eventually the group did not simply await an Apocalypse; it used violence to create one.

No definitive history of Aum Shinrikyō has yet been written, but enough is now known to explore the hypothesis of apocalyptic religious violence. No matter what the parallels with Jonestown and Waco, however, there is a striking difference. Operatives in Aum Shinrikyō murdered some of the sect's recalcitrant members and they wreaked havoc in the world, but the group never engaged in anything remotely like a mass suicide.

A foreshadowed surprise: the Tokyo subway attack

In their dealings with Aum before the Tokyo sarin attack, the Japanese police may have been inhibited by laws meant to prevent the state repression of religion that had occurred in late Meiji and early Shōwa Japan (Reader 1996, p. 77, n. 14). In 1951, toward the end of the post-Second World War occupation, the Japanese government enacted a Religious Corporation Law. As Sheldon Garon (1997, p. 208) writes, this law "effectively protected postwar religions from the type of official interference experienced before 1945." The government retained the right to disband a religious organization that carried out "acts which clearly can be recognized as having violated laws and ordinances and have done considerable harm to public welfare" (quoted in Garon 1997, p. 209), but such a judgment was a matter for the courts, not the police.

Whatever the sensitivity of the Japanese police to religious freedom, with hindsight it seemed obvious to many observers that they should have targeted Aum Shinrikyō before the Tokyo subway attack. For one thing, 20 March 1995 was hardly the first occasion that Japanese people had found themselves subjected to suspicious toxic fumes. On 2 July 1993, about one hundred residents of Tokyo's Kōtō area complained about noxious white smoke escaping from buildings belonging to Aum Shinrikyō. Aum staff refused to allow the authorities to enter the compound and the authorities did not force the issue, perhaps because the buildings belonged to a religious organization.

The authorities were no more effective in dealing with a far more dramatic event that took place in Matsumoto. On 27 June 1994, a specially equipped truck dispersed poisonous gas in the parking lot of a neighborhood supermarket, killing seven people and injuring 200 others. The chemical used in the attack was later determined to be sarin, a substance developed by the Nazis in 1938, but never before known to have been deployed as a weapon. Sarin remains liquid in a closed container, but when exposed to the air releases highly toxic fumes. Extremely small doses can cause serious respiratory troubles, and as little as 10 milligrams can result in paralysis and death.

The police were not able to identify the perpetrators of the Matsumoto attack, but they did have the name of a certain Kōno Yoshiyuki who had given the alert. By coincidence, Kōno worked for a chemicals business, and he had brought some chemicals home for use in his garden. Despite the fact that the wife of Kōno had been asphyxiated and remained in a coma, the media immediately named him as the author of the event. Only later would the authorities establish Aum Shinrikyō's culpability.

A little less than two weeks after the Matsumoto deaths, an incident occurred in a village in the same prefecture. Kamikuishiki, sixty miles from Tokyo, with a population of around 1,700, was where Aum Shinrikyō had established its main headquarters. On 6 July 1994, several residents there complained of nausea, and eye and nose irritation from toxic fumes. Despite good weather, vegetation around Aum buildings had started to wither. The failure of the police to investigate this incident is baffling. The recent Matsumoto sarin attack had occurred in the very town where a case involving Aum members was about to go to trial. True, Kamikuishiki was not close enough to Matsumoto to establish any immediate link, and the nature of the gas in Kamikuishiki could not immediately be determined. But Aum Shinrikyō had been at odds with the villagers and authorities there virtually from the day they arrived, and the group's leader, Asahara Shōkō, had spoken publicly in recent months about the threat of sarin gas attacks.

Eventually the police took samples from the soil around Aum buildings in Kamikuishiki. In November 1994, long before the Tokyo attack, analysis indicated the presence of residual decomposed sarin chemicals. The police then began to link the two incidents (Reader 1996, pp. 78–83). This news came out in Japan's largest newspaper, the *Yomiuri Shimbun*, on the first day of 1995. "Traces of an organic phosphorus compound that could have resulted from sarin were detected in Kamikuishiki, a small village at the foot of Mount Fuji," the paper reported. Making an explicit connection, the article continued, "Police suspect sarin could have been produced in Kamikuishiki about twelve days after Matsumoto's poisoning incident" (quoted in Kaplan and Marshall 1996, p. 215).

Aum Shinrikyō had often reacted aggressively to allegations against it, and its response in this situation was true to form: the sect was the victim of the attack in Kamikuishiki, not its perpetrator. In a press conference on 4 January, Aum distributed a video claiming that some "state power" was responsible, and the tape's narrator maintained that the FBI had used chemical weapons against the Branch Davidian compound near Waco, Texas (Kaplan and Marshall 1996, p. 217).

A little less than two months later, on 28 February 1995, an event occurred that proved decisive. In Tokyo, a group of four or five men used a rental van to abduct a sixty-eight-year-old notary, Kariya Kiyoshi, who was known to be at odds with Aum Shinrikyō. Kariya had been concealing the location of his sister, a former Aum member who had refused to donate land and had then escaped from sect confines. As trial evidence eventually established, Aum operatives kidnapped Kariya, gave him a dose of an anesthetic used as a truth serum and, when he unexpectedly died from the drug, destroyed his body in an industrial incinerator facility in Kamikuishiki. By the time of the kidnapping, police had placed Aum strongly in their investigative sights and they quickly traced the rental van to an Aum member, placed the sect under suspicion for the kidnapping, and initiated a national search for one of its disciples, Matsumoto Tsuyoshi, aged twenty-nine (Brackett 1996, pp. 121–4; Kaplan and Marshall 1996, pp. 227–8).

According to an account that later circulated widely among police and the media, these were the developments that triggered the Tokyo attack. Some Aum Shinrikyō disciples served in the police, and they may have warned Aum leaders that sect properties were to be raided in the search for the missing Kariya. However, Aum's leader, Asahara Shōkō, would hardly have needed inside information. According to one reporter, on around 17 March police leaked word to journalists that some 2,000 police personnel would search Aum Shinrikyō's Kamikuishiki headquarters on 20 March, that is, the very day when the Tokyo subway attack took place. Asahara seems to have gained about the same advance warning (Reader 1996, p. 85; JT 10 December 1997).

Well before the Tokyo gas attack took place, events during 1994 and early 1995 raised strong suspicions about Aum Shinrikyō. Indeed, long before then Aum had a history of antagonisms with neighbors of its communal settlements and with families of its members. As early as 1989 concerned families had formed a group they called the Aum Shinrikyō Victims' Association. Overall, the absence of police intervention before 20 March 1995 is thus a testament to the uphill struggle that opponents of a sect can face. Yet nothing that the police or anyone else might have suspected could have prepared them for the enormity of the action in the Tokyo subway system.

At the peak of the morning rush hour on 20 March 1995, the perpetrators of the attack placed packages containing sarin in five cars on the Hibiya, Marunouchi and Chiyoda subway lines, puncturing the packages with umbrellas as they got off the trains. Authorities received the first reports of casualties at 8:14 a.m. The Kasumigaseki station, where all three subway lines come together, was hit the hardest.

Kasumigaseki serves the heart of the Japanese government bureaucracy: the Ministries of Foreign Affairs, Construction, Transportation, Agriculture, Labor, Finance, Post and Telecommunications, as well as the National Police, the High Court of Tokyo, and the Ministry of the Interior. Several hundred yards to the north are the headquarters of the Tokyo police and the Ministry of Justice. To the south lies the Ministry of Education. Government employees are generally expected to arrive at work at 8:30 a.m., precisely the time when the trains carrying the deadly gas converged on the station.

Subway personnel, police, firemen, emergency assistance teams, and news reporters got to the scene quickly, and they improvised intervention as best they could all morning. Japanese Self-Defense Force specialists did not arrive until 1:30 p.m. All told, twelve people died, and 5,510 eventually received medical treatment. Among them were sixty-eight policemen and forty-eight firemen. Some twenty different subway stations reported injuries. Many people continued to experience symptoms four years later.

After the attack, police raided Aum Shinrikyō so quickly and with such force as to suggest that their action had already been planned. On 22 March, with exceptional media coverage, 2,500 policemen, some of them wearing gas masks, entered the sect's compound in Kamikuishiki, describing the raid as a part of their investigation of the Kariya notary's abduction. They confiscated gas masks and took possession of two tons of chloroform and ethane, and fifteen bottles of ethylene. These basic materials would have been enough to produce 5.6 tons of sarin, a quantity sufficient to kill ten million people. They also seized equipment that could be used to manufacture the gas, as well as sizable quantities of raw materials for producing dynamite. In Asahara Shōkō's safe in the center of the building complex, they found ten kilograms of gold ingots and 700 million yen in cash (roughly seven million dollars; at the time, 100 yen equalled approximately one US dollar). They also found some fifty emaciated individuals whom they concluded were suffering from malnutrition or drugs. At the sect's nearby heliport, firemen discovered an unauthorized storage facility containing more than 2,000 liters of fuel, along with a Soviet-manufactured Mi-17 helicopter that belonged to Maha-Posya, a Tokyo company whose president was Asahara Shōkō.

Four days later, on 26 March, police returned to the Kamikuishiki compound, again equipped with gas masks, this time accompanied by canaries to detect toxic gases. They also raided Aum sites elsewhere in Japan. At one site, in Fujinomiya in the prefecture of Shizuoka, they discovered human bones. On 14 April, police conducted simultaneous searches of 120 Aum buildings throughout the country.

Almost immediately after the attack, the media portrayed Aum Shinrikyō as the likely perpetrators. The shock over what was widely regarded as terrorism ran deep among the Japanese population, yet some people seized on developments that might have seemed to exonerate the movement. For example, they wondered about an incident on 19 April (the same day that, in the United States, a terrorist bomb blew up the Oklahoma City federal building in retaliation for government actions against the Branch Davidians). Even though many Aum Shinrikyō disciples had been arrested by then, someone released an unknown toxic gas in the Yokohama station and around 500 people had to be treated in hospitals.

By mid-May, police had taken approximately 200 Aum disciples into custody. Among them were key figures of the movement's inner circle. Asahara himself remained at large, and the police put out a nationwide wanted bulletin. On 16 May, they finally discovered the guru in a secret room in a building at Kamikuishiki and arrested him.

Overall, during an investigation that lasted a full year, the police served 613 arrest warrants on disciples of Aum Shinrikyō. By March 1996, the authorities were still holding 428 individuals. Gradually they developed incontrovertible evidence that Aum Shinrikyō was responsible for the Tokyo attack. Nevertheless, justice has been slow in coming. A number of the inner circle eventually confessed, but others pleaded not guilty. As of October 1998, three fugitives who had held top positions in Aum remained at large, thirty members were still on trial, and attorneys expected the trial of Asahara Shōkō to continue for years (NYT 11 October 1998, p. A10).

The Japanese media response to these events created something like a cross between Waco, the O. J. Simpson trial, the death of Princess Diana, and the impeachment of Bill Clinton. Fixating on every detail of the emerging story, people in Japan found it difficult to understand why some of their country's brightest, most educated youth had become caught up in a sect that carried out acts of indiscriminate murder. How could scientifically trained chemists and biologists take on such bizarre religious beliefs, and what would lead them to attack their own society? The educational system, in particular, came under scrutiny for failing to promote any critical stance toward knowledge. Observers argued that by emphasizing memorization, schools replicated standardized knowledge but created human automatons who lacked the capacity to think outside bounded information games. So long as these automatons found places within the existing social order, things went smoothly. But when they took up life in a countercultural movement, they easily succumbed to its discipline and demands. This analysis thus raises the question: whence the movement and its demands?

Japanese religion and the origins of Aum Shinrikyō

Aum Shinrikyō emerged in the 1980s in Japan's highly syncretic religious milieu, where an individual may marry in a Christian ceremony, observe Shintō rituals, pursue Chinese healing techniques, and have Buddhist funeral rites after death. In general, however, faith is not deeply anchored and in urban areas religious observance is mostly a matter of social convention.

Shintoism is the oldest of the major religions, officially counted as having some 70.3 million believers. Buddhism arrived in the middle of the sixth century of the modern era, and has some 81.3 million followers, divided among diverse schools and sects, including Zen. Christianity did not make its appearance until the fifteenth century, and had little significance until after the Second World War; today there are fewer than a million Christians in Japan.

In 1868, with the new political order ushered in by the Meiji restoration, the Japanese state established the principle of freedom of religion, yet used Shintoism to supplant the traditional role of Confucian philosophy as the ethical foundation of state officialdom (cf. Weber 1964). Over the course of the late nineteenth and early twentieth centuries, despite supposed religious freedom, certain "new religions" (*shin shūkyō*) faced persecution and dissolution under state authority (Murakami 1972).

After the Japanese defeat in the Second World War, Shintoism was disestablished. Religious persecution by state authorities was outlawed, and various syncretic sects began to flourish again (Garon 1997, p. 209). More recently, paralleling contemporaneous New-Age religious movements in Europe and North America, a wave of new religions swept Japan during the 1980s. The emerging Japanese groups differed in nature and audience from previous religious movements there, and Japanese call them *shin shin shūkyō* or "new new religions."

The origin of Aum Shinrikyō can be found in the efflorescence of the new new religions in Japan. Its founding guru, Matsumoto Chizuo, was born on the southern island of Kyūshū in 1955, the fourth son of a modest family of seven children whose father manufactured *tatami* floor mats. Matsumoto Chizuo was born with glaucoma and was almost completely blind, having only very weak sight in his right eye. From the beginning of his education, he had to go to a school for the blind, and he spent fourteen years in boarding school. In his early twenties, he worked for two months as an acupuncturist in a clinic in Kumamoto, and tried and failed at university entrance examinations, including the highly competitive exam for the University of Tokyo. In 1977 he set himself up in Funabashi, near Tokyo, and continued to practice acupuncture, along with *kyū*, a type of Asian herbal medicine popular in Japan. At the age of 23 he married Tomoko, the oldest daughter of two teachers, who also failed her university entrance exams. Over the course of their marriage, she gave birth to six children, and became an active and central participant in her husband's religious enterprises.

In Tokyo, Matsumoto Chizuo began to show an interest in religion, notably through his involvement in the God Light Association, a new new religion founded by Takahashi Shinji. In 1981, Matsumoto joined a group called Agonshū led by Kiriyama Seiyū, who claimed that those who followed his teachings and yoga practices could obtain superhuman powers to foresee and intervene in the future. Matsumoto participated in a demanding 1,000-day devotional regimen (Reader 1996, p. 21) and discovered that yoga could wake sexual and vital energies, transforming the body and emotions and leading to a flowering of the spirit. However, in June of the following year he was indicted and fined for violating the Drugs, Cosmetics, and Medical Instruments Act by selling unlicensed herbal treatments (namely orange rind in alcohol). This development, according to Brackett (1996, p. 64), profoundly embarrassed Matsumoto and turned him more strongly in the direction of religion.

The basic outlines of Matsumoto's future religious project took shape during this period. In 1984, he opened a yoga school in Shibuya, one of the largest commercial centers of Tokyo. The following year he made his claim of levitation with the famous photo published in the magazine of paranormal phenomena, *Twilight Zone*, showing him seemingly suspended in mid-air in a position of meditation. This impressed many people, and some of them sought Matsumoto out. Through January 1988 *Twilight Zone* published more than a dozen articles on Matsumoto and his yoga training, including some written by the teacher himself. In 1985, Matsumoto also wrote articles for a similar magazine named Mū, after a lost continent supposed to have existed in the Pacific.

By 1984 the teacher had already developed his own movement, Aum Shinsen no Kai (the Aum Congregation of Sages). Surrounded by around fifteen followers, most of them from the yoga school, he threw himself into writing, touring, and developing his organization. In 1986 he published *Chōnōryoku himitsu no kaihatsuhō* (How to develop your secret extraordinary powers). In the same year, he travelled to Nepal and India, and at one point was photographed with the Dalai Lama. While in the Himalayas, the guru later reported, he achieved the final enlightenment. On the basis of this inspiration, in August 1987 he took on the religious name of Asahara Shōkō and changed the name of his movement to Aum Shinrikyō, Religion of the Supreme Truth (for biographical details, see Ishii 1996).

As a goal, Asahara asserted that he had been given the divine mission of establishing the utopian buddhist kingdom of Shambhala, and he proposed in 1988 to build communal "Lotus Villages" across Japan. The first such village was the sect's headquarters, opened that summer in Fujinomiya, in Shizuoka prefecture, near the capital. The goal of the sect was for individuals to rid themselves of bad karma (Brackett 1996, pp. 69–75). Asahara Shōkō borrowed many practices from yoga, and he defined a sophisticated sequence of training and spiritual testing. Together with these practices, regimens of asceticism and fasting were eventually supposed to bring devotees to *gedatsu*, the supreme stage of enlightenment that only the guru had reached.

In August 1989 Aum Shinrikyō obtained legal recognition as a religious organization, thereby gaining tax exemption for all donations and a substantial exemption for other types of income. The movement went on to establish an organizational presence in almost all major Japanese cities. It set up headquarters in Tokyo and a training center in Fujinomiya.

Followers who lived together in community, called *shukkesha* in Japanese, withdrew from the wider world, like monks in other religions. They gave all their belongings to the sect and renounced any bonds to the wider world. As their guru later told them, "In order to establish your new self, you proceed to the stage of 'Detachment.' In this stage, you practice some special meditations in which you offer everything to your guru – your body, your mind, material objects – everything" (Asahara 1993, p. 67).

Over the years, the sect recruited a solid base of 1,115 *shukkesha*, some three-quarters of them in their twenties and thirties, a few in their forties, a smattering of older people, some teenagers, and some children of *shukkesha*. Like other New-Age groups, Aum Shinrikyō appealed to educated youth. In addition, it was particularly successful at recruiting young professionals, many of them technically trained. The group provided them with challenging work, recognition, advancement opportunities, and research facilities that were typically unavailable in the wider society, where they might work in highly formalized Japanese professor-student apprentice relationships or tightly organized corporate structures. No doubt the group also attracted followers who wanted to acquire the superhuman powers that Asahara promised. Whatever their objectives, the most committed followers ended up by withdrawing from society. Overall, Aum Shinrikyō turned away from family ties and traditional Japanese religious practices to build a utopian communal society whose *shukkesha* rejected the materialism of the wider society, replacing it with an extremely ascetic monastic lifestyle. They slept in small cubicles and threw themselves into regimens and initiations supposed to help them achieve ever higher states of mystical enlightenment.

From the group's earliest existence, it invoked strongly millennialist themes. Initially, the ideas were drawn from Agonshū, the sect that Matsumoto had joined in 1981. Agonshū's leader, Kiriyama, had prophesied doom in 1999 unless spiritual action headed it off, and he puzzled over whether he might be the saviour that Nostradamus had mentioned as coming out of the East. Like Kiriyama, Asahara at first offered his movement as a way of heading off the catastrophe: if enough *shukkesha* gathered together, their positive spiritual energy could overcome the negative forces that threatened to unleash the impending crisis. Here, Asahara mirrored the approach of pre-apocalyptic conversionist sects such as Jehovah's Witnesses that seek to gather converts *before* Armageddon arrives. But there was an important difference. Whereas Jehovah's Witnesses continue to live and work in the world at large, Aum Shinrikyō promoted renunciation of the world by converts who would marshall their spiritual energies in cloistered communes. To avert the crisis, 30,000 *shukkesha* were needed. Time was short (Reader 1996, pp. 22–4).

Some families of Aum members who became *shukkesha* found the devotees' radical separation from the world incomprehensible, but in its initial program, the sect did operate within a certain religious logic. Many religions require renunciation of the world on the part of their monks. However, Aum's theology shifted dramatically. No later than April 1990 Asahara came to believe that harnessing the spiritual energy of a large number of followers was not enough to save the world. He spoke to his disciples instead about a mass, indiscriminate death as the only basis for the salvation of humanity. Through death, the guru claimed, the soul could reincarnate at a superior spiritual level.

Reader (1996, p. 43) dates the theological shift even earlier, to 1989. Another scholar, Shimazono Susumu (1995, p. 395–8), argues that by 1985, Aum's guru had already begun dabbling in "the apocalyptic vision of the prewar theorist of 'ultra-ancient history'," Sakai Katsutoki. His prophecy was that Armageddon would come at the end of the twentieth century, to be survived only by a "race of compassionate sages" whose guru would come from Japan. Shimazono argues that Asahara's plan for Aum Shinrikyō to rescue its followers from the fate facing most of humanity dates definitively from 1988.

Indeed, in a January 1988 article in *Twilight Zone*, Asahara discussed the expected 1999 Armageddon. This supports Shimazono's thesis that Asahara had begun to incorporate ideas from the New Testament book of Revelation. By 1989 Asahara was clearly pessimistic about the possibilities of saving the world. His publication *From Destruction to Emptiness: A Sequel to the Day of Destruction* noted that time was running out and, as a result, the proportion of humanity that could be saved was dropping (Brackett 1996, pp. 75–6). Several years later, the claim would be that only Asahara's followers could escape the end of the world. Under the dispensation as it eventually developed, Asahara described "Pho-Wa," a "transfer of consciousness" which "makes it possible for you to reincarnate into any realm you wish at the moment of death" (Asahara 1993, p. 67). Astonishingly, as Brackett observes, "Though the original Tibetan means to lead a soul to a higher level of being, usually at the moment of death, for Asahara and many of his key followers, it had become a euphemism for killing" (Brackett 1996, p. 97). Highly evolved souls could transcend death, and lower souls, namely opponents, could be killed, thereby preventing them from accumulating more bad karma.

Asahara, like his mentor Kiriyama, invoked Nostradamus as a prophet of the approaching end of the world. Like Nostradamus, Asahara Shōkō made public predictions. In one talk, in January 1990, he asserted Aum Shinrikyō to be the most evolved religion in the world, and anticipated attacks on the group by both the police and the wider society. Yet salvation could be attained only by those who had undergone spiritual, psychological, and physical training designed to help individuals withstand the weapons used during Armageddon, which Asahara sometimes described as the coming Third World War. Actual *shukkesha* of Aum Shinrikyō alone would be saved. The way was difficult, as only Asahara Shōkō understood: "Frankly," he wrote later, "there are too many religious organizations which preach 'you only need faith to be happy after death'. It is, in fact, not that easy" (Asahara 1993, p. 56).

If, at the beginning, the idea was to develop superhuman powers through the practice of yoga, as time passed the spiritual goal became more complicated. In Asahara's elaboration of Buddhist ideas, while preparing for Armageddon, pursuit of personal enlightenment required extreme asceticism. It was necessary for followers not only to separate themselves from the everyday world but to reject it. The only means to reach salvation was through meditation. The proper path was to observe the rituals and stages of initiation proposed by Aum Shinrikyō.

That path required large sums of money. At lower levels, the sect operated like a school, with registration and course fees. Writer Egawa Shōko observed that everything had a price on it:

> Garbled prospectuses are sold: 2 ¥ per B4 sheet, 1.5 ¥ per B5 sheet . . . the video tape of Asahara Shōkō preaching costs 15,000 ¥, the video tape "The secrets of the Himalaya yoga," 100,000 ¥, recordings of religious music, from 10,000 to 30,000 ¥, holy water, 4,000 ¥ for 3 liters. . . . There is a personalized orientation to holy yoga for 10,000 yen per

hour, the analysis of destiny, 30,000 ¥, an audience with Asahara, 20,000 ¥. Everything was defined within a system of fees.

(Egawa 1991, p. 84)

Disciples could also purchase 200 c.c. of Asahara's bathwater. Another initiation involved drinking a vial of what was supposed to be the guru's blood with its purportedly special DNA, the effects of which were probably produced through the addition of hallucinogenic drugs. The famous helmet first appeared in 1990. A device invented in the sect, it had electrodes intended to connect the user to brain waves emitted by the guru. The person wearing the helmet was supposed to be able to reach the same state of meditation as the master, at a rental cost of merely 1,000,000 ¥ per month (Brackett 1996, p. 73). "One had to have the helmet," Takahashi Hidetoshi (1996, p. 38) writes, "for the 'Perfect Salvation Initiation' ritual."

In a number of ways Aum Shinrikyō operated like other religious sects that grow affluent by marketing spiritual enlightenment. However, its extremely ascetic practices marked a decidedly different path from peddling the soft mysticism of personal self-realization. The practices and the life of *shukkesha* were originally designed to yield transcendence, but transcendence became linked with survival in the face of a rapidly approaching disaster that promised to wipe out the vast majority of humanity (Mullins 1997, pp. 316–17). It was this decidedly apocalyptic aspect of the theology that pointed the sect in the direction of militarization. Eventually the group's higher echelons effectively launched a holy war against the state and the society-at-large. The theological foundation for these dramatic changes emerged as early as 1988, and it took full form by 1990. Why, then, this apocalyptic turn?

The public trajectory: failure in politics and success in religion

In January 1990, Asahara Shōkō publicly announced that he and twenty-five of his followers would participate in legislative elections the following month as candidates of the political party just formed by Aum Shinrikyō, *Shinritō* (Party of Truth). Political action by a religious group was nothing new in Japan. One group, *Seichō no Ie*, had been politically active since the end of the Second World War, and, from 1958 onward, it became a recognized supporter of the Liberal-Democratic party's right wing. Another religion, one that Asahara considered his major rival, was the famous Buddhist-inspired *Sōka Gakkai*. Founded in 1930, it developed politically significant ties first with the moderate-conservative *Kōmeitō* party founded in 1964, and later with the powerful conservative New Frontier party, *Shinshintō*, established in 1994. With sixteen million followers, the Sōka Gakkai became an important political force (Nakano 1996; Garon 1997, pp. 209–11).

Once Aum Shinrikyō announced candidates, it began acting like a political

party. Its staff planned the campaign. The sect's followers made campaign donations totaling around one million yen, a modest sum for a Japanese campaign
but an important start for a new party. Their candidates went to meet voters,
sometimes accompanied by important disciples. They organized street parades,
rallies and demonstrations, clothed in their white religious garb, sometimes
wearing masks so that they all looked like their guru, Asahara. Lacking any
clear political program, they held out the promise of a better world. However,
the number of votes that Aum candidates received was abysmal. They all lost.
The effort to imitate other sects and establish connections to the wider society
through politics was a complete failure.

Did this stinging setback provoke Aum's spiral of violence? Some observers
eventually identified this moment as the key to the change in orientation of the
movement. As Reader put it,

> One is tempted to speculate that this rejection, when in Aum's eyes
> Japanese society spurned the chance to be saved (or perhaps, in Aum's
> view, was too stupid, too mired in the swamp of contemporary
> decadence to be saved), might well have pushed Aum's leadership into
> feeling that society was damned and should be abandoned.
>
> (1996, p. 45)

During the trials that stemmed from the Tokyo subway attack, several former
disciples confirmed that a dramatic shift took place at this time.

However, three points ought to be considered. First, the financial viability of
Aum hardly seems to have been threatened by the campaign; on the contrary,
the group had well established conduits of income from course fees and donations of its members, and after the defeats it continued to expand its real estate
holdings and even to start new businesses. Second, the number of devotees who
became *shukkesha* reached an all-time high of 246 in 1990 despite the political
defeat at the beginning of the year (Reader 1996, p. 29). Third, as we have seen,
Asahara began to harden the apocalyptic aspects of his theology well *before* the
election defeat in February 1990.

Moreover, despite the failure at the ballot box, it is not self-evident that Aum
Shinrikyō really lost ground by running candidates in the election. The sect's
efforts to reach out during the political campaign gave an instant new visibility to
the movement. After the election debacle, Asahara Shōkō continued to cultivate
his public image. He became increasingly widely known through his frequent
appearances on television, especially in religious debates. Asahara had a certain
talent, as a number of observers recognized. Always speaking in measured tones,
he advanced relevant critiques of his religious adversaries without lowering the
level of the discussion. Until then, religious topics had rarely been addressed on
television. The debates aroused the interest of the public, and therefore of television producers. Asahara's ability to contradict tradition-bound conventional
religions even attracted young religious practitioners who had waited a long time

for a critique that they dared not initiate themselves because of their own hierar-chies' strictness and intolerance. To the wider public, Asahara's language seemed accessible and modern. His examples were evocative. In the debate format, his skill at speaking, the substance of his critiques, and the originality of his religious ideas brought viewers to his side. With his fame growing, Asahara became sought after as a lecturer. He made the rounds of the most prestigious universities in a tour late in 1992. By the time of the attack on the subway on 20 March 1995, there would not be many Japanese who had not heard of Asahara Shōkō.

However, even if the election did not weaken Aum Shinrikyō, the group certainly consolidated its apocalyptic stance in the aftermath. Some weeks after the defeat in the 1990 elections, a key event occurred in Aum's short history. The sect organized a seminar for disciples in Ishigakijima, in Okinawa archipelago. In the media at the time, partly on the basis of the political failures, there was speculation that Aum Shinrikyō might commit mass suicide at the gathering (Sayle 1996, p. 62). However, despite logistical problems, the success of the event was resounding. During the seminar, some five hundred participants decided to join Aum Shinrikyō. It was said that almost two hundred of them renounced the world and joined the community of *shukkesha*. In the sect this date came to be regarded as a turning point. People would speak of "before" or "after" Ishigakijima. In the election campaign, Aum had sought to obtain power by political and legal means, but had failed in this attempt to reconnect with the wider social world. In the aftermath, what followers took to be the success of Ishigakijima resounded as a true validation of both the sect's doctrines and its guru, who treated the event as an incontrovertible personal triumph. Yet the triumph took a new direction.

At Ishigakijima, Asahara announced a shift away from a Mahayana path of Buddhism (the so-called "great boat" that holds out the promise of salvation for everyone). In its place, he offered his own special interpretation of Vajrayana Buddhism, a tantric path of salvation only open to the elect who are willing to submit to the program of meditation and discipline required to attain enlight-enment. Asahara associated this theological shift with an apocalyptic survivalist motif. According to Reader (1996, pp. 45–6), the communal sites were no longer just retreats; they became shelters from nuclear holocaust. As Asahara's Ishigakijima speech spelled out the connection between meditation and survival,

> we have to secure a place where we can protect ourselves from bodily harm, where we can live and continue our ascetic practice, no matter what kind of weapon, whether that be nuclear weapons, or bacterial weapons, but where we will be protected no matter what kind of weapon is thrown against us. . . . From this day, from this moment on you'll have to dedicate yourselves to even stricter practice, and quickly raise yourselves to the stage where you are prepared for death at any time.
>
> (Aum-published text quoted in Brackett 1996, p. 84)

At the very moment when Asahara alluded to bacterial weapons, the sect was initiating a historically unprecedented project to develop a capacity for biological warfare; eventually the program would involve a trip to Zaire to try to obtain the deadly Ebola virus (NYT 26 May 1998, p. A1, 10). As a follower later reported, he believed Aum Shinrikyō was becoming "the last fortress of Buddhism" (JT 13 November 1997).

With its stricter and narrower theology, Aum grew more slowly in the two years after 1990, attracting only forty-three new *shukkesha*. However, by 1992 Asahara Shōkō and key aides had begun to organize a branch of the sect in Russia, at a time when a variety of religious movements were seeking to establish themselves there. According to media estimates, Aum's Russian converts numbered nearly 30,000. In Japan, over the year and a half beginning in January 1993, there was also significant growth: some 524 devotees became *shukkesha*. Overall, in the years following 1990 Aum increased in wealth, members, and property.

In 1989, the movement had taken ownership of seven plots of land situated in the commune of Kamikuishiki, in the prefecture of Yamanashi. Over the next five years, sect members constructed around thirty major buildings. Eventually, the value of the properties would be estimated at 100 million yen. Many *shukkesha* moved to Kamikuishiki, especially after the holdings became the sect's communal headquarters in the early 1990s. Overall, from 1989 onward, Aum Shinrikyō acquired approximately 3,000 hectares of land across Japan, valued at 2.25 billion yen. The movement gradually established a presence in many areas, including most of the large cities.

Asahara Shōkō had grand projects. Given that *shukkesha* were no longer supposed to work outside the group, and given the property acquisitions, money was an essential requirement. The sect quickly became financially successful, mainly through the donations of believers, but also through lucrative business enterprises. Asahara surrounded himself with highly educated *shukkesha* advisors, and together they built an economically successful sect that started a computer retail business, a fitness club, a telephone-dating club, and a chain of "*bentō*," or boxed-lunch shops, some cheap noodle restaurants, and a child daycare center.

In short, from all appearances, despite its failure in the 1990 elections, Aum Shinrikyō became a moderately successful religious organization in the following years and leveraged this success into substantial financial growth. Yet it was in these years of prosperity and growth, beginning immediately after the February 1990 elections, that the group began to act concertedly on its apocalyptic theology, to the point of arming itself, developing biological and chemical weapons, and using them. The central puzzle about Aum Shinrikyō is thus how to explain this development. As we will show, the apocalyptic turn did not come simply as a result of the elections, nor solely as the elaboration of a nascent apocalyptic theological position. A dynamic of conflict with the wider world was taking hold for more tangible reasons.

Figure 3.1 The Kamikuishiki compound of Aum Shinrikyō, with Mount Fuji in the background. It was here that many of the group's clandestine acts of violence took place, and that sarin was manufactured.

Source: Kyodo News International

First victims

There were numerous complaints and allegations about Aum Shinrikyō over the years, but the sect staved off any public accounting prior to the Tokyo subway attack. Indeed, the attack, as well as a number of previous acts of violence committed by the sect, may have been intended to forestall precisely such an accounting. Like many new religions in the contemporary period, Aum Shinrikyō was vulnerable to charges that grow structurally out of recruiting young people to paths that separate them from their families. But Aum Shinrikyō's inner circle of leaders carried out acts far more violent than any committed by the other mystical movements and apocalyptic groups that it most closely resembled. Opponents who began to organize against Aum Shinrikyō had far more to worry about than the typical complaints against religious movements of breaking up families, brainwashing, and extorting money.

The first known Aum death came in September 1988 when Mashima Teruyuki, a devotee reportedly thinking of leaving the sect, died during a demanding regimen of training involving immersion in baths. His death may have been accidental. But even if this is the case, Asahara is accused of ordering his closest aides to destroy the body and cover up the fact that the death had occurred.[1] This death, accidental or not, led to another that was clearly murder. A follower named Taguchi Shūji knew about Mashima's demise, and it kindled his own doubts about Aum Shinrikyō. In February 1989, Aum staff executed Taguchi for criticizing Aum's doctrines and training methods, and for stating that he intended to leave the community (Reader 1996, p. 28; Kaplan and Marshall 1996, pp. 35–6). As Brackett observes, the cover-up of the original death created a secret bond of criminality among those who knew about it (1996, p. 87). In turn, the murder of a person who might reveal the secret established a precedent for using violence to protect the organization from any threat against it.

Even more daring violence arose out of events that began a few months later in 1989, when a network of families began to mobilize against Aum Shinrikyō. The sect made intensive use of psychology as well as powerful yoga techniques, and it attracted individuals who, in seeking enlightenment, sometimes became strong devotees, ever ready to pursue the next stage of enlightenment. These general conditions do not differ dramatically from other new religions such as the Hare Krishna movement and the followers of the guru Rajneesh who eventually settled in a remote area of Oregon. However, they are the generic conditions under which anticult movements arise, and in 1989 such a movement began against Aum Shinrikyō. Some of the families were concerned that they had been cut off from contact with *shukkesha* relatives. Others sought to get back money that they or a relative had given to the movement.

A freelance writer involved in human rights issues, Egawa Shōko, received a phone call from the mother of a sect member and put the woman in contact with a young Yokohama attorney acquaintance of hers. The attorney, Sakamoto

Tsutsumi, had previously worked with parents seeking custody of their children against one of the best established and earliest of the new religions, Reverend Sun Myung Moon's Unification Church, long the object of anticult efforts in Japan. The "Moonies," of course, were one of the religious movements on which the classic anticult-movement profile of a "cult" had been formulated (Bromley and Shupe 1979, Barker 1984). Attorney Sakamoto started working with Aum families in May of 1989, and began to gather evidence against the sect in June. The following month he negotiated with Aum officials and successfully brokered a meeting between the concerned mother and her Aum daughter, held on 3 August at the sect's Mount Fuji headquarters. After that, Sakamoto began to pursue a case against the sect for the return of one million yen to a man who had paid for an initiation in which he drank what was supposedly Asahara's special blood but experienced no particular supernatural effects for the expenditure.

In October of the same year, Aum came under the scrutiny of the anticult journalism that had sprung up as a genre in Japan during the mid-1980s with campaigns against the Moonies and a group called *Kōfuku no kagaku* (The Science of Happiness). On October 2, the *Sunday Mainichi* magazine began publishing reporter Hiroiwa Chikahiro's seven-part exposé of Aum Shinrikyō, detailing accusations that the sect separated individuals from their families and engaged in financial extortion through such devices as the Asahara blood-drinking initiation. The articles galvanized an outpouring of letters to the editor, and the magazine brokered connections of the families with one another and with Sakamoto. On 11 October, Sakamoto convened a meeting of families with grievances against Aum, thereby obtaining further information, more leads, and more connections. A few days later, the attorney gave a telephone radio interview accusing the sect of fraud, deception, recruiting minors as members, and cutting them off from their parents. By then, the attorney had contacts with some twenty-three families. Out of that confluence, the Aum Shinrikyō Victims' Association was founded on 21 October 1989, with legal representation by Sakamoto (Reader 1996, pp. 37–40; Brackett 1996, pp. 12–15; Kaplan and Marshall 1996, pp. 37–43).

Around the same time, the television network Tokyo Broadcasting System (TBS) taped an interview in which Sakamoto criticized Aum Shinrikyō. Somehow, possibly through a disciple working for TBS, sect leaders learned about the existence of this tape. Representatives of Aum showed up at the television network headquarters, demanded to see the interview in advance, and obtained an agreement from the network not to broadcast it, perhaps by promising an exclusive interview with Asahara Shōkō.

In the confluence of the radio interview, the magazine exposés, the suppressed TBS interview, and the formation of an organization with legal counsel that was pursuing a series of cases against the sect, Asahara is alleged to have sent three trusted Aum representatives to meet Sakamoto in his law offices on 31 October. There, the four got into a heated discussion over the magical potency of the DNA in Asahara's blood, with Sakamoto steadfastly maintaining

92

that no scientific tests had ever established its special power. At the end of the confrontation, Sakamoto informed the Aum visitors that he planned to file suit to challenge Aum Shinrikyō's status as a religious organization under Japanese law (Brackett 1996, pp. 15–17).

If Aum needed any further evidence, this meeting confirmed Sakamoto's common cause with the earliest organized opposition to Aum Shinrikyō as a cult. The group's application for official religious status, though filed in April 1989, had been approved only in August, and not without opposition. The Tokyo prefecture that was considering the application received complaints from a number of families that Aum Shinrikyō recruited *shukkesha* out of the ranks of minors (in Japan, individuals under twenty years old) and young adults with promising futures; once the young people joined the group, the families charged, they cut off all communication with their families. Presumably on the basis of these protests (which Aum regarded as the work of "a certain lawyer representing the discontented families of Aum members") and perhaps under some political pressure, the Tokyo prefecture initially turned down Aum Shinrikyō's application. Indeed, this difficulty in obtaining recognition as a religious organization may have led Asahara in July 1989 to seek political clout by fielding Aum candidates in legislative campaigns (Shimazono 1995, p. 398; Reader 1996, pp. 35–7, 44).

Sakamoto's threatened lawsuit against Aum came in early November, when the group's religious status still fell under a one-year probationary period. At the time, the sect was continuing in its plan to field candidates in the February 1990 elections. Sakamoto had hoped that negotiations with Aum would prove fruitful but, as the young attorney informed freelance writer Egawa Shōko, the sect's lawyers did not act like attorneys dealing with another attorney but as Aum delegates (Reader 1996, p. 39). The day after Sakamoto met with the Aum delegation, he gained permission from the former Aum member to pursue a suit for the return of the one million yen spent on the blood ritual (JT 2 August 1995). Meanwhile Asahara received word from the Aum delegation about how their meeting with Sakamoto had gone, and it is alleged that he ordered the attorney brought to a sect compound. Aum's inner circle tried several times to catch Sakamoto by himself, but failed. Finally, in the early morning of 4 November 1989, operatives abducted Sakamoto along with his wife and their one-year-old son, and brought them all to the Aum Shinrikyō settlement at Kamikuishiki. There, close associates of Asahara strangled the two adults and suffocated the child. They crushed the teeth of the lawyer to make identification more difficult, wrapped the bodies in blankets and took them away to bury in three separate places in the mountains, distant both from one another and from any Aum communes.

Sakamoto, his wife, and their child had disappeared with hardly a trace. Relatives and the attorney's co-workers noticed the family's absence immediately, but it was not until 7 November that Sakamoto's mother and one of his co-workers went to the family's apartment. Finding signs of foul play and an Aum Shinrikyō badge, they notified the police, who did not make the disappearances public until 15 November (Brackett 1996, pp. 20–1). Sakamoto's colleagues in his law office quickly came to suspect Aum Shinrikyō, but the police seemed deaf to the lawyers' requests that they investigate the group. Asahara went ahead with a planned trip to Europe in November without the authorities' intervention. In an article in the weekly magazine *Shūkan Bunshun* on 7 December, the writer Egawa revealed Sakamoto's dealings with Aum, and some religious-movement opponents of Aum Shinrikyō publicly denounced Asahara and his sect as responsible for the abductions. In this climate, the sect sought to explain away the Aum Shinrikyō badge found at the scene as planted by someone who wanted to make them take the blame for the crime.

Sakamoto's colleagues were not willing to let the matter rest, and they organized meetings across Japan, seeking any information about the missing lawyer and his family. Gradually they mobilized the entire legal profession; in March 1990, the Japanese Bar Association established an office for the Sakamoto case. The next month, the Victims' Association demonstrated in front of Aum headquarters. Sakamoto's mother pushed to get the case solved and received wide public support. Egawa Shōko published more accounts of Aum Shinrikyō in 1991 and 1992, criticizing the group for its pursuit of donations and detailing the circumstances, such as were known, of the Sakamotos' disappearance. But for all the concern, police did not conclude the Sakamoto investigation until 1995, after the Tokyo subway attack.

Given what was known at the time of the abductions about the conflict between Sakamoto and Aum Shinrikyō, many people have asked why the authorities did not aggressively investigate the sect, and why they failed to produce results. Did the organization of the police into different levels pose difficulties of coordination and cooperation? Were the police incompetent? Or did they make a deliberate choice not to pursue the matter? Did the authorities seek to avoid accusations of persecuting a religious organization? Or had Aum Shinrikyō infiltrated high levels of power? There is still no clear answer to these questions, but in September 1995 Kunimatsu Takaji, the chief of the national police, publicly acknowledged that if the police had reacted more effectively in the Sakamoto investigation, the Matsumoto and Tokyo poison gas attacks might never have taken place.

In the end, Asahara and six of his disciples were indicted in the Sakamoto case. One of them, Okazaki Kazuaki, confessed at Asahara's trial that he had fled Aum after the Sakamoto murders. From hiding, in February 1990, he revealed to the court, he had begun carrying out a plan to extort money from the sect by threatening to reveal the murders to the police. As a result of his scheme, Okazaki received some 8.3 million yen in hush money from the group (JT 18 April, 21 June, 5 September 1997).

It is highly likely that only Asahara, his closest followers, and the defector Okazaki knew what had happened to the Sakamoto family. Aum Shinrikyō in effect established a "spiritual hierarchy" (Hall 1978, 1988) in which those deemed closest to enlightenment were those closest to the guru. In Aum, status was signified by the colour of clothing devotees were allowed to wear at various levels. This hierarchy had the effect not only of grading enlightenment, but also of compartmentalizing knowledge. Rank-and-file members almost certainly did not know about, much less participate in, the group's most clandestine and violent activities. Outside the highest levels, most devotees probably acted with the "substantive rationality" of foot soldiers: they knew what they were doing within their own spheres, but had no idea of how their actions fitted into the larger scheme of things. The sect's doctrines took such a strong apocalyptic cast that when devotees did understand something of the larger picture, they could interpret their actions as part of the group's larger effort to survive the coming Armageddon. But even with the Apocalypse, many devotees reacted in disbelief when finally confronted with the inner circle's agenda. The majority of devotees, especially the *shukkesha*, probably would not have supported such actions.

Overall, compared to either Peoples Temple or the Branch Davidians, the apocalyptic orientation of Aum Shinrikyō was initially relatively underdeveloped. However, it was there, and events led to its elaboration. Early on, Aum Shinrikyō brought a siege mentality upon itself by the cover-up through murder of a devotee who knew about the possibly accidental death of another member. Given the sect leaders' secret guilty knowledge, the opposition that they faced in 1989 and 1990 must have seemed extremely threatening. The efforts by families to prevent the sect from gaining official recognition as a religious organization, writer Egawa Shōko's brokering of an alliance between Aum relatives and the attorney Sakamoto, the media exposés, the formation of the Aum Shinrikyō Victims' Association with Sakamoto as its attorney planning to sue to revoke the sect's religious status, and defector Okazaki's extortion threats to go to the police – all these activities spelled trouble for a growing religious organization that was covering up a murder, undergoing the probationary period for religious organizations, and preparing for the February 1990 legislative elections.

The murder of Sakamoto eliminated an opponent of Aum who was by all accounts effective in the law and tenacious in pursuit of his goals. Yet here lies a decisive difference between Jonestown, Waco, and Aum Shinrikyō. The two groups in the United States could not possibly have covered up their violence against opponents, for it was highly public. Aum Shinrikyō, on the other hand, carried out its horrible crime without getting caught, and it continued for more than five years without coming to any major public reckoning. During this time, Aum's course increasingly came to approximate the pre-apocalyptic warring sect that engages in a quasi-military struggle with forces of the established social order as a manifestation of its struggle to save humanity and establish a utopia in the wake of the apocalypse.

Sectarian radicalization and rejection of the social order

Aum Shinrikyō continued to arouse opposition after 1989, in part because of suspicions about its role in the Sakamoto family's abduction and presumed murder, and partly because the group generated controversy in villages and towns where they established communal settlements. After Aum started a center in Namino, Kyūshū, on the southern island where Asahara was born, residents formed an association to oppose the sect's presence; ultimately opponents paid the sect 920 million yen to leave the village. Similar strong opposition came from the Aum Shinrikyō Countermeasures Committee in the community of Kamikuishiki, where residents complained about all-night construction, truck traffic, and the mantras that seemed to come constantly blaring from loudspeakers. Along with the opposition in local communities, Aum Shinrikyō also faced slack recruiting in 1991 and 1992, and when the sect began to exert stronger pressure on devotees to attract new recruits, families' complaints to the police increased (Reader 1996, pp. 46–9, 71–2; Brackett 1996, pp. 84–5; Kaplan and Marshall 1996, p. 60, 148). Conflict on multiple fronts became a routine fact of the group's existence. However, the responses of Aum were anything but routine.

From early 1990, the movement entered a new phase, which ultimately ended in the sarin attacks. Over a period of five years the sect radicalized its beliefs, armed itself, and tightened its internal organizational linkages as it prepared to fulfill its mission during Armageddon.

Who would take part in the struggle? Asahara asserted that Japan and the United States would be the main protagonists. But how did Aum Shinrikyō fit in? Here, the guru increasingly gravitated toward a right-wing paranoid view of the world that other social movements had previously used to mobilize mass followings, sometimes with devastating consequences. He embraced Nostradamus and the Bible's book of Revelation. His theological shading of Buddhist thought invoked a doctrine of creating superhumans through meditation. He justified eliminating the bad karma of the less evolved through murder. And he asserted that only the saved would be left standing after Armageddon. All these views, especially when taken together, led in a direction that Adolf Hitler had entertained, of creating a civilization based on a master race. Indeed Asahara seems to have admired Hitler and his vision of a thousand-year reich (Reader 1996, p. 58).

In the 1990s, Asahara began to describe a vast conspiracy that included not only competing Japanese religious groups, the emperor, and crown princess, but also the usual suspects of conspiracy theories in the West: the Freemasons, Jews, a United States government dominated by hidden forces, and the world government that these forces conspired to establish (Reader 1996, pp. 67–9; Brackett 1996, pp. 107–8; Kaplan and Marshall 1996, pp. 218–20). In the vision of the guru, the greatness of Japan was being eroded by the corruption of Japan itself, by the west, and by an emergent world government. Only the pure and disciplined devotees of Aum Shinrikyō would survive the coming holocaust.

Indeed, Asahara became ever more precise about the exact ways in which the prophecies of the end times were to be fulfilled. Initially expected to arrive around the year 2000, the apocalypse was eventually predicted for an earlier date, first in early 1997, then in November 1996. Asahara pointed to the fall of the Soviet Union as a sign of its approach:

> The peak of materialism as the result of the expansion of man's worldly desires . . . will appear together with the peak of spiritualism. Let us look at today's situation: we have reached the peak of materialism; socialism has collapsed and only materialism seems to thrive. I have made the following prediction. . . . The genuine spiritualists will grow full and shine like the sun, while the genuine materialists will be collected to be burned.
>
> (Asahara 1992, p. 129)

In the university lectures that he gave in October and November 1992, Asahara predicted that ABC (atomic, biological, chemical) arms would destroy 90 per cent of the urban population; the only means of surviving would be to become "superhuman," a state that could only be attained through spiritual training (Shimazono 1995, p. 402). To ensure survival beyond the apocalypse would require preparation, but this was not just a matter of sect members getting ready to hunker down in sanctuaries while the events of the last days unfolded beyond their doors. By December 1993, the guru was pressing his followers to prepare for the struggle of the final war, Armageddon. In March 1994, in the course of a talk, he predicted, "there is going to be collusion between the Americans and powerful Japanese, and it will have the effect of killing a number of Japanese people." The same month he claimed that "deadly gas and drugs have been used against us." In April, he predicted that his own death would be caused by a fatal gas like sarin. During a radio broadcast distributed by Aum Shinrikyō on 1 January 1995, Asahara Shōkō seemed to draw the date of the apocalypse even closer than before. "After this year," he predicted, "Japan is going to face immense changes that will lead to the Third World War and to Armageddon."

Within the movement Asahara fed a bellicose rhetoric that created the illusion of war. Sect members considered many survival schemes over the years, including underwater cities. They would have to endure terrible heat during Armageddon, and *shukkesha* prepared by practising intensive immersion in hot water. In addition, the sect would be required to defend itself, and this led to a search for arms equivalent to those that would be used against it. Anticipation of World War III ended up absorbing all other doctrines. Aum's leaders claimed to be alone in understanding the urgency of the sect's mission as the surviving vessel of humanity. In their vision, Aum Shinrikyō's only obligation was to the destiny that derived from the supernatural powers that the group had mastered. The approaching end of the world, which they considered certain, justified Aum's program of intense spiritual and physical training, and legitimated a technologically sophisticated program of biological and chemical weapons production. Nothing, it seems, could slow down this sectarian machine of war produced in a cloistered imaginary world through intense religious discourse and practices.

Providing the movement with capacities of violence and state power

Aum Shinrikyō's plan to initiate Armageddon with biological and chemical warfare first surfaced in March 1990, almost immediately after the failed election attempt. Initially the group concentrated on biological weapons. Over the next five years they launched at least nine attempts to spread deadly diseases, attacking the Japanese Diet (the legislature), the Imperial Palace, Tokyo's streets, and the United States naval base at Yokosuka. Frustrated because their early efforts failed to produce epidemics, in 1992 Asahara began to focus on chemical warfare (NYT 26 May 1998, p. A1, 10).

Even if unfolding events dictated the means, times, places, and targets, the gas attacks in Matsumoto and Tokyo could not have taken place without intensive preparations. A follower brought back scientific information necessary for the manufacture of sarin from the United States in 1992, and research on the gas was initiated in March 1993. Tsuchiya Masami, then twenty-eight years old, had studied chemistry at the most modern university in Japan, Tsukuba. He acted under the authority of the man eventually designated as the sect's minister of science and technology, Murai Hideo, who reported directly to the guru. Triangulation of testimony at the Tokyo subway trials suggests that Asahara Shōkō ordered Murai to prepare to produce toxic gas on a mass scale, and that Tsuchiya rose to the challenge. He conducted simultaneous research on several types of toxic gas and submitted his conclusions: sarin was the easiest to manufacture, mainly because the raw materials could be bought without much difficulty.

Tsuchiya publicly "predicted" that gases such as sarin would be used during the Third World War. He is alleged to have developed sarin production in close collaboration with Endō Seiichi, thirty-two years old, who became minister of health, along with the eventual vice-minister of science and technology, Watanabe Kazumi, thirty-four years old, a computer engineer and graduate of the famous Tokyo Institute of Technology. The sect also used its facilities to produce several hundred kilograms of mustard gas, and it pursued research concerning production of other types of toxic gas, including VX gas, originally developed by Great Britain in 1950, and considered to have a toxicity a hundred times greater than sarin (NYT 18 July 1998, A5).

Beginning around the middle of 1993, the movement began to use various drugs. Aum Shinrikyō's chemists produced amphetamines, as well as hallucinogens such as LSD. These drugs were especially used during religious rituals to heighten the spiritual experiences of devotees seeking transcendent experiences (JT 17 August, 17 November 1995). They also manufactured several pharmaceutical products for use in the movement, notably thiopental sodium or "truth serum" (JT 6 September 1995). This drug may have been used for social control of recalcitrant disciples and individuals who attempted to leave. Moreover, the sect's inner circle started to suspect that the police or other spies had infiltrated the movement, and they are alleged to have used thiopental sodium to ferret them out. All in all, the sect's chemical production program seems to have encompassed drugs used to produce feelings of ecstasy, control members, and interrogate offenders, as well as poisons prepared to kill those deemed enemies (Reader 1996, p. 31; Brackett 1996, pp. 97–8; Kaplan and Marshall 1996, pp. 162–5).

By June 1994, Aum Shinrikyō had amassed a capacity for chemical warfare on a level previously known only to governments, which claim the legitimate right to monopolize the means of violence. In a sect holding *de facto* powers exceeding those of many states, Asahara took a logical step. He restructured the organization. In effect, Aum Shinrikyō became an undeclared state within a state, with its own authority and control structure, through which responsibilities were distributed and actions planned, organized, and carried out. Under Asahara Shōkō as ultimate authority, the sect bureaucracy consisted of some twenty ministries and agencies, including Asahara's own "household agency" akin to the Imperial Household Agency of the Japanese Emperor (Brackett 1996, p. 104). Donations to the sect came increasingly to be organized like "tax farming," a practice by which governments sometimes contract out authority and quotas for tax revenue (JT, 22 October 1996). The new structure strengthened submission to the guru and weakened horizontal lines of communication, and its form conveyed the image of Aum Shinrikyō as an organization ready to take charge after the chaos of Armageddon arrived. On the outside, Aum maintained an amazing range of connections, including alleged ties to organized crime and *shukkesha* who served in Japan's Self-Defense Forces.

Participants in Aum's *de facto* management team, all of them *shukkesha*, took titles as heads of the ministries, agencies, and commands. Their youth and education are striking. The great majority were less than thirty. Most had advanced degrees or expertise in technological and scientific areas. They included trained chemists, physicians and lawyers, and a former researcher at the National Agency for Space Research. Educated in some of the most prestigious Japanese universities, they came from elite strata of Japanese society.

The broad base of Aum Shinrikyō's members participated in an apocalyptically tinged mystical sect that operated as an other-worldly spiritual hierarchy, but this member-base supported (and in turn was organized by) an elite cadre participating in a proto-state that increasingly operated as a warring sect. The principal perpetrators of violence came from within the tightly bounded state-patterned management team, which controlled action, demanded that its participants maintain secrecy, and enforced discipline within its ranks. As though they served in a private army, Aum operatives later claimed to have carried out orders because they feared punishment or death if they refused (JT 14 February 1998).

From transcendence to transgression

From the late 1980s, Aum Shinrikyō's leaders carried the hidden but suspected stigma of murder, but until 1995 the group was never charged with any significant crime. Rather like the participants in the 1950s Mau Mau rebellion in Kenya, who were told that magic prevented their opponents' bullets from harming them, the inner circle of Aum Shinrikyō seem to have developed a naïve hubris. They acted as though they were either invisible or omnipotent, or both. Once the sect began producing chemical and biological weapons, it moved even beyond violent lawlessness, in effect irreversibly renouncing any wider claims upon it. The formation of a state within a state confirmed this position in quasi-legal terms: with an autonomous government, the movement no longer recognized any laws beyond its own. Even for the *shukkesha* who knew nothing, practically speaking, to go back was impossible. The dramatic approach of an agonizing Third World War increased solidarity within the only community whose members understood how to prepare for what was going to happen. The emergency elevated the movement above ordinary principles and rules. And it required new training, new and more frequent rituals, and more offerings.

Aum Shinrikyō anticipated the coming Third World War, and its leader envisioned the group on the other side of the Apocalypse, in a life after the death of this world. But the guru did not guide his followers like a prophet searching for a promised land, nor did he herd them along like a shepherd tending his flock. Asahara acted like a supremely powerful emperor toward his army, enforcing discipline.

As Brown (1996, p. 111) observes, "The vast majority of members of Aum joined willingly, and stayed willingly." Media treatments of "cults" conventionally focus on the cases of coercion from above, but the far more striking thing in Aum is how completely many members internalized the rationales of the group, even to the point of seeing apostates and unsaved family members in the light of sect doctrines. Sectarian resocialization, confinement, violence, abductions and murder, all could be justified in these terms. Although Asahara described the coming Armageddon on a grandiose scale, Aum Shinrikyō waged its apocalyptic war as a series of strategic efforts to control internal and external opposition.

Apocalyptic war would suffer no criticism and no retreat, and Aum Shinrikyō could entertain no breech of discipline. If disciples came to doubt, and especially to voice their doubts, they were to be considered traitors. And if they thought about leaving the ranks of the movement, like deserters, they would be severely punished. Those who tried to escape sometimes found a neighbor in Kamikuishiki who would help them (JT 22 March 1998), but if they were captured they were forced to return, held captive, and punished. Within the movement, the extreme measures of social control were legitimated as the steps necessary to "save" followers who strayed from the path and "lost their way." In some cases, members even tried to force parents into the movement in order to shield them from the apocalypse to come (Reader 1996, pp. 51–2).

Within the movement, order was strictly maintained. From early on, Asahara capitalized on Buddhist doctrines of total devotion to the path of salvation revealed by the guru. On this basis, the group developed its spiritual hierarchy so that those who conformed became elevated in status. *Shukkesha* alone would be saved, but even among them an elaborate set of initiations and rituals led followers to ever higher aspirations, and thus to strict conformity with the demands of the sect. Doubt could only be error, and so those who voiced any skepticism were assigned "special trainings."

Extending textbook commitment and control mechanisms (Kanter 1972; Hall 1988) to conditions of apocalyptic war, Aum Shinrikyō came to embrace the routine use of violence. It also developed routines for eliminating evidence. The death of Ochida Naoki in 1993, after a training exercise of hanging by the feet, may have been accidental. However he died, his body, like that of a number of other hapless individuals, was reduced to ashes in the industrial incinerator that the sect had installed in Kamikuishiki in May 1992. In 1994, after some twenty disciples left the sect, Aum's minister of home affairs, Niimi Tomomitsu, established the "Agency for the New Disciples." It was this arm of Aum that carried out abductions and held dissidents under conditions of house arrest. Strict internal discipline was enforced to the point of obsession. Those who maintained contacts with the outside were denounced. Following widespread Japanese belief concerning the importance of blood for character and interpersonal relationships, in Aum those who didn't have the right blood type were subjected to special surveillance as unreliable individuals likely to weaken the Buddha's teachings.

The ultimate recourse was murder. Attorney Takimoto Tarō, an opponent who had very detailed knowledge, later asserted that the total number of Aum murders, including the subway deaths and all other incidents, could reach fifty (Takimoto and Fukushima 1996, p. 3). One murder, of a disciple named Ochida Kōtarō, offers particularly stark testimony about the cruelty of sect leaders. Ochida, along with his wife, had joined the movement as *shukkesha* in May 1990, and he became a pharmacist in the sect's hospital. But, in January 1994, he left Aum Shinrikyō, reunited with his wider family, and confided to them that he had seen partially burned human bones and remains at Kamikuishiki. He was forcibly kidnapped and brought back there. He then discovered that a forty-nine-year-old woman was being held in the building named Satyam 6.[2] Hoping to assist her in escaping, he sought help from the woman's son, Yasuda Hideaki, who had recently left Aum. As the two were about to secrete the woman away from the group late at night at the end of January 1994, they were discovered in Satyam 6, handcuffed, and taken to Satyam 2. In the offices of Asahara Shōkō, it is alleged, Asahara told Yasuda that if he killed Ochida, his own life would be spared. According to court testimony, Yasuda executed his friend in February 1994 in the presence of some ten people, including Asahara and his wife. Asahara then gave orders to burn the body in the incinerator (Reader 1996, p. 50; Kaplan and Marshall 1996, pp. 113–17; Brackett 1996, p. 172).

Other clearcut murders and certain suspicious deaths occurred the same year. In April, an eighty-one-year-old woman receiving treatment in a Tokyo hospital was transferred to Aum medical facilities, where she began receiving thermotherapy treatments. She died from a heart attack some days after her arrival, according to the report of an Aum physician, but not before having donated her house (valued at 120 million yen) to the sect. Her body would never be found. In July of the same year, Tomita Toshio, accused by the movement of being a spy, was strangled in Kamikuishiki. His body disappeared in the incinerator complex. In August, Nakamura Tōru, who had joined the movement in January 1989, died at the age of thirty-two after suffering burns caused by a prolonged immersion in excessively hot water.

If there were dangerous individuals within, there were also plenty of enemies beyond the sect's realm. The 1989 murder of the Sakamoto family provided the basic model of how to deal with opponents, but the technology for murder and disposal of human remains advanced considerably. In May 1994, disciples placed sarin in the car of attorney Takimoto Tarō, who was participating in a case against Aum Shinrikyō, seriously poisoning him. The freelance writer Egawa Shōko was another target. She had brought attorney Sakamoto and the families together in 1989. In 1992, she published two books on Aum Shinrikyō, detailing the guru's early sexual advice and describing the atrocities that defectors had experienced while in the sect (Kaplan and Marshall 1996, pp. 158, 175–81). In September 1994, she found a parcel left at her door during the night. It contained the toxic gas phosgene. Takimoto and Egawa both became convinced that perpetrators of these attacks were members of Aum Shinrikyō, and they went to the authorities.

According to Kaplan and Marshall (1996, pp. 186–7), Egawa's complaint was the event that finally led police to connect Aum Shinrikyō with the sarin gas attack in Matsumoto. If this is so, the attempted attack on Egawa backfired badly, finally giving her a way to convince police of the danger that the sect posed, and establishing the basis on which the authorities would direct their suspicions towards Aum Shinrikyō so quickly after the Tokyo subway sarin attack.

Aum Shinrikyō's inner circle presumably did not learn that it had become connected to the Matsumoto gas attack until the news came out in the press on 1 January 1995. But both before and after, they continued their quiet, deadly war against opponents. Over the course of several weeks, in December 1994 and January 1995, sect operatives attacked three people. Mizuno Noboru, aged 84, had been helping five apostates sue the sect to get back some 46 million yen in donations. One night while putting out the garbage, Mizuno was sprayed with VX gas. He survived the assault. However, some days later, a young businessman from Kansai, Hamaguchi Takahito, was less lucky. On a street in Osaka a commando squad of seven disciples attacked him with VX. Hamaguchi never belonged to the sect, but he had frequented its headquarters, and the Aum leadership concluded that he was a police informer. Hamaguchi went into a coma and died less than two weeks later (Kaplan and Marshall 1996, p. 212).

Then there is the case of Nagaoka Hiroyuki, father of an ex-*shukkesha* and the founder and president of the Aum Shinrikyō Victims' Association. On the very day in early January 1995 when Aum was accusing its opponents of gassing sect properties, Aum operatives sprayed Nagaoka with VX in a parking lot. He had to be hospitalized but he managed to live, keeping quiet about the incident out of concern that news of it might have a chilling effect on supporters of the anticult movement (Kaplan and Marshall 1996, p. 218). The same month, a sect commando team abducted, murdered, and incinerated the notary Kariya, and it was through clues from this abduction that police finally closed in on Aum Shinrikyō. But not before the sect unleashed urban chemical warfare in the Tokyo subway system.

Taking stock of the violence

To explain Aum Shinrikyō's turn toward public violence, there are two critical questions to address. First, why did they engage in any violence at all? Second, how did the shift from murder to *de facto* terrorism occur? As we already have seen, the initial decision to engage in murder seems to have grown out of an accidental death and the effort to cover it up. In turn, this murder placed the group in the position of adopting an aggressive posture toward opponents like Sakamoto and the Aum Shinrikyō Victims' Association. Aum had always had a latent apocalyptic orientation, and this orientation grew in importance in dialectical interaction with the group's murders of opponents in 1988 and 1989. However, the question remains: does Aum's apocalyptic ideology and its struggle against opponents explain the shift toward the quasi-militaristic posture of a warring sect that would attack society-at-large?

The critical point in the shift probably came early in 1990, when Asahara Shōkō and his lieutenants initiated development of biological and chemical weapons. The genesis of this decision remains murky. Further investigation may yet reveal links between Aum Shinrikyō and clandestine international intrigues of espionage, especially through its Russian connections, which possibly helped Aum Shinrikyō obtain equipment and supplies for its quasi-military operations (Reader 1996, p. 75). But in any event, the early shift toward a war footing weakens some explanations of what tipped the group toward executing the Tokyo subway attack.

One hypothesis suggests that in March 1995 the movement received advance warning about police plans to raid Kamikuishiki, and that the sect launched the Tokyo subway attack to divert attention from itself. Aspects of this hypothesis are not implausible. Certainly advance intelligence about an impending raid would explain the hurried dismantling of the Kamikuishiki sarin production facilities. But it is highly likely that the sect's leaders knew from the newspaper reports in January 1995 that the police had begun to make connections between the sect and the Matsumoto gas attack in June 1994. It is thus difficult to understand why Aum's inner circle would have thought that attacking the Tokyo subway would divert attention. With the group already under suspicion, at the most it would have bought some time. Moreover, the stockpiles of sarin had been in Kamikuishiki for some time. Whatever the proximate strategy behind the Tokyo attack, the sect clearly had prepared for something of the kind for years.

A second hypothesis suggests that the Tokyo subway attack amounted to an attempted *coup d'état*. The choice of the place of the attack and the precision of its timing at morning rush hour seem plausibly to have been aimed at a carefully selected target, namely officials working in governmental offices. Under this hypothesis, the attack was meant to destabilize the state, prevent it from functioning, and, maybe, seize political power. This view gained wide support in Japan, and perhaps widespread belief had its own consequences for the political situation. However, the coup hypothesis is not really convincing, at least as anything more than Asahara's apocalyptic sectarian fantasy (which is described in JT 22 October 1997).

In the first place, the coup hypothesis does not explain the sect's other violent actions: the abductions, murders, and earlier deployments of gas. More to the point, for any *coup d'état* to succeed, at the time of the attack Aum Shinrikyō would have had to have called into play previously established political alliances in order to create the appearance of broader support for the action. In particular, leaders of a serious coup attempt would want to establish contacts with governments capable of extending recognition to a new regime. Even if a coup attempt were not this well thought out, its perpetrators might have been expected to make their political program known, or at least reveal the basis of their opposition. Yet nothing along these lines characterizes Aum Shinrikyō at the time of the Tokyo attack. On the contrary, following what had become by then its standard line of projecting its actions onto others, the group claimed that the "authorities are the perpetrators" of the attack, and that Aum Shinrikyō was being framed (Kaplan and Marshall 1996, p. 148). In a European press release, dated 21 March, Asahara Shōkō maintained that a recent report of the group's supposed plan to commit mass suicide,

> evidently demonstrates their intention of killing us and making it appear to be a mass suicide. Suicide does not exist in the teaching of Buddhism; we reject suicide. Therefore, if it is reported that our order committed suicide, understand that we were killed by the Japanese state authorities.

In a separate radio broadcast from Russia monitored around the same time, Asahara announced to his followers, "It is time for you to carry out the plan of salvation. Let us prepare to meet our death without any regrets" (Mullins 1997, p. 318). However unnerving these statements, and whatever lay behind them, they are not the claims of a man intent on leading a *coup d'état*. Perhaps Asahara envisioned a diehard struggle of martyrdom, or maybe he really did envision a mass suicide and planned, as he had before, to project the blame onto others for what Aum Shinrikyō would carry out. But in any event, the inner circle of Aum Shinrikyō were not politicians, and their actions in 1995 do not resemble an attempted coup.

In the final analysis, the only hypothesis that makes sense centers on the beliefs of the sect and the years of conflicts between it and opponents in the

Figure 3.2 On 25 March 1995, five days after the Tokyo sarin attack, a devotee in the
sect's New York City headquarters sits facing photographs of Asahara Shōkō
and a sign that lists as the first of its ten commandments, "Do not kill, but
love." The vast majority of sect members had no knowledge of the violent
acts perpetrated by the group, and many continue to proclaim its innocence.

Source: AP/WORLDWIDE PHOTOS

wider society. The actions of the group were instrumentally rational only within
the narrow frame of the group's increasingly apocalyptic struggle against what its
leaders portrayed as external forces of evil. There was no contradiction between
beliefs and actions but, rather, articulation. And the powerful connection
between beliefs and actions was rendered necessary by the group's construction
of dramatically urgent circumstances.

The inner circle of the movement – in the first instance Asahara Shōkō –
had announced their doctrines all along. From the beginning, the kingdom of
Shambhala had been at the heart of their beliefs. But as time went on, reaching
Shambhala became an opportunity for the few rather than the many, and it
became mapped onto an apocalyptic struggle that would precede it. This apocalyptic eschatology gained power in light of certain events, in particular the sect's
early murder of an insider who might blow the whistle on the group, and its
murder of the Sakamoto family in the midst of a pitched external campaign of
opposition. After these early events, Aum Shinrikyō never lacked external

opponents, mainly the freelance writer Egawa Shōko, the victims' association, the lawyers, and longstanding residents in the communities where it established its settlements.

As the years passed, certain signs (including the fall of the Berlin wall in 1989, the 1991 Gulf War, and finally, the Kobe earthquake in early 1995) strengthened Asahara's view, or his claims to followers, that the end of the world was closer than he had previously thought. At first the mission of Aum Shinrikyō consisted of saving the world from the prophesied apocalypse. Later, the movement construed itself as the only group capable of surviving the apocalypse (Asahara 1992, p. 136). After the electoral failure of 1990, in a tragic reformulation of Buddhist ideas, the world at large became nothing more than an illusion. In the illusion of Aum Shinrikyō, the group had to triumph in its war against illusion so that its own reality could prevail. The increasingly devastating violence sustained that illusion internally and projected it into the wider world.

From violence to debates

Even after the Tokyo subway attack, when the police already had zeroed in on Aum Shinrikyō, acts of violence continued. On 30 March 1995, an attempt was made on the life of the chief of the Japanese National Police, allegedly by an Aum member who was a police officer. More gas attacks took place, or were barely foiled. Soon after Asahara Shōkō's arrest in May, a package bomb exploded in the office of the governor of Tokyo. Most tellingly, before Asahara was captured, he prophesied that April 15 would be a day of grave significance for Japan, especially for Tokyo. In the climate of fear that prevailed at the time, Tokyo became a ghost of its normal bustle (Reader 1996, p. 88). Asahara thus demonstrated the power of symbolic violence to reach far beyond its direct targets.

How far events in the first half of 1995 – the Kobe earthquake followed by Aum's campaign of terror – had deeper effects on the mass psychology of Japanese society is difficult to tell. A government poll conducted in December of that year showed confidence in Japan's capacity to maintain peace and stability had dropped significantly from twelve months earlier (JT 10 March 1996). What Walter Benjamin(1940: 263) called "chips of messianic time" shot through a nation that, in the years immediately thereafter, went into a crisis of public confidence.

During the Aum Shinrikyō trials over the next three years (scheduled to last years more) television cameras were not allowed in most of the courtrooms, but media coverage was enormous. Japan faced an unexpected boomerang effect. Across the country, hardly a day went by without images and stories about Aum Shinrikyō. The sect's properties became tourist attractions. Huge crowds rushed to visit Kamikuishiki. Fan clubs devoted to Aum spokesperson Joyū Fumihiro sprang up. Even before the trials began, the press interviewed members of the inner circle, former followers, and true believers on almost a daily basis. In part to counter public doubts about Aum's guilt, newspapers, magazines and television painted often excessively demonized profiles of key Aum members, offering meticulous details of their alleged crimes. The incredible horror received so much coverage that when the public was finally able to see and hear the disciples at the trials, many Japanese people had difficulty establishing any meaningful connection between the real human faces of the accused individuals and the crimes for which they were being tried, and they could not come to believe that the defendants were guilty.

In many respects, the case of Aum Shinrikyō is neither culturally, socially, nor religiously distinctive. New religious movements have arisen around the world; they are hardly specific to Japanese culture. Moreover, Aum Shinrikyō gained a following in societies other than Japan, most importantly Russia. Aum's often well-educated followers were disproportionately oriented toward science, medicine, technology, and engineering, but the broad social strata of its recruits did not differ markedly from a number of New-Age religious movements of the same generation in Europe, the United States, and Asia. The total devotion to a charismatic religious leader has been widespread in such cases, but *per se* it certainly does not necessarily result in violence. At one moment or another, many new religious movements have undergone crises of real or imagined persecution. In any number of cases, treatment of children and the broken ties between both minors and adults and their families are objects of tensions between sects and the wider society. The adepts of apocalyptic religious movements often believe that they belong to a sacred community which exists above the real world. In these respects, nothing distinctive about Aum Shinrikyō allows us to conclude that a similar episode could not happen sometime in the future. In other words, Aum cannot be dismissed as a unique case, either on the basis of some purported essence of Japanese culture or by comparison with other new religious movements. Its distinctiveness lies in how its apocalyptic theology developed in relation to its conflict with opponents, the media, and the state. Here, Aum Shinrikyō closely approximates a general pattern of apocalyptic religious violence.

To be sure, the sect's trajectory differs from that of Peoples Temple or the Branch Davidians in three important ways. First, the genesis of extreme violence came with an incident of murder within the sect itself. Second, the murders of the Sakamoto family went unsolved for years, thus heightening the apocalyptic mentality within the group and emboldening its leaders in their continuing conflicts with opponents. And third, the group did not commit mass suicide at the end.

The first difference shows that the entry point into the channel of apocalyptic religious violence is variable and contingent. Aum demonstrated a capacity for violence *before* it became an object of concerted external opposition. In turn, committing one act of violence established a precedent for subsequent violence, and concern over keeping this secret probably heightened the group's strong stand against external opponents when they did emerge. There is no reasonable basis for conjecture about what would have happened if Aum had never received the kind of opposition that began in 1989. The group's leaders demonstrated their willingness to undertake violence and, presumably, they would have been willing to engage in violence again, should they have deemed that circumstances warranted it. Structurally, Aum generated opposition on so many fronts that it is difficult to imagine the group *not* becoming the object of countermovements. Yet just as clearly, Aum violence became inextricably linked with opposition. The dynamic of violence from 1989 through 1995 always involved strategic actions that the sect either took against its opponents or used to try to keep authorities from closing in on them.

The second difference – the fact that the Sakamoto murders remained unsolved for years – demonstrates that conflict between a sect and its opponents is highly variable in its dynamics and its outcome. Still, the parallels are striking. Like Peoples Temple and the Branch Davidians, Aum Shinrikyō directed violence almost exclusively toward its opponents and, as in the two other cases, it was actions of Aum's opponents that led authorities to close in on the group. In this light, what seemed like public terrorism at the end developed out of the group's practice of strategic violence. Previously Aum had consistently used violence to eliminate internal and external opponents; as events came to a head, this more focused strategy broadened to the creation of generalized terror (cf. Reader 1996). Yet just as clearly, Aum Shinrikyō had acquired biological and chemical weapons, along with a helicopter, that ultimately might have been used to unleash an even grander apocalypse than the chaos they inflicted during their reign of terror. Compared to the two American groups, Aum Shinrikyō was far better prepared to create the holy war that its charismatic leader prophesied.

In short, even in light of the first two differences, Aum Shinrikyō's trajectory of apocalyptic religious violence was remarkably similar to those of Peoples Temple and the Branch Davidians: all three cases centered in a group with an apocalyptic ideology becoming involved in conflict with cultural opponents, the media, and state authorities as surrogates of the enemy in the battle of Armageddon. Thus the third difference between Aum and Jonestown and Waco is all the more striking. It would be wrong to essentialize "mass suicide" as a coherent type of event that always plays out according to the same script. Nevertheless, it is clear that Aum Shinrikyō's members never came close either to any pitched battle or to mass suicide, despite Asahara's call to "carry out the plan of salvation." Given the striking other parallels with Jonestown and Waco, the question is, why not? Two hypotheses suggest themselves, one structural, the other having to do with the cultural specificity of the group.

Structurally, both Peoples Temple and the Branch Davidians established other-worldly sectarian communities where they intended to survive beyond their prophesied apocalypses. To be sure, both groups armed themselves, and struck out violently against opponents who came to their doors. Aum Shinrikyō was also geared to survival after the apocalypse. However, by comparison to Peoples Temple and the Branch Davidians, the leadership circle of Aum came more strongly to resemble that of a pre-apocalyptic warring sect. This inner circle could not marshall any extended war against the established order, in part because it was cut off by its own wall of secrecy from the wider membership, which participated in an other-worldly spiritual hierarchy that marketed mysticism as apocalyptic transcendence. Isolated within isolation, the inner circle of Aum did not just seek to defend the sect *during* the Apocalypse; it prepared an arsenal of mass destruction that could be used to precipitate the public disaster that would *be* the Apocalypse. But Aum does not seem to have sought any final decisive showdown, and although Aum operatives continued to commit acts of violence in April and May 1995 (even for a brief time after Asahara himself was arrested), structurally they were in no position to call on the wider base of devotees either to pursue the struggle or to carry out mass suicide.

Cultural reasons perhaps reinforce the structural ones. Partly the refusal of suicide may have had to do with Buddhist theology, as Asahara once maintained. In addition, however, suicide carries a particular resonance with memories of samurai culture in Japanese society, one that connects it with honor in a different way from in the West. The true believers of Jonestown and Mount Carmel took stands that they construed as something like martyrdom. For them, death was more honorable than submission to opponents who sought to exercise jurisdiction over their communities. But in Japan, suicide may echo what Eiko Ikegami (1995, pp. 103–13) calls the "self-willed death" sometimes chosen by samurai warriors who failed their followers. The relationship between religion and samurai warrior culture has reflexive echoes, as has been noted by Robert Bellah (1970, p. 182; see also Collins 1997, p. 857): "The buddhist monk in his selfless devotion to his religious duties has been taken as an ideal for the warriors." In the meaningful construction of samurai honor, the person who is guilty of failing to fulfill the expectations of others, particularly his or her family, sometimes will commit suicide to absolve the family from dealing with the living source of its disgrace. In effect, this kind of suicide is an admission of responsibility, or in legal terms, guilt, and it is an act that certain Aum perpetrators of crimes considered (JT 11 December 1997). However, if other individuals among Aum's perpetrators of violence were acting within the cultural logic of the samurai, they may have rejected suicide precisely as a way of denying any dishonor in what they had done.

For that matter, the group itself sees no dishonor in the crimes of which it is accused. As the Public Security Agency – the main intelligence office of Japan's Ministry of Justice put it – "There has been no word of repentance or apology." The Japanese government failed in its bid to outlaw the sect, but the US State Department has designated Aum as a terrorist group, and Japanese authorities monitor certain known Aum individuals and operations twenty-four hours a day. Despite all the opposition and surveillance, however, Aum has continued to hold seminars, operate its computer businesses and web site, attract old followers back into the fold, and attract new ones, both in Japan and abroad. In December 1997, it counted some 2,200 members in Japan. Rumors circulate that the idol of certain Japanese teenaged girls, the handsome and charismatic spokesman for the sect, Joyū, will take control as leader of the group once he has served his time in jail for perjury and forgery (JT 30 December, 31 December 1997, 20 March 1998; NYT 11 October 1998, p. A10).

In contrast, in the wider population the stigma associated with Aum Shinrikyō became enormous. Anticult organizations with names like the "Defense Council for Countermeasures to Damage from Aum Shinrikyō" sprang up. Former members of the sect often found themselves rejected in the wider society, refused jobs and housing, and disowned by families embarrassed to admit having an Aum member among their number. In turn, some families of devotees found themselves ostracized by their neighbors, and moved to new communities.

There are obvious reasons for the social reactions in the sheer terror that Aum unleashed. But there may be deeper reasons as well. Japan reached the height of material abundance in the early 1990s, but did not always provide its young people with a stake in that abundance or the cultural basis to enjoy it. An intense devotion to work remained the order of the day. Nagaoka Hiroyuki, the head of the victims' association whom Aum members sprayed with VX in January 1995, testified poignantly on the parallel between Aum and the pyramidal hierarchical organization and restricted horizontal communication of some large Japanese firms. At the trial of one of the assailants who tried to murder him, Nagaoka recounted his career as a typical Japanese corporate employee. He worked long hours and spent little time with his family. His company transferred him and his family from city to city. Ultimately, Nagaoka came to the realization that his son had joined Aum Shinrikyō because the boy felt rootless in relation to his family and his schooling. With a change of heart, the father quit his job. When the son left Aum Shinrikyō in January 1990, he told his father he had returned, "because you have changed." For all Nagaoka's opposition to Aum Shinrikyō, he came to regard the sect as less than alien to Japanese society:

> I spent many years as a salary man. Every time I got promoted, they made me take a training session, a virtual confinement in a hotel, and when they were over, I felt that I could die for the company. When I remember my feelings in those days, I can understand that people can be made to think it is right to kill.
>
> (quoted in *Asahi Shinbun* 10 September 1997)

The fear and stigma surrounding Aum Shinrikyō may not have come so much from confronting something beyond comprehension as from looking at a distorted mirror image of Japanese society that people found uncomfortably understandable. Yet the Japanese were hardly alone in their cultural introspection. Six months before the Tokyo subway attack, in Switzerland and Québec, strange events of ritualized carnage had begun to raise similar issues for francophone societies.

4

THE MYSTICAL APOCALYPSE
OF THE SOLAR TEMPLE

John R. Hall and Philip D. Schuyler

At one o'clock in the morning on 5 October 1994, investigating judge André Piller was serving a stint as night duty officer in the Judge's Registry in Fribourg, Switzerland, when the telephone rang. "It was the police," Piller told us later. "They said, 'Your intervention is requested at Cheiry for a fire.'" Half an hour after the phone call, Piller arrived in Cheiry, a hamlet about thirty kilometers southwest of Fribourg. On a hill overlooking the village, the barn of La Rochette farm was completely engulfed in flames. While volunteer firemen tried to save the structure, Piller and his colleagues entered the farmhouse. They quickly found that this was no ordinary fire. Canisters of propane and garbage bags full of gasoline sat hooked up to detonation devices that hadn't gone off – yet. Then, Piller reported, "We saw this Monsieur with a plastic bag over his head. Albert Giacobino. We said to ourselves at first that this could be – could be! Conditional! – a suicide with a fire." There were only two problems with this hypothesis: although Giacobino had apparently

Aside from scholarly and journalistic sources, this chapter draws on interviews with former Temple members, government officials, and other individuals in Switzerland and Québec, and from documents in the archives of the Centre d'Information sur les Nouvelles Réligions (CINR) in Montreal. The authors are grateful for the advice and encouragement of John Bennet. We also thank the many people involved in this project, most of all: those who agreed to be interviewed; Annabelle Koch for research assistance; Jean-François Mayer for consultation; Bertrand Ouellet, the director of CINR; reporters – especially Jean Luque in Switzerland and Eric Clement and André Noel in Montreal – for courtesies extended during the course of research; Susan Palmer and Thomas Robbins for their editorial engagement; and Anne-Marie Tougas for providing archival materials on the Solar Temple. The research for this chapter was supported by the UC Davis Faculty Research Council and *The New Yorker* magazine, and we thank them both.

Periodicals and magazines consulted include: *l'Actualité* (Montreal), *Agence France Presse*, *Le Devoir* (Montreal), *The Gazette* (Montreal), *L'Hebdo* (Geneva), *L'Illustré* (Lausanne, Switzerland), *Le Journal de Genève*, *Le Journal de Montreal*, *Le Matin* (Lausanne, Switzerland), *Le Monde*, *Photo Police* (Montreal), *La Presse* (Montreal), *24 Heures* (Lausanne, Switzerland), *Le Soleil* (Québec), and the *Toronto Sun*.

been killed by a bullet to the brain, there was no gun near the body, and no hole in the plastic bag.

Searching long into the night, police eventually discovered a hidden salon where ten or fifteen briefcases lay open on the floor. In them investigators found papers that mentioned something called the Order of the Solar Temple. The room looked as though a meeting had been in progress. "But that raised a question," Piller noted. "Where are these people?" Finally, around four o'clock that morning, just as Piller and his colleagues were ready to quit for the night, they discovered a secret door in the wall of the salon; behind it was a narrow corridor with more incendiary devices. At the end of the corridor, the men entered a room. There lay eighteen bodies, dressed in silk capes and arranged in a circle, radiating outward like the spokes of a broken wheel. Beyond the circle, a door opened into a small, octagonal, chamber with mirrors on the walls and three more bodies on the floor. In a small room next door, yet another body lay alone. Altogether, there were twenty-three dead, twenty of them shot with a single gun, about half of them with plastic bags over their heads.

Piller and his colleagues had barely absorbed the shock of their discovery when they received news from a resort town about sixty kilometers away, Granges-sur-Salvan, where three vacation villas had caught fire. The houses belonged to Camille Pilet, a retired sales director of the Piaget watch company; Joseph DiMambro, owner of a chain of jewelry stores; and Luc Jouret, a homeopathic doctor and former Grand Master of the Order of the Solar Temple (OTS). The police connected the two events when they found a car registered to Joel Egger, a resident of the torched farmhouse in Cheiry, parked outside the compound at Salvan. When the flames died down, investigators discovered twenty-five bodies scattered around two of the three chalets; most of them were burned beyond recognition.

Police in Québec, Canada, heard the news from Switzerland the next morning and realized that there must be a connection to a strange fire in Morin Heights, a resort town in the Laurentian Mountains near Montreal. There, on the morning of 4 October, only hours before the events in Switzerland, a blaze had engulfed a complex of luxury condominiums owned by the same men – Pilet, DiMambro and Jouret – and a woman named Dominique Bellaton. A Swiss couple, Gerry and Colette Genoud, had perished in the fire with no obvious signs of violence. After the news from Switzerland, on October 6, police returned to the Morin Heights complex and found three more bodies hidden in a storage closet. Antonio Dutoit, a Swiss citizen, had fifty stab wounds in the back. His British wife, Nicky Robinson Dutoit, had been stabbed eight times in the back, four times in the throat, and once in each breast. Their baby boy, Christopher Emmanuel, just three months old, had been stabbed six times in the chest, resulting in twenty gashes to his heart. According to police reports, Mrs Dutoit and the baby had been "bled white".

News analysts were quick to compare the deaths in Switzerland and Québec to the mass suicide and murders at Jonestown in 1978 and the fiery carnage at Waco

Figure 4.1 A secret sanctum of the Solar Temple in the basement of a farmhouse in the village of Cheiry, Switzerland, where the authorities discovered the bodies of eighteen people on the morning of 5 October 1994.

Source: AP/WORLDWIDE PHOTOS

in 1993. Much the same connection was made by whoever wrote four letters with return addresses of "D. Part" and "Tran Sit Corp.," postmarked the morning after the fires and mailed to sixty journalists, scholars, and government officials world-wide. One letter, addressed To Those Who Love Justice, noted "a particularly troubling coincidence" between the Waco standoff and a 1993 raid by the Sûreté du Québec against Luc Jouret and two associates, Jean-Pierre Vinet and Herman Delorme. The writers maintained that their group had been subject to "systematic persecution" by authorities on three continents. Nevertheless they defined their own deaths as a "Transit, which is in no way a suicide in the human sense of the term."

In already tragic company, the Order of the Solar Temple seems truly bizarre. Whereas Peoples Temple and the Branch Davidians included mostly ordinary folk, like Aum Shinrikyō, the Ordre du Temple Solaire was hardly a sect of the dispossessed. Many of its participants were quite wealthy and socially established, and most others participated in the New-Age culture and economy that flourishes in postindustrial cities, resort areas, and other venues of the relatively educated new middle class. Among the dead in the October 1994 "Transit" were Robert Ostiguy, a wealthy businessman and mayor of the Québec town of Richelieu; Jocelyne Grand'Maison, a business correspondent for the *Journal de Québec*; Robert Falardeau, an official in the Québec Ministry of Finance; and

113

Guy Berenger, a French nuclear engineer. The roster of known survivors and associates was even more illustrious, including Alexandre Davidoff, nephew of the cigar manufacturer, and Edith and Patrick Vuarnet, the wife and son of the French skier and sportswear manufacturer, Jean Vuarnet. Michel Tabachnik, a distinguished orchestra conductor and student of Pierre Boulez, had often lectured to the group (although he denies ever being a member). These kinds of people could easily fit in at the Chamber of Commerce or a ski club; they might be expected to embrace rationalism or mysticism, perhaps yoga or Tai Chi, but never Armageddon.

Initially, the Swiss police suspected that the leaders of the group might not be found among the dead. Police were unsure of the whereabouts of several members of the group, including Camille Pilet, 68, the wealthy former Piaget representative, and the prime suspects in the Morin Heights murders, Joel Egger and Dominique Bellaton. The police detained Patrick Vuarnet, who had mailed the Transit letters from the Eaux-Vives post office in Geneva on Joseph DiMambro's orders. Two days after the fires, André Piller issued warrants for the arrest of Luc Jouret, the charismatic master of the group, and DiMambro, the presumed financial director. News reports began to portray the two as international racketeers who had amassed an enormous fortune – $93 million in Australian banks alone – through spiritual confidence games, money laundering, and gun running. In this scenario, the cult became a gang and the deaths became part of a plot to dispose of the Temple's inner circle and make off with the loot.

But within a week, Swiss authorities announced that the gang suspects – Pilet, DiMambro, Egger, Bellaton, and Jouret himself – were all indeed dead. A month after the fires, identifications were announced for the last bodies, including Line Lheureux, an anesthesiologist from the Caribbean island of Martinique, and Jean-Pierre Vinet, a former executive at Hydro-Québec, the state-run power company. Swiss police confirmed that twenty of the victims, all of them found at Cheiry, had died of gunshot wounds. Among the rest, some had probably died of smoke inhalation and others, perhaps, of a drug overdose or poison. At a lurid press conference the same month, the Sûreté du Québec played to the most sensational aspects of the case. Their spokesman interpreted the symbolism of each of the knife blows that had killed the Dutoits and declared categorically that the infant Dutoit, Christopher Emmanuel, had been killed because he was "the Antichrist." Joel Egger and Dominique Bellaton had perpetrated the Morin Heights killings and then boarded a flight for Switzerland. From there, Jouret and company had intended to depart for Sirius, the Dog Star.

The October 1994 Transit was not the last attempt to reach Sirius. Over a year later, on the winter solstice of 1995, sixteen more people associated with the sect died in a similar ceremony in a wooded mountain area in France, near the Swiss border. And five more adepts died in a third Transit, held near Québec around the spring equinox of 1997.

The significance of the Transits will continue to be contested. From one perspective, the people who died under Temple auspices must be dismissed as either selfish cynics or hapless postmodern fools. In a different view, the events suggest one or another clandestine plot. From a third direction, the deaths are seen as the product of "cults" enacting some vision of the Millennium. These possibilities are not necessarily contradictory. They all attach to the dynamics of countercultural religious movements and their uneven relationships to an established social order.

Many countercultural religions offer mystical association or quietistic community for individuals who, as Max Weber aptly put it, "cannot bear the fate of the times" (1946: 155). But in the most volatile apocalyptic sects, charismatic prophecy gives "religious" meaning to an anticipated cataclysmic end of the world as we know it. The Solar Temple developed a quasi-Catholic mystical theology not unlike Aum's quasi-Buddhist doctrines about moving from this world to the next, and even though it lacked the strongly apocalyptic Protestant (and in Jones's case, crude communist) sensibilities of Peoples Temple and the Branch Davidians, it ended in murder and mass suicide that bore a striking resemblance to the violence of Jonestown and Waco. However, as with Aum Shinrikyō, the affluent, mostly post-Catholic society of francophone Europe during the early 1990s hardly seems the place where apocalyptic anxieties could take hold among people like those associated with the Solar Temple. Would it not be an exaggeration to understand the Temple Solaire in terms of a cultural struggle like those that swirled around Peoples Temple, the Branch Davidians, and Aum Shinrikyō? On the face of it, and for multiple reasons, the Order of the Solar Temple does not seem a likely candidate for apocalyptic violence. It is thus important to consider whether the deaths of people associated with the Solar Temple resulted from a dynamic similar to the conflicts at Jonestown, Mount Carmel, and in Japan. If not apocalyptic murder and mass suicide, what was it? And if it was apocalyptic violence, how can its occurrence be squared with the generic narrative model that describes the other three cases? To answer these questions, we need to explore both the historical filiations of the Temple Solaire and the actual trajectory of its unravelling.

The countercultural movement as a hybrid reordering

At their most successful, countercultural movements influence the cultural orderings of society, by producing new meaningful accounts of existence and new forms of social organization. To the degree that such cultural innovations yield a competitive advantage to their advocates, on whatever basis, they pose a serious threat to the existing social order. The pathways, degree of resistance met, and success of any such reordering as it diffuses through society will vary. Thus, there are vast differences between the hierarchical, bureaucratic diffusion of Catholicism through Europe and the Americas, the sectarian congregational spread of Protestantism, and the early growth of Mormonism as a sort of patriarchic proto-ethnic group. Nor can these developments be understood simply as alternative channels of diffusion: they simultaneously embody the principles of the innovative cultures and forms of social organization themselves.

Wondering whether the Temple Solaire was caught up in such a process, we met a surviving member, Louis-Marie Belanger, on a cold, snowy day in February 1995, in a bar in the little Québec town of Sainte-Anne-de-la-Pérade on the north bank of the St Lawrence River. Louis-Marie Belanger lives on after the deaths of others in the Temple Solaire, but he seems to telescope history by transcending time. As Louis-Marie tells it, the Temple Solaire of our era met the same fate that befell the original Knights Templar whom they took as their inspiration. "What's the difference between the Middle Ages and now?" he asks. "None. Maybe the way it's done is a little more subtle. The result is the same . . . . We had to close too, because we were publicly banished. Flushed out, you know. we've been flushed. Right there." – The Middle Ages? The way it's done? Banished? – "Check in history books," says Belanger.[1]

In the twelfth century, when Christian soldiers "took the cross" (from which, the word crusade) as a promise to make a pilgrimage to the Holy Land, the Order of Poor Knights of the Temple of Solomon was formed to protect Jerusalem and the pilgrimage routes. Based at the site of the temple of Solomon, the knights took religious vows, and they obtained sanctification of their order by the Church of Rome with the help of St Bernard, the Abbot of Clairvaux. Not that Bernard was particularly enamored of the knights' religious fervor. "You will find very few men in the vast multitude which throngs to the Holy Land," he observed, "who have not been unbelieving scoundrels, sacrilegious plunderers, homicides, perjurers, adulterers." Europe, St Bernard suggested, would be better off without such men, most of them badly educated and illiterate, drawn from the lower echelons of the feudal order's warrior class. As Knights Templar, they could serve the Church in the unseemly duty of killing infidels. But this was a difficult point. Whereas medieval theologians had previously insisted on keeping the carnage of war separated from the direct works of the Church, Bernard produced a fusion: "For Christ! hence Christ is attained. . . . The soldier of Christ kills safely: he dies the more safely. He serves his own interest in dying, and Christ's interests in killing!" Thus wrote the man whom Dante, in *The Divine Comedy,* had intercede with the Virgin Mary on behalf of the pilgrim who had finally arrived in Heaven seeking God.

During their years of glory during the twelfth and thirteenth centuries, the Templars wore a white mantle (symbolizing innocence) with a red cross (affirming their readiness for Christian martyrdom). Under the leadership of a Grand Master, they established cohesive fighting cadres and organized other military ranks of troops under their command. From their early duties maintaining strongholds and protecting pilgrimage routes to Jerusalem, the Templars developed an ever more widespread organization that helped finance the religious Crusades with support from feudal nobility. So many donations flowed in that the Templar order became adept at property speculations and banking functions, such as protecting, transmitting, and loaning funds, services that they began to provide for dukes and kings. Chartered directly by the Pope outside any authority of the bishops, the Templars also established lay memberships in the order, in some instances operating a sort of parallel religious organization that collected dues and offered the sacraments, even to men and women who had been excommunicated from the Church. By the end of the thirteenth century, the Order of the Knights Templar had become something of a hybrid corporate conglomerate; operating outside the religious and feudal orders, it combined military and security operations with banking, money lending, and the dispensing of salvation.

Unfortunately for the Templars, however, their organizational successes overreached their military prowess. The infidels won in the Levant, inflicting a series of defeats on the crusading forces that culminated in the disastrous loss of Acre, on the Mediterranean coast of Galilee, in 1291. Many martyrs attained Christ in that battle, but the defeat raised a thorny theological question. Why had the forces of righteousness under God failed? Because the Templars lacked any solid base in medieval society, and because the order was powerful yet secretive, they became suspect. Perhaps the Templars were not truly servants of Christ but something much more sinister. The money lending had always offended feudal sensibilities. "Atrocity tales" that began to circulate described the Templars as greedy, corrupt in matters of honor, and foolhardy in the Crusades. Rumors surfaced that they were sodomites. The king of France, Philip the Fair, dispatched undercover agents to infiltrate the Templars, and in 1307 he ordered an amazing feat for its day, the simultaneous arrest of every known Templar in his kingdom. Two months later, the Pope, Clement V, demanded that other European monarchs undertake similar mass arrests.

Once locked up, Templars found themselves accused of having denied that Christ is the son of God. The tortures to which they were subjected ended only when they confessed to this heresy and disavowed their allegiance to the Knights Templar. Some knights committed suicide rather than repudiate a religious military order governed by a strict Rule, but hundreds broke down and admitted to defiling the Cross. Later, when it seemed they might actually get a fair trial, fifty-four knights recanted their earlier confessions. But before any new trial could be organized, a Church provincial Council in Paris sentenced them to death for this "relapse" into heresy. On 12 May 1310, amidst protestations of innocence to the end, the fifty-four were burned alive at the stake. Four years later the Grand Master himself, Jacques de Molay, denied the charges against the order, and he and a provincial leader of the Templars were burned at the stake in Paris, on a small island in the Seine. Within the year, Philip the Fair and Clement V were both dead, victims, legend has it, of the curse placed on them by the Grand Master for their infamy. Dante's pilgrim later found Philip the Fair in purgatory, in the area devoted to avarice.

What are we to make of the possibility that countercultural religious movements engage in hybrid reordering of the social fabric? There is at least a *prima facie* case for understanding the medieval Knights Templar and their fate in light of this thesis. They concocted an innovative hybrid religio-military-financial organization outside the existing order that, if left unchallenged, might have led the nascent European power complex to develop in an entirely different direction, towards a sort of religiously sanctioned military capitalistic socialism. By comparison, the Temple Solaire of our day has not been nearly so central to the axis on which historical development turns. But Louis-Marie Belanger's seemingly romantic allusion to a distant past should not be lost on us. This man, holding forth over coffee in a bar in Sainte-Anne-de-la-Pérade, Québec, wearing a white t-shirt, red v-necked sweater, and black nylon jacket, claims an affinity with the medieval Knights Templar that seems like the commitment of a true chevalier. Louis-Marie shows neither relief nor open regret that he wasn't asked to take part in the Transit, and he refuses to judge his fellow Templars. "Maybe they are a little more conscious than I am," he suggests, "and they knew things I didn't know." To the world at large, a group that claims murder and suicide as a "Transit" will seem incomprehensible. Yet the sincere and reflective faith of Louis-Marie Belanger gives pause to wonder what that small number of seekers from our era did find in the Temple Solaire.

The salvation resonance of the Solar Temple

To succeed even modestly, a countercultural religious movement must offer a formula of salvation that resonates with the existential needs, interests, and anxieties of its audiences. This cultural resonance may develop because of a decline in the relevance or availability of previous salvation formulae, and it may be amplified by the emergence of new felt needs for salvation on the part of audiences, who are sometimes themselves members of newly emergent or changing social strata. This, in broad strokes, is the story that Max Weber told of the Protestant reformation in modern Europe, where an ethic of self-denial and self-regulation resonated deeply with the spiritual and worldly anxieties of diverse classes participating in the emerging urban capitalism.

No one now suspects that the Temple Solaire will bear the same sort of significance for the postmodern world that Protestantism held for modernity. But neither is it very satisfactory to say that the hapless participants in the Temple Solaire were victims of an elaborate con game, for charlatanism does not necessarily distinguish flash-in-the-pan cults from movements that attain a world historical significance. As Weber (1978, p. 242) remarked, the founder of Mormonism, Joseph Smith, "may have been a very sophisticated swindler (although this cannot definitely be established)." The question thus becomes, what kind of con game, with what possible appeal?

To understand the deep resonance of l'affaire Temple Solaire with age-old cultural tensions of religion, we can go to Catholic Switzerland, in the canton of Valais, below the Great St Bernard Pass, near Granges-sur-Salvan, where the inner core of the Temple Solaire took their October 1994 "Transit." The roots of faith in Valais run deep. The town of St Maurice is named for the leader of martyred Roman legionaires who refused to worship the Roman god Mercury. A church grew up around their tombs, and it amassed a great treasure from the huge numbers of pilgrims who visited the holy site in the middle ages. Today, the church suggests much about Catholicism. Its stained-glass windows and sacred reliquaries offer clues about how the medieval Roman church regarded Judaism as blind to salvation through Christ, and how it incorporated astrological symbols of the planets, the moon and the sun into its pantheon. But today, its sanctuary is empty except for a handful of Sunday tourists. Only four candles are burning at a chapel altar. The Catholic Church has worked hard to rekindle the allegiances of Catholics with increasingly secular orientations, most notably with the Vatican II reforms that dropped Latin from the Catholic mass. In Europe, this strategy does not seem to have succeeded, and in the process, the Church has given up the sense of mystery and tradition that the Latin mass marked, and lost some of its most traditional followers to schismatic sects.

The same bifurcation also occurred on the other side of the Atlantic. Once as Catholic as the Pope, Québec underwent *"la revolution tranquille"* in the early 1960s. "People left the church massively," remembers Daniel Latouche, a researcher at the Institut National de Recherches Scientifiques in Montreal. The Québecois are still part of a Catholic tradition, argues Bertrand Ouellet, the director of Montreal's Centre d'Information sur les Nouvelles Religions (CINR). But given the exodus thirty years ago, "they only have memories of the Catholic church before Vatican II. And when they arrive at the period of life where the great questions come out again, they have nothing, zero, zip for an answer, and they search elsewhere." Ouellet muses, "Formerly, there was one great religion, like a garden that was fully cultivated. Well, we chopped down the garden, and now things sprout up everywhere. It's not a spiritual desert, it's a forest. A jungle."

Indeed, CINR has files on as many as three thousand groups in Québec: Eastern, New Age, fundamentalist, mystical, worshippers of extraterrestrial life, the whole gamut. Most of them are perfectly peaceful. And they are not just found in cities where the New-Age bookstores flourish. As Luc Chartrand, a journalist for the newsmagazine, *l'Actualité* notes, "If you go out of Montreal, in the small towns, you'll find a surprising amount of everything exotic – acupuncture, Tai Chi, this Japanese massage, Shiatsu."

The Temple Solaire does not draw its cultural inspiration from the East, but from European Catholicism and its countercultures. Not only did the Solar Temple invoke the medieval Knights Templar, they also became adepts of the longstanding Rosicrucian heresy that claims, as one seventeenth-century French poster put it, to "rescue our fellow men from the error of death."

Over the centuries, a series of mystics, prophets, and charlatans have taken up the mantle of the Knights Templar and reported contacts with the "Unknown Superiors" reputed to make revelations to Grand Masters of the Rosy Cross. Both traditions have inspired secret societies dedicated to chivalry, alchemy, and the gnostic wisdom of the ancient Egyptians and Essenes, heralded either as the "true" Christianity or a far more encompassing spiritual tradition. Eventually, masonic fraternities began to claim descent from the martyred Templars and the Order of the Rose and Cross as a way of substantiating their ancient heritage. These claims fitted easily into the odd Masonic mix of esoteric lore, enlightenment philosophy, egalitarian conviviality, and "aristocratic" status-graded membership. In the secret masonic world, the Enlightenment became subject to magical erasure through esoteric wisdom that held out the promise of bridging the Western dualisms between science and religion, reason and faith, spirit and sexuality. Just as surely, secret organizations became venues of political intrigue. By the nineteenth century, conservatives (and later, fascists) facing unruly rising social classes began to use the lodges to reaffirm the old order, virtue, authority, and the aristocracy of a master race. Yet radicals just as readily drew on the esoteric traditions to invoke reason, community, and a revolutionary theory of "synarchy": a utopian plan to establish a technocratic oligarchy of Templar initiates.

Over the last two centuries, hundreds of neo-Templar and Rosicrucian orders have formed, dissolved, and reformed. Religious movement scholar Massimo Introvigne has valiantly attempted to trace the lines of schism and fusion among these groups (1995). The task is not a simple one, for the history of concrete events has become mixed with imaginary history. Here, the wall of secrecy surrounding the enchanted inner Masonic world is also a mirror, reflecting anxieties of the everyday outer world. Thus, whenever the Masons surface in the news, fact and rumor and belief are quickly woven into contradictory conspiracy theories. In the popular imagination, clandestine struggles unfold between vast but submerged apparatuses of secret organizations, from the Catholic lay group, Opus Dei, to the Trilateral Commission. This hidden world of intrigue feeds both the semiotic fantasy of Umberto Eco's novel, *Foucault's Pendulum*, and the populist paranoia of Pat Robertson's *The New World Order*. Whatever their truth, assertions spill back into the wider course of events.

The man who would launch the Ordre du Temple Solaire, Joseph DiMambro, moved in this murky world for forty years. At one time or another, he was closely associated with the Rosicrucian order AMORC, and with the Sovereign and Military Order of the Temple of Jerusalem, a neo-Templar society. (Both groups deny that he was ever a member.) Tracing the arrows on Massimo Introvigne's chart, one can easily imagine DiMambro rubbing shoulders with members of the Mafia, the Italian Masonic lodge P2, and the private Gaullist police organization, Service d'Action Civique. On the other hand, there is no proof for any of these connections.

There is, in fact, very little solid information about DiMambro's life. Born in the south of France in 1924, he is known to have been a jeweller. In 1972 he was convicted of fraud for impersonating a psychologist and passing bad checks. Around the same time, invoking the longstanding mystics' fascination with Egypt, he established a communal group called La Pyramide at a farm near Geneva. When the farmhouse caught fire in 1979 (a possible insurance swindle), he started a group called the Fondation Golden Way in a Geneva mansion. By this time, DiMambro had become quite friendly with Julien Origas, reputedly a former Gestapo agent in Brest, and the founder of the Renewed Order of the Temple (ORT), a group that combined Templar and Rosicrucian ideas. DiMambro also came under the influence of Jacques Breyer, a French alchemist.

The main ideas of the Temple Solaire trace to the crucible of neo-Templar and Rosicrucian movements in Switzerland and southern France (Introvigne 1995; Mayer 1996). Julien Origas had participated in the broadly Rosicrucian post-World War II milieu of French mysticism, where claims circulated about the existence of "Ascended Masters" who possess the gift of eternal life, moving in and out of historical existence either in material bodies or as specters. In particular, Origas was in touch with a quite accomplished esoteric practitioner named "Angela," who claimed to be a reincarnated fusion of Socrates and Queen Elizabeth I of England. Through her, Origas began to establish stronger contacts with the Ascended Masters of the Grand Lodge of Agartha.

The other clearly evident source of the Solar Temple worldview was Jacques Breyer. In French freemasonry circles during the 1950s, Breyer met Maxime de Roquemaure, who claimed to carry the true esoteric legacy of the original Knights Templar through a branch of the medieval order that had survived over the centuries in far-off Ethiopia. Together they founded the Sovereign Order of the Solar Temple, based on apocalyptic ideas about a "solar Christ." Breyer even published a book on the subject, *Arcanes Solaire; ou, Les Secrets du Temple Solaire* (1959), followed by a 1964 book on the relation between alchemy and *The Divine Comedy*, Dante's famous poem in which, at the very end, the pilgrim arrived in heaven finally glimpses "the Love that moves the Sun." In the early 1980s, as one former Temple member recalls, DiMambro, Origas, and Breyer were "three chums who spoke of esoteric things."

The homeopathic doctor who became central to the Solar Temple, Luc Jouret, entered the DiMambro–Origas–Breyer orbit in 1980. Born in the then Belgian Congo in 1947, Jouret had received a medical degree from the Free University of Brussels in 1974, practiced conventional medicine for a couple of years in the Belgian countryside, and then discovered homeopathy in India while on an expedition to learn the medicines of the world. In the late 1970s and early 1980s, he established a homeopathic practice, first in Belgium, then in France, just across the border from Geneva. There, Joseph DiMambro invited him to speak at Golden Way.

In turn, DiMambro arranged for Jouret to meet Julien Origas, and in 1981 Jouret joined the Renewed Order of the Temple. At some point, following the path of Origas, Jouret was ordained as a priest, in his case by a dissident Roman Catholic "self-proclaimed bishop" (*Agence France Presse*, 4 April 1996). When Origas died in 1983, Jouret took over ORT as Grand Master. Forced out in a schism within a year, he took more than half the membership with him. By that time, Jouret had tied his fate to DiMambro. In 1984 they founded the Ordre Internationale Chevalresque Tradition Solaire, later called the Ordre du Temple Solaire, with Jouret again as Grand Master.

The alliance with DiMambro opened a new world of possibilities to Jouret. In effect, he became the front man who provided channels to a Templar- and Rosicrucian-inspired secret society via an integrated, holistic vision of the New Age. In his public persona, Luc Jouret was strongly centered in his homeopathic

Figure 4.2 Luc Jouret, a homeopathic doctor born in the Belgian Congo, became highly successful at lecturing in a charismatic style that introduced the public to the outlines of the Solar Temple's esoteric theology. This undated photo was released by the Sûreté du Québec after the first collective suicide by members of the group, in October 1994.

Source: AP/WORLDWIDE PHOTOS

medical philosophy, an approach that proved attractive to francophone audiences on both sides of the Atlantic. Under the sponsorship of Club Amenta and Club Archedia, organizations that he helped found in the early 1980s, Jouret travelled a lecture and conference circuit of hotels and universities in France, Belgium, Switzerland, Martinique, and Québec, making presentations on topics like "Love and Biology," "Christ, the Sphinx, and the New Man," and "Old Age: The Doorway to Eternal Youth." Jouret's publications and lecture cassettes, and tickets to his symposia were sold through a network of health food stores and New-Age bookstores, and he became something of a phenomenon. At one 1987 lecture in Lausanne, Swiss religious historian Jean-François Mayer counted more than six hundred people in the audience, some from as far away as Belgium and Brittany.

With his deep, soothing voice and dark, penetrating eyes, Jouret was, by all accounts, a riveting speaker. Herman Delorme, for one, was tremendously impressed when a girlfriend invited him to attend a Jouret lecture in Montreal in 1990. According to Delorme:

> You start listening and by God, you know, you just all of a sudden feel so attracted to what he is saying. You talk about the universe, you talk about how man is made of four ingredients and how the stars are made of these same four ingredients. Then you go back to Egypt and Egyptology, and then somewhere along the line comes the possibility of extraterrestrials. And it goes on and it goes on like that. But the more you hear, the less you understand, and therefore, the more you want to know. You slowly get caught up in the web.

Out of the hundreds who came to the public lectures, usually a handful were at least tempted by the web, and Jouret and his associates gave them special attention. Those who were interested in the "art of living" could join one of his clubs, each of which specialized in a different area, nutrition and organic gardening, or music and theater. For those drawn to more spiritual matters, Jouret had something else to offer. After Herman Delorme attended his second seminar, he was called up on stage, and Jouret told him, "If you make the first steps, I'll make sure that you make the other ones." "Well," Herman said, "I had no idea what he meant, but it sounded so great, you know, coming from him. I felt like I had been singled out. He had that ability to make you feel important, and it was important to me to feel that way."

In Jouret's vision, the practice of homeopathy connects with the unity of all energies. "In the interior of the physical body there blooms a vital force, a vital energy which was there before Man's physical appearance on earth," he asserted. In turn, every pathology results from a disruption of the vibrations of vital energy, manifested in symptoms. But the homeopathic practitioner is not interested in clinical symptoms. What matters is the Sick Being. As Jouret concluded on one of his cassettes, "You are not sick because you have a disease; you have a disease because you are sick."

Given the vibratory unity of all things, it was an easy jump from homeopathy to environmentalism, and from there to ecological apocalypse. Pollution, Jouret said, affects the earth in the same way that a bad diet affects the human body; it disrupts the vital energy. In fact, pollution is not merely "the exterior degradation of the Planet, of Life as such," it is "an exterior reflection of a pollution much deeper inside Man – mental pollution, emotional pollution, and, at the extreme, an authentically spiritual pollution."

Against this grim vision Jouret counterposed the transition from the Age of Pisces to the Age of Aquarius. However, the passage would not be as peaceful as the 1960s vision. We face "a kingdom of fire, in which everything will be consumed." For those who survive and cross over, the Age of Aquarius will bring new laws, new ways of thinking, and new vibratory harmonies. In the meantime, Jouret intimated, controlling the vital force will not only assure victory over disease and pollution in this world, it can completely liberate us from the human condition.

Vital force or no, with the Ordre du Temple Solaire hardly begun, Jouret already began to feel restrictions on his freedom in Europe. According to Jean-François Mayer, Jouret was quite upset that his name was publicly mentioned in connection with Origas's Renewed Order of the Temple, a group identified as "very dangerous" in a 1984 publication put out by the Center for Documentation, Education, and Action Against Mental Manipulation, a French anticult organization. That same year Jouret told Mario Pelletier in Montreal that Europe was old and worn out, its land filled with millions and millions of bodies, and too many vibrations of war and violence. Across the Atlantic, Jouret revealed to followers, Québec was blessed with a broad granite plate and a strong magnetic field that would protect the area from earthquakes in the coming cataclysm. By 1984, he and DiMambro had decided to establish a base in North America.

It was around this time – back in Switzerland – that Rose-Marie and Bruno Klaus met Luc Jouret, when Bruno consulted the doctor on the advice of a friend. Bruno thought he had a bad earache, but Jouret found something far worse, a "cancer" that he proceeded to "cure." After that Jouret liked to remind Bruno, "You should be dead. You owe me your life." Bruno seemed to take this literally, and he became a devoted follower. Sometime later, the Temple astrologer, a former hairdresser named Marie-Louise Rebaudo, saw major changes in Bruno's chart; planetary alignments revealed that he was to move to Québec to help start a 350 acre "ark of survival." "We were leaving Pisces and going toward Aquarius," Rose-Marie recalled. "Europe was going to be burnt up, and we needed to escape to another continent. They said they wanted one hundred people, enough to repopulate the world afterward."

The survival farm was in Sainte-Anne-de-la-Pérade, on the north shore of the Saint Lawrence River, two-thirds of the way from Montreal to Québec City. The group's headquarters was an old orphanage where Jouret's Club Amenta also established a kind of New-Age retreat called Le Center Culturel du Domaine du

Sacre-Coeur. Advertising flyers from the late 1980s announce programs on various disciplines in "the science of life," as well as chamber music concerts and "spectacles." In addition to half a dozen members of the group who actually lived in the house, others who had moved to town took their meals there nearly every day. Once a month, members of the Ordre du Temple Solaire came from all over Québec for a meeting on the night of the full moon.

Gatherings both in Québec and Europe also marked the transits of the earth around the sun. Jean-François Mayer recalls attending such a bonfire held in the French Savoie countryside near Geneva to mark the 1987 summer solstice. "The only ceremonial part was the fire, and people came from several sides, each with a torch, and put it in. And there were also some instructions: we had always to turn around the fire only clockwise." During the event, Mayer remarked to a Temple representative, "Oh, this is ritual." "Well, no," the man replied, "Real ritual, it's something much more."

Deemed worthy, the Temple seeker gained the opportunity to experience deeper spiritual truths. But the experience came not through meditation, as in Aum Shinrikyō's Buddhism. "Come on!" says Louis-Marie. "You may meditate, you may meditate, but you don't pass your life meditating. You need your bread and butter on the table, dammit." Nor does personal prayer establish the direct communication with the Divine that the Protestant reformers had championed. The central device was the time-tested practice of ritual. Like traditional Catholicism, indeed, like all religions that ritualize the mysteries of the Divine, the Order of the Solar Temple could distribute its core religious experience even to people who were not "musical" in esoteric theology or in the disciplining of the mind in the pursuit of transcendental illumination. What the Order offered was a mystical *mood* available to the many, not just the spiritually gifted.

By 1990, the rules of the order described an organization under the absolute authority of a secret inner group called the Synarchy of the Temple. There were three major degrees: Brothers of the Court, Chevaliers of the Alliance, and Brothers of Former Times, each with three internal ranks. On the occasion of one ritual, men and women wearing white mantles with a red cross over the breast file slowly, two by two, into a round room. Each couple bows before a candle standing on a mirrored triangular pedestal in the center of the chamber, and then the pairs split to form two lines along the wall. Suddenly, from beneath their robes, the chevaliers pull forth long epées. Raising the swords in unison, they bring the cruciform hilts to their faces, then stretch their arms outward, pointing the blades toward the light.

The event is a Solar Temple initiation ceremony, recorded on a video seized by the Québec police. As the sound track switches from Lohengrin to Gregorian chant, two white-mantled Templars lead in a man in a business suit. The escorts take a new robe and surplice from an altar and carefully place them around the initiate's shoulders. He then kneels before a priest, his hands on the altar next to a red rose and a Bible held open by a sword. The priest picks up the sword and dubs the initiate on his right shoulder, his left shoulder, and the top of his head.

After the ceremony ends, the members file out of the sanctuary, two by two, into a long corridor. At the end of the corridor, one can barely see a mirrored door slide open. The video closes with a closeup of Luc Jouret giving a priestly benediction (followed by a fullscreen shot of a fireplace, crackling warmly).

Behind the mirrored door lies the inner sanctum, a small round room just large enough for a handful of people to stand. At a ceremony with forty people, perhaps only three or four would be admitted to the room, leaving the others to wait outside, sometimes for hours. The chosen few saw and heard the Ascended Masters, emanations of eternal life who dispensed gnostic wisdom and practical advice. Police in Québec and Switzerland have mentioned holographic projections in the crypts, and Temple survivor Thierry Huguenin talks of "montages." Probably only Tony Dutoit, DiMambro's longtime technical assistant, knew how all the special effects really worked, and he was murdered at Morin Heights. However they were created, the projections, together with the robes, candles, incense, and music, created a powerful sacred tableau.

Initiates not only encountered the divine, they joined an eternal chain of reincarnations. DiMambro especially seems to have promoted this idea. "He made me believe that I was a great reincarnation of Bernard de Clairvaux," Thierry Huguenin told us. "Whether or not one believes in reincarnation," he argued, "you have to admit that man lives with emotions, and you know that one can have an experience as a child and remember it at eighty. And you can imagine, if you do believe in reincarnation, that there is a memory, a cellular memory, which, across time and space, comes back home to live in man." Thierry remembers seeing the last grand master of the Knights Templar, Jacques de Molay, and almost all the apostles of Christ. "And then, Egypt, well, there we had a lot. Akhnaton, of course, was DiMambro. DiMambro was Akhnaton, Moses, Cagliostro, Osiris. He used to say, 'You understand, in all my incarnations I always had to fight, because my spiritual development was always so far in advance of the time when I was living.'"

Inside the Order, according to Huguenin, Luc Jouret had no special status; he simply had a job to do, like everyone else. Jouret was the Grand Master, but DiMambro was the secret master, unknown to the outside world. "He was one of the last on earth," as far as Louis-Marie Belanger is concerned. "Maybe one of the last conscious persons on Earth. It's that simple."

"So, could you feel his energy?"

"The only thing I can answer: you're just next to me, I don't need to touch you. And something may happen – that depends on the Big Guy up there. We're channels. So if a channel opens, fine. That energy can go through. But if you don't have anything to get from me except words and ideas, we won't be channeling, that's all. You take that radio on that FM dial, how can you catch the message on 107 point 5 if you're stuck at 92 point 3?"

The Temple Solaire is a hybrid that transcends neat modern distinctions between science and religion, reason and faith, spirit and sexuality, technology and popular culture. Jouret played on wide interests in homeopathic medicine to unveil a theology of health and environmental consciousness that would counter the ecological apocalypse. These ideas became wedded to other "New Age" motifs – astrology, numerology and time travel – that themselves have been persistent elements in both the syncretic symbolic codes of European Catholicism and the "invented traditions" of Knights-Templar and Rosicrucian mysticism. The Solar Temple's neo-traditional Catholic countercultural world-view eliminated any sharp distinction between life and death, and it extended the pantheon of eternal figures like the Saints into the world of everyday life by the visits of the Ascended Masters. In a world beset by secular influences even within the Church itself, the Temple Solaire resurrected enchantment.

In all of this, the Temple Solaire appealed almost entirely to people of franco-phone Catholic background who felt that the Church had become increasingly irrelevant to the felt New-Age concerns of postmodern Europe and Québec. However, its principle innovation – erasing the firm boundary between life and death – resonates with similar religious ideas that have a wider following. In Texas, a woman named Annie Kirkwood reports on her conversations with Mary, the Blessed Virgin (1991), who operates as something of an Ascended Master herself, offering advice on how to move back into the spirit world after physical death. And the leader of the Church Universal and Triumphant in Montana, Elizabeth Clare Prophet, also sometimes talks about the possibilities of moving in and out of this world. Apparently, the image of heaven as the reward for the faithful upon death is no longer compelling for those who believe in reincarnation. The Temple Solaire may not be the avatar of a dramatic cultural reordering, but it reflects a broader New-Age reconstruction of religious meanings that has gained the attention of a substantial audience.

The struggle for cultural legitimacy

However marginal countercultural religious movements may appear, they must have a certain power and appeal in wider society, for they are treated as though they pose a real threat, and alternately subjected to ridicule and repression. Like the medieval Knights Templar, such groups are "utopian" in the specific sense that their ascendancy on a wide scale would entail a dramatic reordering of culture, power, and social relations. In the extreme case, an established church may suffer a loss of legitimacy at the hands of states that side with a counter-cultural move-ment, as was the case with the Protestant reformation. Given this potential, it is hardly surprising that the trajectories of counter-cultural religious movements are often shaped by conflicts with an established social order. As we have seen in the cases of Peoples Temple, the Branch Davidians, and Aum Shinrikyō, these conflicts sometimes play out as struggles between the group and a loose alliance that develops among cultural opponents (including former participants and distraught relatives of members), mass media stories that frame issues of moral deviance, and modern states that have absorbed the "religious" function of enforcing cultural legitimacy. In all these three cases, the conflict resulted in

127

deadly violence. Yet is there really any comparison? Was the Temple Solaire actually subjected to "systematic persecution" as the Transit letter claimed?

The leaders of the Temple Solaire worked assiduously to promote a public image of high cultural legitimacy, meeting in the best hotels and holding seminars at rented halls in universities. Yet the public facade protected a secret world, and it turned out to be a fragile construction.

A trickle of defections that began in the 1990s left the Solar Temple potentially subject to embarrassing revelations by its apostates, and cut into the financial vitality of the group (Mayer 1996). The person who ended up causing the group the most trouble, Rose-Marie Klaus, was the exception who proves the rule of the group's appeal to a culturally Catholic audience. "Mysticism," says Rose-Marie Klaus with considerable distaste. "All this tra-la-la and all those robes. It's a thing very far from Protestantism. Luc Jouret depended on the Masters, but they didn't exist. I never believed in that. I am too Protestant for anyone to tell me that there's something else besides God."

Louis-Marie Belanger thinks that Rose-Marie Klaus was "a pain in the neck all the way," but he did like one thing about her: "she was able to say what she believed in, right in your face. She said once, 'I'm gonna put you into trouble.' She said that to Jouret; I was there." Belanger adds, "And she did." Six months after arriving in Sainte-Anne-de-la-Pérade, while her husband Bruno, a lapsed Catholic, grew more deeply involved in the Order, Rose-Marie had pulled back. Nevertheless, she continued to live with Bruno in a house just down the street from Sacre-Coeur. But then, as Rose-Marie remembers it, Bruno came home one day and announced, "The Masters have decided. I am going to live with another woman." Upset, Rose-Marie called upon Luc Jouret to mediate, but his solution followed a Temple formula of "cosmic" coupling that ignored the boundaries of earthly marriage. In other words, Luc set Rose-Marie up with another man. "But, ouf, it didn't work," she says. "Six weeks. Because I saw later that this man went with other women, the women had other men. It was very mixed up."

Mostly, married couples separated if one partner did not want to follow the other into the Temple. Otherwise, both husband and wife participated, either as a couple or in "cosmic" arrangements. But for years, Rose-Marie neither followed her husband nor left Sainte-Anne-de-la-Pérade. "I had a foot inside, but always one outside," she says. After repeatedly trying to get her husband back, however, Rose-Marie says she eventually gave up. Her complaint was financial as well as marital. "I said I won't do it any more. I can't. I'll be ruined." Sometime in 1990, she began talking about her troubles with friends, including a police officer whom she had met through her daughter's school.

One of the friends suggested that Rose-Marie contact Info-Secte, a privately funded organization in Montreal that works, according to its leaflet, "to help families of cult members and ex-members of cults." Info-Secte (or Info-Cult, as they call themselves in English) defines a "cult" as "a highly manipulative group which exploits its members and can cause psychological, financial and physical harm." Info-Secte had close ties to the Cult Awareness Network (CAN), an organization that operated on a much larger scale in the United States. A similar group, l'Association pour la Defense des Familles et de l'Individu (ADFI) has branches around France, and on the Caribbean island of Martinique, but not in Québec. "We are the equivalent," says Yves Casgrain, research director at Info-Secte.

When Rose-Marie Klaus came to their offices around 1991, Info-Secte already knew a little about the Temple Solaire from scattered, unsubstantiated complaints. Klaus told Casgrain about her separation from her husband and her troubled efforts to recoup her investment in the farm at Sainte-Anne-de-la-Pérade. Casgrain recalls Rose-Marie Klaus also telling him "that there were problems." The farm project was going bankrupt, investors were losing money, and Robert Falardeau, an official at the Québec ministry of finance, had replaced Luc Jouret as Grand Master at Sacre-Coeur. However, she didn't provide enough detail or corroboration for Info-Secte to go public with accusations. Rose-Marie Klaus was pursuing a lawsuit at the time, says Casgrain, so "she would never unpack her bags for us." But Casgrain soon learned more from another source. On 10 September 1991, the president of ADFI in Martinique, Lucien Zécler, sent a circular to Info-Secte and other organizations in Québec requesting information about the Temple Solaire.

Zécler's letter cited the 1984 anticult publication connecting Jouret to the Renewed Order of the Temple and to Julien Origas, "alias Humbert de Frackembourgde, former head of the Gestapo at Brest." The leaders of OTS, Zécler concluded, "sit at the extreme right of God." He also described the Order's message of planetary catastrophe. "Only 'elect' beings who will be able to change forms can 'regenerate' humanity and save it," Zécler reported, and he quoted a 1991 Temple bulletin announcing, "the countdown is locked in." The immediate threat, from Zécler's point of view, was that Jouret had been trying to persuade wealthy and influential Martiniquans to sell their possessions and depart the island for Québec, where the Temple was constructing an "arch" to the new world. Indeed, Jouret had convinced several Martiniquans to invest in complex real estate deals in which he, DiMambro, and other Temple entrepreneurs traded property among themselves, their initiates, and a variety of shell companies.

"We have come to the conviction," Zécler's letter ended, "that the only way to save the relatives of our friends and stop the hemorrhage is to unmask this organization in its noxious practices." This letter did not get many responses from Québec, but one of them proved fruitful. A little over a month after he sent it, on 20 October 1991, Rose-Marie Klaus composed a four-page handwritten letter, and Info-Secte sent a copy to Zécler. Addressing herself "to all [in] this beautiful world who hope to have a better life here in Canada, believing in Luc Jouret, Grand Spiritual Master of the Order of Templars," Klaus echoed the themes of "the elect" and "the arch" mentioned in Zécler's letter, sarcastically suggested how "urgent" it was for her readers to invest in "this 'monument' of manipulation, deception and mystification," and closed by offering to "give you other information, or to meet you."

"It was Casgrain who said to us that if we got in touch with Mme Klaus, she was ready to give us a lot of information," Lucien Zécler recalls. Rose-Marie received a typed letter from Zécler dated 17 July 1992. "Dear Madame," it read, "In October, 1991, Info-Cult provided our association against cults with a photocopy of a letter that you were willing to write to denounce the swindle in which you and your family have been victimized by the Temple Solaire." Public opinion in the Antilles and metropolitan France would benefit from learning about the "actual machinations" of Jouret and the order, Zécler wrote, and he asked Klaus for written permission "before undertaking the necessary steps." Whatever Klaus did in response, in October 1992, she received another letter from Martinique. "A woman wrote to me and she said, 'Spend Christmas with us, in the heat, and we'll discuss the affair. And we want to go to the press to say that it must stop, because the police do nothing. It's necessary to publish.'"

By the end of the year, Klaus had completed her divorce from her husband, receiving a $150,000 settlement from OTS. In the court's reckoning, this amounted to half the money that she and her husband had originally put into the project. But the settlement did nothing to diminish Rose-Marie's bitterness; if anything, it freed her to amplify her denunciations. She continued to assert that the Temple Solaire had taken her money. With ADFI-Martinique paying for the plane ticket, Klaus travelled to the Caribbean island in December of 1992. During a stay of about two weeks, she spoke to the Rotary Club. Stories about her appeared in *Frances Antilles*, the newspaper of the islands. "After the visit of Mme Klaus," says Zécler, "there was a film that we produced, and the Templars calmed down. As for the project of departure to Canada, they put that in the background." The campaign of ADFI-Martinique to "unmask" also seemed to produce other results. From what Zécler heard, some Martiniquans "went to Canada to demand the money that they had invested in the project. Because they realized finally that Jouret had fooled them."

To this point, the Solar Temple had managed to keep increased internal dissension and apostasy outside the public eye in Europe (Mayer 1996, pp. 55-61). The developments in Martinique revealed what a determined opponent could do to fuel public controversy. And indeed, the apostate career of Rose-Marie Klaus soon became connected to a different chain of events in Canada, already in motion. At Sainte-Anne-de-la-Pérade, Luc Jouret had been replaced as Grand Master, as Klaus told Info-Secte. The change occurred in 1990 or 1991, when Jouret began to put more urgency into his already apocalyptic message, and people in the group increasingly responded by questioning his common sense. "He was maybe right, okay?" Louis-Marie Belanger told us. "But he didn't take it, to be pushed aside. 'Cause he was a man of pride, you know." Jouret's solution was to found a new group, called l'Academie de Recherche et Connaissance des Hautes Sciences, ARCHS, a pun on Jouret's favorite images of an ark of survival and a bridge to the future. In the schism, he took a number of loyalists with him, just as he had done after the ORT schism in 1983. His key ally, Jean-Pierre Vinet, a vice-president at Hydro-Québec, helped Jouret move into a new field: giving seminars as a "management guru." In 1991 and 1992, Jouret gave lectures on such topics as "Business and Chaos," and "The Real Meaning of Work." By early 1993, as many as fifteen officials of Hydro-Québec had become members of ARCHS.

Vinet and Jouret asked Herman Delorme to become president of ARCHS, but that turned out to be an honorary title with no more meaning than the knightly ranks within OTS. "One day I managed to get a little private session with Jouret," Herman recalls, "and he says, 'Herman,' he says, 'You're where you're supposed to be, so just do what you're supposed to do without question.' And you'd do it."

In November 1992, Vinet asked Delorme to get him a pistol with a silencer. Vinet explained that he needed protection, but he didn't know how to shoot, and he wanted to practice without alerting the neighborhood. Taught to obey, Herman sought to honor this request, first approaching Daniel Tougas, a policeman whose wife had attended several of Jouret's lectures. Tougas could provide pistols but not silencers, so Herman turned to his karate instructor, who suggested a student in one of his courses "who had done some time on a drug charge or something." That man, Bernard Gilot, turned out to be a police informant.

At about the same time, the Sûreté du Québec (SQ) later reported having learned of a man identifying himself as "André Masse" who made calls to various government offices, threatening to assassinate the Minister of Public Security, Claude Ryan, and several Parliamentary deputies. The Sûreté du Québec has never been able to find any information about "André" or the organization he claimed to represent, Q-37, whose name was supposedly derived from the thirty-seven Québeckers who made up the group. The SQ asserts, however, that at the time, their investigators saw a possible connection between Q-37's threats and Herman's interest in buying guns. Following this slim lead, the SQ obtained a warrant to tap Delorme's phone, then Vinet's, and then those of other members of OTS. When the Sûreté searched a villa in St Sauveur owned by Temple member Camille Pilet, Jouret and Pilet got wind of the investigation while on a trip to Switzerland. They engaged a Montreal attorney, Jean-Claude Hébert, to look after their interests, but Hébert was unable to learn the reason for the search.

News of the investigation never got back from Pilet and Jouret to Vinet and Delorme, who were proceeding with their plans to buy weapons. Gilot, the police informant, kept stringing them along until the police arranged for him to come back to Herman with a sting.

> He showed me pictures of AK-47s and tanks and Isuzus – what you call them? – Uzis. And I was telling myself, what do I have to tell these people to get a simple little handgun with a silencer? And here they are, asking me all sorts of questions. "How big a group are you?" Of course, you know, we're about thirty. "You serious?" Of course we're serious, we're all business people. "Do you have any political ideology?" [Herman

chuckled.] I hate politics! But then you can interpret that as I hate politicians, or I'm gonna shoot politicians. They would interpret everything that I said according to what they *thought* was going to happen.

Herman finally settled on a set of three pistols and a vague agreement to "buy a ton" later. He made the pickup on Nun's Island in Montreal on the afternoon on 8 March 1993. Forty-five minutes later, as he was pulling off Highway 74 near his home, he was ambushed by a SWAT team and forcibly arrested. Within hours after police picked up Delorme, they took Jean-Pierre Vinet into custody and issued a warrant for the arrest of Luc Jouret, who was in Europe at the time.

Three days after the arrests, Rose-Marie Klaus appeared on the front page of the tabloid *Journal de Montreal*, scowling and holding up a white robe with a red cross. "I Lost One Million," the headline declared. A week later, *Photo Police*, the Québecois equivalent of the *National Star*, turned up the volume. Next to a picture of Rose-Marie in the same pose, the headline promised "What They Haven't Told You About THE HORROR OF THE ORDRE DU TEMPLE SOLAIRE." The revelations in these stories – and in interviews with other newspapers, radio, and television stations – turned out to be a repetition, with some inflation, of Rose-Marie's allegations to Info-Secte in 1991.

The news coverage continued for over a month, and some of it was more balanced. Active members defended the group in several articles, and the citizens of Sainte-Anne said that they had no objections at all to OTS. For its part, the Sûreté du Québec kept insisting that, while gun laws had been broken, they had found no evidence of terrorism or arms trafficking. Claude Ryan himself put out an appeal for public "prudence" on the subject of sects. Yet even while printing such statements, the newspapers continued to characterize OTS as a doomsday cult bent on stockpiling arms. A number of commentators, including Yves Casgrain of Info-Secte, could not resist making a comparison to events in Waco, where the government siege of the Branch Davidians had just begun.

The arrests also set off an investigation within Hydro-Québec, and that too was closely watched in the media. The examiner's report confirmed that Jouret had given lectures at Hydro-Québec facilities, that fifteen employees had been members of OTS or l'ARCHS, and that other employees had attended meetings. The report concluded that any financial improprieties had been marginal, but Jean-Pierre Vinet lost his job. (A year later, in March 1994, OTS and Hydro-Québec were linked again when two transmission towers were blown up. The SQ released a letter that claimed responsibility on behalf of OTS. The writer, however, betrayed an ignorance of both OTS style and the details of the bombings, and the police dismissed the letter as a hoax.)

Jean-Claude Hébert thought he could win an acquittal on the weapons charges; in fact, afterwards, he still doubted the legality of the warrants and phone taps. Jouret, however, didn't want any publicity. "They were very preoccupied by a question of image," Hébert said of Jouret and Pilet, whom he visited in Switzerland. "At that period, they had the wind in their sails, and I could understand that the negative publicity put out in Canada might come down in France, in Switzerland, in Martinique, and spoil his whole network of activities." When the case came to trial in July 1993, the Crown Prosecutor accepted a plea bargain, and Jouret's hearing lasted just forty minutes. The judge's decision repeatedly asserted that the weapons had been purchased for defensive purposes and that the defendants had already been abundantly penalized by the media. He sentenced Jouret, Vinet, and Delorme each to one year of unsupervised probation and a fine of $1000 to be donated to the Red Cross.

Outside the public eye, in key police circles the gun incident became framed as illegal arms trafficking, and it triggered a chain reaction of official investigations. Within two days of the arrests, the Sûreté du Québec publicly announced an inquiry into financial aspects of OTS. Australian police opened a parallel inquiry later in 1993. An Interpol bulletin went out, alleging that Joseph DiMambro and a woman confidant, Odile Dancet, took part in two banking transactions in Australia of $93 million each. French authorities initiated an investigation in 1994, delaying the reissue of the passport belonging to Joseph DiMambro's wife, Jocelyne. By March 1994, the Royal Canadian Mounted Police were cooperating with Australian Federal Police inquiries concerning possible money laundering. Swiss authorities also received bulletins from Australia.

The initial "Transit" took place in October of 1994, more than a year after the gun incident and the negative press stories centered on the claims of Rose-Marie Klaus. The organizers of the Transit never fully understood the extent of the investigations into their doings, but they had their suspicions. Their Transit letters clearly assert the belief that the group was the target of a conspiracy, and the beleaguered tone of their writings is unmistakable: "We do not know when they can close the trap on us again . . . what days, what weeks?" (Mayer 1996, p. 100). Joseph DiMambro did know about the delay in the renewal of Jocelyne's French passport. On 4 October 1994, he gave Patrick Vuarnet his own and Jocelyne's passports, along with a bitter letter of complaint to send to the French interior minister, "Very dear Charlie" Pasqua (who himself has been associated with Interpol and Service d'Action Civique).

The Transit letter, "To those who value justice," never mentioned the rumors of money laundering that circulated on the Interpol network. But it did air suspicions that a "pseudoplot" had been concocted as a pretext for moving against OTS by connecting the order with a Québec terrorist group, Q-37, that had never been mentioned publicly before the gun arrests.

By 1995, SQ sergeant Robert Poeti would say, "Q-37, as far as we're concerned, never existed. It was a joke, a guy who called. There are people who are deranged, who do this. We are convinced that the one who made the calls had nothing to do with the Ordre du Temple Solaire. Nothing at all." If so, we are left with an irony of history, that a mere coincidence should have drawn together police action, the Temple's most formidable dissident, and cultural opposition to the group in the mass media.

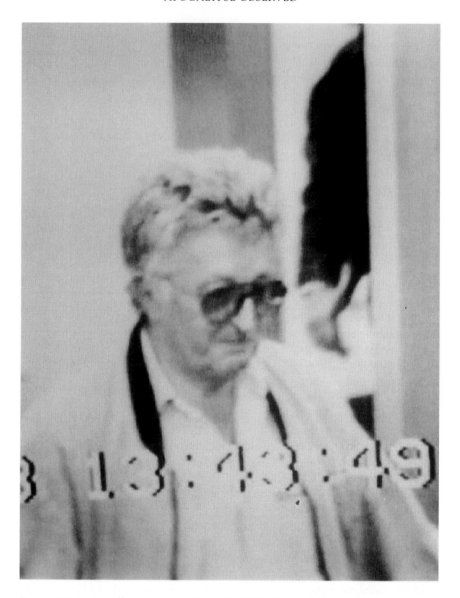

Figure 4.3 A surveillance photo of Joseph DiMambro arriving at Brisbane airport, Australia, late in 1993, released by the Australian Federal Police. DiMambro did not know about the money laundering investigation that was under way, but the Transit letters clearly indicate that Temple members believed themselves to be the object of a conspiracy that included government agencies.

Source: AP/WORLDWIDE PHOTOS

We are not in a position to know fully about either the events surrounding Rose-Marie Klaus's denunciations of the Temple Solaire or how the Sûreté du Québec came to unleash a full-scale gun-running investigation of individuals seeking to buy several pistols with silencers. Perhaps the purchase of arms in 1993 really was ordered to protect survivalists from attack during the Apocalypse, as Vinet somewhat lamely asserted to Jean-Claude Hébert. Perhaps there had been no plan for a violent Transit in Québec, only the original plan to survive the end times on a solid granite plate. Perhaps. But if plans for the end times ever had a more benign interpretation, the situation changed dramatically after the scandals erupted in March 1993. Herman Delorme never spoke to Jouret again after the gun incident. "But," he said, "Vinet told me about Luc and a couple of others – desperate. It was downhill all the way from there. His mind changed, he was a tired, tired, tired, disappointed, disillusioned person."

The multiple constructions of Templar reality

Countercultural religious movements often traffic in reconstructions of cultural meanings that create tensions with more conventional views of reality. These tensions are especially volatile in an apocalyptic movement, which may locate itself either *within* the Apocalypse, as a warring sect engaged in a struggle between the forces of good and evil that amounts to the Apocalypse enacted, or beyond it, as a post-apocalyptic other-worldly sect that seeks to escape "this" world to establish a tableau of "heaven on earth" beyond the evils of the secular world.

Peoples Temple and the Branch Davidians advanced strongly apocalyptic ideologies that alternated between escape to a heaven-on-earth versus confrontation with their adversaries, with no other mystical element than the imagery of the Bible's Book of Revelation (especially important to the Davidians, who nevertheless were far from mystics). In the Temple Solaire, like Aum Shinrikyō, a more complex set of tensions presents itself between the two apocalyptic orientations and the collective search for transcendence in a *mystical association* devoted to meditation or other procedures designed to produce enlightenment and ecstasy (Hall 1978). Thus, three alternative constructions of reality came into play at various junctures: a mysticism of eternal transcendence that nevertheless intervenes in this world; an apocalypticism of escape from impending disaster by establishing a colony "beyond" the "old" world, on the granite bedrock of Québec; and an apocalypticism of persecution by forces that could not countenance their countercultural movement. The tensions among these alternative constructions came to a head in the "gun incident" and the campaign against the group channeled through the person of Rose-Marie Klaus. These events seriously destabilized the operations of the group, but to date, there is no evidence that they derived from any conspiratorial campaign of persecution involving collusion among law enforcement and cultural opponents. Indeed, although investigations of the group were continuing at the time of the initial Transit, they amounted to nothing like the direct state assertion of jurisdiction at Jonestown and Mount

Carmel. The Solar Temple as a whole never faced any proximate visible threat. However, for the Temple's principals to sustain the collective honor of their enterprise, they had to construe their failure as the consequence of persecution and resolve the crisis in a way that affirmed their mystical powers. The cultural formula to do this was already in their possession, and they may have planned to use it even before the troubles with Rose-Marie Klaus and the gun incident.

The Solar Temple had long held to a secret doctrine of soul travel between earthly existence and eternal transcendence, and even in the absence of persecution, their theology might have been developed toward warranting a "Transit," which would look like mass suicide in earthly terms. The most esoteric of Temple doctrines claimed to bridge the gulfs of separation between this world and other realms, between the historical present and other times, between finite life and infinite immortality. If you worked through the complex charts and alchemical formulations in Jacques Breyer's 1959 book, *Arcanes Solaire, or the Secrets of the Solar Temple,* you would grasp the relation between eternity and cycles of history; then you could move from one to the other. Many of Breyer's formulations are based on ancient wisdom concerning triangles (the two-triangled Star of David, Breyer claims, derives from a revealed religion that preceded Jews, Aryans, or Celts). In one diagram, the triangle's apex is "disincarnation": beyond material existence. The base of the triangle rests on the line of historical time. Along the triangle's sides, sages can move from incarnation to disincarnation, carrying the Solar Depository in and out of historical time, *if* they coordinate their actions with rare dates of high energy.

For the age of Pisces, the phases of the astrological cycle on the bottom side of the triangle are defined by rays representing the colors of the rainbow, which radiate from the apex. With seven colors, each having a temporal projection of 308 years, the age of Pisces "granted to our Elementary Human Species" lasts 2,156 years. A foldout chart directly aligns Pisces with the Apocalypse of St John the Divine, beginning with the birth of Jesus Christ. The last phase, beginning with the revolutions of 1848, is divided in half, with the first half ending in the year 2002. Leading up to this moment, "After Struggles on all Planes, Union achieved between Sulfur and Mercury. (Grand Monarchy. Temple. Apotheosis. Truth.) 'Fire!'" Breyer enthuses, "Ask God: that Israel (among others) convert to Christianity, now that we have reached the *End of Time!*" On another chart, the "End of Incarnation" is calculated to the year 1999.8 (all dates are only approximate, Breyer notes, based as they are on mere mundane calculation). On a third chart, he points out that Jesus was born four years before the year 1 M.E., and concludes, "The Grand Monarchy ought to Leave this world around 1995–96."

In 1986, the Temple's astrologer, who wrote under the name of Marilou de Saint-Aignan, grandly described an "evolution toward the state of God" and the opening of "a door to the infinite." The astrologer foresaw man's "voyage across the stars." "Through plutonian influence," she asserted, "he ought to be able to undergo the disintegration of the physical body so that he may set free the foundation of his soul." But the seeker had to steel himself: "The absence of fear in facing the events, however painful they may be, is evidence that he is on the right path." Much the same narrative could be found in *Voyage Intemporel: Terre Ciel Connection*, a photo-comic book published in 1982 that could be found for sale at Luc Jouret's lectures.[2] And these ideas are part of a wider francophone New-Age culture awash with ideas of immortality, reincarnation, time travel, and astral voyages.

In the early 1990s, Herman Delorme reminds us, "There was talk of this "departure" for Sirius." This indeed was the location of the "Great White Lodge" mentioned in one Transit letter. Another of the letters, "Transit for the Future," alludes to a brotherhood of thirty-three Rosicrucian Elder Brothers who once lived their own terrestrial lives, but now use "assumed bodies to manifest themselves in this world and to accomplish the Divine Plans" (in New-Age language, they are "walk-ins"). Because their message was rejected, the Elder Brothers decided to leave this historical period of Earth. However, before going, they gathered together people enlightened enough to cross the Apocalyptic end of our era and initiate the New Age. As the author of a Transit letter put it, "We leave this Earth to rediscover, in complete lucidity and freedom, a Dimension of Truth and the Absolute, far from the hypocrisies and oppression of this world, with the end of producing the embryo of our future Generation."

"October the 4th, 1994," mused Herman Delorme.

> Add up the numbers, one by one, and see what we come out to. The fourth, okay, and the tenth month. Four plus one is five plus zero is still five, plus one is six, plus nine is fifteen, and nine is twenty-four. Twenty-four plus four is twenty-eight, two and eight is ten, one and zero is . . . one. One is a new beginning.

There was, in fact, a new moon that night, coming into phase just as the planet Mars entered the house of Leo, the polar opposite of Aquarius. The significance of this passage may be explained in a cassette tape found on the door of the farmhouse at Cheiry, but Swiss police will only say that it is the voice of a woman, talking about astrology. Either way, said Herman, "I think everything was well calculated in advance."

There are two widespread and mutually contradictory myths that have served as backdrops for speculations about the Temple Solaire's Transit: that the group was rolling in money and that they executed the Transit because of a financial crisis. Television mini-series, movies, and pulp books about the Temple Solaire will doubtless spin conspiracy theories based upon both. The first myth, stemming from the famous legend of the $93 million, originated from an Interpol bulletin about banking transactions between Switzerland and Australia, which Jouret, DiMambro, and Pilet visited frequently from the late 1980s on. Commenting on reports of these transactions after the events of October 1994, Pascal Auchlin, a journalist with the Swiss weekly *l'Hebdo*, reminded readers of the legend of the original Templars' treasure. Pierre Tourangeau of the Canadian

Broadcasting Company announced the treasure as fact, and speculated that such huge amounts could only be garnered through drug smuggling or international arms trafficking, and that an operation on that scale could not succeed without the collusion of government officials. (When asked to back up these claims, a Radio Canada spokesman was reported by *Le Devoir* to be "mute as a carp.") Later, reporters at *La Presse* in Montreal became captivated by Introvigne's genealogical chart, connected DiMambro and Giacobino to the infamous Italian Masonic lodge P2 and the Gaullist Service d'Action Civique, and suggested that all fifty-three deaths might be the result of a massive Mafia hit. After a year and a half of investigation, Swiss authorities reported that they never found evidence of money-laundering or anything remotely approaching $93 million. Even so, with the seemingly limitless capacity of Templar and Rosicrucian chronicles to absorb conspiracy theories, the failure to find the big money will no doubt be used to draw the Temple into a far-flung network of intrigue that may even include governmental cover-ups.

The second myth is that the group around DiMambro and Jouret took their own and others' lives because of imminent financial disaster. According to this scenario, the gun incident precipitated a wider defection of members (which had already begun with the schism in 1991), and the example of Rose-Marie Klaus encouraged not only Martiniquans but other disaffected members to try to get their money back. Thierry Huguenin claims that he had filed a criminal complaint as well as a civil suit against DiMambro and his wife, and that others were after them as well. However, they still held a considerable amount of property at the time of their attempt at transhistorical travel, and cash does not seem to have been a problem. Even if the group around DiMambro had been forced to sell off some property at a loss, they could have continued their lavish life for some time to come. In short, they did not face any financial crisis in the short term.

What they did face was the loss of something that had been an obsession: the honor and good name necessary to sustain their network of enterprises. Even though the SQ investigation yielded only three handguns with silencers, it unleashed ruin for Jouret, DiMambro and their inner circle. Under the glaring spotlight of bad publicity in Martinique and Québec, the lucrative career of a charismatic public lecturer itself became a scandal, closing off a major avenue of legitimation, recruitment, and cash flow. The growing bubble of an expansionary movement burst after March 1993, and the change of circumstances seems to have precipitated a crisis of morale. Jean-Claude Hébert remembers going to visit Jouret in Switzerland after the gun raid. "That's what started to destroy his pedestal. And he experienced it as an enormous anguish," says Hébert. "Frankly, he was frightened by what had taken place. I think that in his mind, it was perhaps the beginning of the end." The Swiss authorities concur that though the idea of a Transit dates from 1990, psychological preparation did not begin until 1993 (*Le Monde*, 5 April 1996).

The Sûreté du Québec seems to accept the idea that at least the core group of

Templars truly calculated a departure for Sirius. Indeed, the SQ has argued that if its investigators had not stumbled on the plan to buy guns, the murders and suicides would have taken place in Québec in the spring of 1993, with perhaps twice as many participants. Building on the Temple theory that higher consciousness feeds on other consciousness, one Sûreté informant explained that one hundred people would have provided enough fuel for a non-stop Transit to Sirius. Because their plans had been frustrated in 1993, the theory goes, they could only gather fifty-three, and so needed to make a stopover in another solar system.

The SQ also offers a theological explanation for the murder of the Dutoits in Québec before the Transit in Switzerland. In this account, the family's fate was sealed in the summer of 1994, when Tony and Nicky had the temerity to name their newborn baby Christopher Emmanuel. DiMambro had not wanted the Dutoits to have a child in the first place, and he regarded the name as an usurpation of his own daughter's name. Emmanuelle DiMambro was a "cosmic child" (supposedly conceived when Joseph pointed a magical sword – with a battery-powered light – at Dominique Bellaton's throat). "She was the Avatar who was going to rebuild the Temple and prevent the Apocalypse," according to Lt. Richard St Denis of the SQ. The Sûreté insists that the Dutoit baby was the "Antichrist," Emmanuel versus Emmanuelle, and they report having found a written ritual procedure according to which "the Antichrist had to be killed by two knights with a stake." Investigators maintain that they found the stake along with the baby enclosed in a plastic bag. (Thierry Huguenin disagreed with this analysis. "There was an Antichrist," he claimed, "but it was a boy, and he's still alive." Louis-Marie Belanger was skeptical about the entire ritually saturated account. Concerning the stake, he argued, "Somebody put it there after. Come on.")

We must take the Sûreté's analysis with a grain of salt, for the simple reason that their interaction with the Solar Temple was not simply an investigation after the fact of the murders. At least from the Temple viewpoint, the SQ was part of the plot against them. In one of the Transit letters that denounces the "deceitful accusations" levelled against the group in France, Australia, Switzerland, Martinique and Canada, the writers reserve their most bitter venom for the Sûreté du Québec and the "pseudoplot" of the Q-37 investigation. They claim that systematic persecution on the part of government agencies, in league with the Mafia and Opus Dei, has pushed them to leave this earth. "We accuse them of collective assassination," the letter concludes. Small wonder that Québec authorities prefer a theological interpretation of the Transit.

The rhetoric of persecution in the letters suggest that the firearms arrests in 1993 did not delay the Transit, but rather hastened it. Perhaps the group intended to fight its way through the cataclysm, not flee it, and the pistols Delorme purchased really were intended to protect the survivalists from attack. In any event, one of the letters calls the departure of the Order "premature." As it was, at least according to Breyer's calculation of the Apocalypse; the clock was ticking, but there was still time before the End of Time. Even at the End, it should be noted that other groups, most famously the nineteenth-century

American Millerites, seeing their long anticipated and precisely dated Apocalypses come and go, have then either recalculated, or lost the critical mass of support for their movement. In the case of the Solar Temple, Breyer's calculations left considerable room for revisionist flexibility, and other theological resources oriented the group toward post-apocalyptic survival on earth.

We are not in a very good position to conduct the experiment with History that would inform us of what would have happened if the followers of the Ascended Masters had not believed themselves to be the target of a conspiracy. As Casaubon, the Templar scholar and narrator, remarks in Umberto Eco's novel, *Foucault's Pendulum*, "Counterfactual conditionals are always true, because the premise is false." What we do know is that after the scandals erupted in March 1993, Jouret and his group found themselves in dramatically altered circumstances. There are also rumors that DiMambro was in poor health; he had cancer, people say, of a sort that Jouret could not cure. In his last days, Piller suggested, DiMambro

> could have reached the end of his rope. He could be at the end in terms of health. He could be at the end in financial terms. He could be harassed by people who want money. He could be at the end on the level of the sect – there was a loss of members, loss of support, abandonment by his close relatives.

Perhaps, seeing his life near its end, DiMambro orchestrated the Transit as an effort to dispose of his enemies and salvage personal and collective honor in the face of an earthly organizational future that could promise only further decline.

The distribution of the bodies and their manner of death lend considerable support to the outlines of Piller's explanation. The Dutoits were obviously murdered, but probably not because their son was the Antichrist. According to several sources, Tony Dutoit had become disillusioned with the group in the early 1990s, but he continued to work for DiMambro because he needed the money and because his wife, Nicky Robinson, was also deeply involved, making robes for the chevaliers and serving as governess for Emmanuelle DiMambro. When Tony Dutoit began openly questioning DiMambro's motives and procedures, however, his family was exiled to Québec. There, Dutoit had begun to reveal the backstage secrets of crypt electronics. That betrayal might have been enough to lead to his condemnation as a traitor. Clearly, those who orchestrated their own departure were not above murder if they could rationalize it as "justice."

Collette and Gerry Genoud just as obviously committed suicide. According to the Sûreté du Québec, they had assisted Joel Egger and Dominique Bellaton in the murder of the Dutoits on September 30, and then spent the next four days cleaning up the evidence and preparing for departure. Then they set the timers on the incendiary devices and laid themselves out on their beds, dressed in their robes and medals. Both Genouds were sedated but still alive when the fires began in the Morin Heights villas, and Gerry, at least, was apparently conscious, and still ready to make the Transit.

The bodies of Collette and Gerry Genoud were never reclaimed by their families. They were laid to rest on 12 December 1994 in a communal plot of the Laval Cemetery, in St François. Frances Houle, spokesperson for the coroner's office, explained, "In all such cases, people are buried without a religious service, because no one knows their religious convictions. They are not cremated, in case someone comes someday to reclaim the bodies and bury them somewhere else."

The four children and three teenagers who died in Switzerland – the twelve-year-old cosmic child named Emmanuelle DiMambro, three others at Salvan and three at Cheiry – were murdered, in legal terms and in emotional terms as well. The question that remains is whether their parents knowingly participated in the events and brought the children along. That happened in seventeenth-century Russia, when the Old Believers locked themselves in churches and set them on fire (Robbins 1986), and it happened again in 1978, in Jonestown, Guyana, when women brought their babies up to receive the cyanide poison.

The death at Salvan of Joseph DiMambro's twenty-five-year-old son may mark something equally as twisted: murder for the sake of appearances. If, as reports suggest, the young man had distanced himself from his father, his presence at Salvan brought the family back together in death. However, evidence suggests that a number of Jouret and DiMambro's associates were not unwilling participants. Most of the twenty-five people dead at Salvan were evidently loyalists or longtime members. They included Luc Jouret, his woman friend, Carole Cadorette, and Joseph DiMambro, his wife, mistresses and secretaries, and their children. Also found there were Joel Egger and Dominque Bellaton, the presumed Morin Heights murderers, Egger's mother Bernadette Bise and his wife Annie, as well as Jouret's Canadian ally, Jean-Pierre Vinet, and his companion Pauline Lemonde. Herman Delorme recalls the last time he saw Vinet. "I'm leaving definitely," Jean-Pierre told him in July 1994. "You probably will never see me again. You don't have anything left to accomplish, but I do." Others made similar foreboding comments before their deaths. Martin Germain gave a will to one of his daughters. "Take it," he told her. "One never knows what might happen." His wife, a surviving daughter recounts, told her that "One day they were going to depart for Venus, and there was no reason to be sad when they disappeared."

Some transits are worse than others, it would seem. Joseph DiMambro gave Patrick Vuarnet a short fifth letter printed in the same computer font as the other four. "Following the tragic Transit at Cheiry," the letter says, "we insist on specifying, in the name of the Rose + Cross, that we deplore and totally disassociate ourselves from the barbarous, incompetent, and aberrant conduct of Doctor Luc Jouret." It continues, "he is the cause of a veritable carnage which could have been a Transit performed in Honor, Peace, and Light." Twenty-one of the twenty-three dead at Cheiry died of gunshot wounds after having received powerful sleeping pills; some had three or more bullets to the head. The two others died of suffocation, although eight other bodies were found with plastic bags over their heads (perhaps intended to accelerate the incineration of their faces). Some died much earlier than others and their bodies were moved after death. Several showed signs of struggle.

It has been widely reported that Albert Giacobino, the principal investor in the Cheiry farm, and his friend Marie-Louise Rebaudo, the group astrologer, were both disenchanted with the Solar Temple, and trying to recover investments. A group of Canadians, including Robert Falardeau, Jocelyne Grand'Maison, and Robert Ostiguy, came to represent the group in Sainte-Anne-de-la-Pérade. (Indeed, Louis-Marie Belanger insists that Falardeau, Grand'Maison, and Leopoldo Cabrera Gil, a Spaniard from the Canary Islands, were the only members among the fifty-three who still belonged to the official Ordre du Temple Solaire.) At least some of the Canadians are thought to have gone seeking a reconciliation with Luc Jouret, but Jouret seems to have had other plans. Ostiguy's wife, Françoise, was said to have gone to "ransom" her husband. Jouret's ex-wife, Marie-Christine Pertué, may also have been invited to Cheiry for more personal reasons. (Jouret and she had married in the early 1980s, but they divorced after their only child died in infancy.) Three of these people, Swiss authorities concluded, were murdered for revenge.

Yet many who died at Cheiry clearly had close or enduring ties to the core group. Jocelyne Grand'Maison had been a member of the Renewed Temple before the Temple Solaire was started. Camille Pilet, the organization's chief financier, was there, as was 70-year-old Renée Pfaehler, one of the founding members of Golden Way and a vigorous recruiter for the group. Several of the dead had direct family ties to individuals who died at Salvan, or belonged to networks that went back to the founding of Golden Way in 1979.

Since all the dead at Cheiry were clearly assassinated, the question remains of whether they submitted freely. Notwithstanding the foreshadowing of departure, there are considerable pressures to declare a judgement of wholesale deceit, trickery, and murder. Friends, associates and relatives understandably find it disconcerting to believe that people whom they thought they knew well could have hidden such enormous aspects of their lives. They rightly remain incredulous that anyone could ever wittingly have participated in such a farfetched project as the Transit plan to effect a transmigration of living souls. Some small dignity might be salvaged for the dead if it could be shown that the they had been murdered. However, precisely because the organization emphasized secrecy, the accounts that people who are now dead gave of going to "sign papers" cannot be fully credited as proof that they were tricked.

Evidently, people died at Cheiry under a variety of circumstances, from murder to suicide, with shadings in between. Even those who went willingly may have been duped, expecting a spectacular Transit, only to be surprised by a bullet to the brain. Yet the possibility remains that a number of those shot to death joined in the voyage, as the Transit letters state, "in all lucidity and all liberty." During the investigation into the deaths, a beautiful woman in her forties came into Piller's office, dressed in a dark red cape, draped in necklaces and little crosses. She was devastated, she told Piller, that she had not been summoned to the Transit. And Piller replied, "'Transit? Twenty out of twenty-three with bullets in their heads? What kind of a Transit is that?' She answered me, 'Listen. They all wanted the Transit, but they didn't have the courage to go. I might not have had the courage either, and I would have been happy if someone had helped me. If it was necessary. Why not?'"

In Transit

We cannot rule out the possibility that the Ascended Masters continue to walk amongst us. Despite all the information amassed about the Solar Temple since October 1994, secrets and intrigues remain hidden. The shadowy events that contributed to the sense of destabilization within the Temple Solaire, the ambiguity of evidence about a secret organization, and the opportunities for conspiracy theorizing all ensure a continuing flow of wildly conflicting speculative scenarios. Investigators and journalists, academics and scriptwriters all try to contain the irrational, to force the affair into some matrix that makes sense. By manipulating symbols, we try to capture the spirits, like tourists taking photographs of the natives. At the moment of photographic success, natives lose control over their souls. But when we develop the Temple Solaire film, the negatives are luridly overexposed, or simply blank. In its bizarre and tragic failure, the Transit established an almost impenetrable veil of secrecy.

As in the fourteenth century, the visible order has disappeared in flames. But the Transit letters insist, "The Rose + Cross has not finished surprising you." True, some former members are trying to move on. Having failed to settle with DiMambro over wages he claimed, Thierry Huguenin has tried to recoup his losses by publishing his memoirs and consulting on a television film. In Granby, Québec, Herman Delorme considered joining Creations, a multilevel marketing scheme with spiritual overtones. But Lucien Zécler, the anticult activist, asserted that OTS in Martinique would reform itself quietly, under a new name. And why not? After all, according to the Transit letters, "their name or the label of their organization matters little. We will say simply that they appear and disappear at a precise time, always at critical moments of civilization."

In the Manoir Ste Anne in Sainte-Anne-de-la-Pérade, the juke box seemed to grow louder as night fell on the icy world outside. Reminded that the letters mailed by Patrick Vuarnet justify the attempted Transit because the world wasn't ready for the truth, Louis-Marie Belanger allowed, "Well, in my opinion, they're not wrong." His pause was punctuated by pool balls colliding with one another. "Maybe they are a little more conscious than I am. And they knew things I didn't know." Belanger would continue on his spiritual path alone. "The thing is," he remarked,

you don't need to be in an order, a Templar order, to be a Templar. Whatever you do, when you're on the path of spirituality, you're always facing yourself in the mirror. You're alone, even if you're four hundred members around the world. See, it's your soul, your consciousness, and that's it. But I think the Big Guy out there is so just in his creation, that if you need a little help when you're making a step, he'll make it up to you.

Anyone who still believes in Transit need not despair. Because of "a just law of magnetism," the authors of the letters mailed from Eaux-Vives proclaimed, they will be able to "call back the last Servants capable of hearing this final message." From their new state of being, they "hold out their arms" toward anyone who turns out to be "worthy" of joining them. The rest of Earth's peoples, trapped in the mundane world of time, have their Love and wishes of Peace as we face "the terrible ordeals of the Apocalypse."

How long into the future servants will be called back remains to be seen. After the winter solstice in 1995, near Grenoble, French authorities found a circle of fourteen charred, bullet-ridden bodies of people associated with the Solar Temple who had not made the initial Transit. Three were children. The others included Patrick Vuarnet and his mother, Edith. Near the fourteen lay the bodies of two other Templars: a French immigration inspector and a French police official. Apparently they had shot the others before starting the fire that would consume the whole group after they had shot themselves. Police later found notes in four homes of the dead describing wishes to "see another world."

Given that the leaders had all supposedly died in October 1994, this "Transit" produced a strong public response. Both French and Hydro-Québec officials voiced concerns that the secret order had infiltrated government agencies, and France formed a government watchdog group to "battle against the dangers of cults." Authorities temporarily removed a child from the home of her mother, a known Temple associate before 1994. In Québec, Yves Casgrain of Info-Secte warned that the sect probably continued to operate underground, and Herman Delorme predicted that ten to twelve people might be caught up in a new suicide at the summer solstice of 1996 (nothing happened). Police in France undertook preventive roundups involving scores of suspected Temple members; they apparently feared another collective suicide on each new moon, equinox, or anniversary of the dates when the fifty-four medieval Knights Templar and their last grand master, Jacques de Molay, were burned alive at the stake at the beginning of the fourteenth century. Even the close police surveillance could not prevent Rose-Marie Klaus's former husband Bruno, another man, and three women from taking their lives in a burning house in a Québec village during the spring equinox of 1997; police had last had contact with them the previous summer solstice. Three teenaged children of the deceased were given the choice, and decided not to attempt the Transit (New York Times, 24, 25, 28 December 1995; Le Monde, 4, 22 March 1996; Washington Times, 11 March 1996; Agence France Presse, 3 April 1996; International Herald Tribune, 24, 25 March 1997).

For all our own sciences and religions, we do not know what happens to the souls of the deceased. Atheist, agnostic, or believer, our attitudes toward death are matters of faith. Uncertain of the alternative, most of us do our best to prolong life. We may disagree about capital punishment and war, abortion and assisted suicide, but we find murder and suicide among the young and the healthy to be an unconscionable assault on religious and humanistic values alike. If the letters of Transit bear faithful witness, however, death for the believing Adepts was not the final frontier but rather a ritualized journey to be undertaken when transcendent purpose called for it, willingly, with noble spirit, without remorse or fear. By choosing the Transit, the true believers among those who died affirmed their faith by enacting a demonstration.

From the seventeenth century onwards, Rosicrucian societies have claimed to reverse the Fall, offering their secret knowledge to transform human existence from its presently mistaken paths, promising immortality as the reward for breaking through the mantles of illusion. This assault on modern religion and science offers a ready explanation to those of us whom Herman Delorme describes as "disconnected" from life, family and work. The most alienated among us can convince themselves that they have no home in our world because they are really members of an eternal brotherhood. The disbelief in the outer world sustains the boundaries that divide them from us. The Transit letters mailed from Eaux-Vives reject an apocalyptic struggle with detractors who would label them as a cult, and they refuse to sully the wisdom of the ages with transitory struggles against some latter-day inquisition. Martyrs, argued St Bernard de Clairvaux, sacrifice their lives to a higher cause. Immortals do not make such a sacrifice. They have no life to give. They simply return to eternity.

Reflections

Did the Transits of the Solar Temple members amount to apocalyptic religious violence similar to what occurred at Jonestown, Mount Carmel and in Japan? To answer this question, it would be helpful to know what would have happened if the followers of the Ascended Masters had not believed themselves to be the target of a conspiracy. Although, as Umberto Eco's Casaubon argued, there can be no definitive answer to a counterfactual question, certain elements can be disentangled. At Jonestown and Mount Carmel, the violence began with murder of outside opponents, and in Aum Shinrikyō, it began with the murder of a member who knew about the cover-up of the death of a devotee. The first Transit of Solar Temple faithfuls followed this pattern, beginning with the murder of the handyman who knew the secrets of the technology used in the crypts to create fantastic sensations during "visits" from the Ascended Masters. Even without Rose-Marie Klaus and the gun incident, if the Temple had attempted a Transit, this family with knowledge of organizational secrets might still have died.

A central question, then, is whether the Temple would have attempted its initial Transit in the absence of the negative publicity from Rose-Marie Klaus and the gun incident. The Sûreté du Québec asserted that they prevented an earlier Transit by their arrests, whereas the Transit letters describe the departure as "premature." This very description acknowledges the plan for Transit, independent of external opposition, a plan that can be tied to Jacques Breyer's (1959) calculation that "The Grand Monarchy ought to Leave this world around 1995–96," that is, around the time of the second Transit, at the winter solstice of 1995.

If the Solar Temple were to follow some version of Breyer's script, the plan would not be to wait passively for an external sign of the Apocalypse, but to take action to "leave this world" at a specific point in time in order to feed upon the presumed convergence of harmonic energy force fields. It is thus not completely implausible that the initial Transit could have taken place even without either the specific elements of apocalyptic conflict that did occur (i.e., the gun incident, the efforts of Rose-Marie Klaus brokered by Info-Secte, the resulting media coverage, the trial, and subsequent investigations) or some alternative crisis that might have been precipitated by actions of other apostates in the wings (e.g., Europeans, Martiniquans, the Dutoits).

How, then, would a hypothetical non-confrontational Transit be understood within the sociology of religion? This question brings us to core issues about the meaningful structures of mass suicide, apocalypticism, and mysticism. By considering it, we can come to a clearer understanding of the parallels and differences among the episodes of violence associated with Peoples Temple, the Branch Davidians, Aum Shinrikyō, and the Solar Temple.

On the one hand, a Transit seems contradictory to any logic of mysticism as an ideal type (that is, considered as a cultural logic in and of itself), since mysticism does not acknowledge either time in its social construction or a strong dualism between this world and some eternal world (Hall 1978). On the other hand, the model of religious violence we have presented characterizes apocalyptic mass suicide as bound up with issues of collective legitimacy in the face of mobilized public opposition. A counterfactual "pure" Transit of the Solar Temple in the absence of perceived external threats (as opposed to the first Transit that actually occurred) approximates neither this model nor the ideal typical logic of mysticism. Mysticism has other routes to eternity than physical death, and without a manifest social opposition, mass suicide lacks any apocalyptic raison d'être.

These theoretical considerations about ideal typical logics suggest that the specific hybrid character of the Solar Temple has to do with how it combined apocalyptic and mystical elements. As we have seen, the theology in Aum Shinrikyō combined these two elements by shifting the Buddhist idea of seeking transcendence into an apocalyptic transformation that legitimated violence against the less evolved. The Solar Temple, by contrast, did not offer its rank-and-file participants any practice such as meditation that would yield direct mystical experience. The production of religious experience in the Solar Temple depended on a spiritual hierarchy in which a mystagogue, acting as priest, served as an intermediary between divinity (the Ascended Masters) and the audience of religious seekers. Believers took the role of clients who received a mystical experience produced through participation in ritual.

146

But here another puzzle arises, for what can be called "client mysticism" is a staple of New-Age spirituality, found in other Templar and more strictly Rosicrucian groups, tarot readings, and ritual practices under diverse other auspices. Yet there is no obvious theological reason to anticipate mass suicide or any other form of collective death among Rosicrucians in contact with Ascended Masters. Thus, even in client mysticism not so dissimilar from the Temple's, physical death as a *sine qua non* seems odd. Either death is illusory, and transcendence (i.e., the Transit) doesn't depend upon it. Or in the realist zen Buddhist view (which Aum Shinrikyō rejected), death is the end of life that closes off the possibility of transcendence. There are indications that the Solar Temple theology finessed these alternatives by the thesis that the trauma that seemed like death in the Transit wasn't really death at all; it was only the wrenching shift from quotidian to eternal reality by Ascended Masters whose existence eclipses life and death in any humanly understood terms. Yet any such claim begs the question of why previous Templar and Rosicrucian adepts had not found suicide necessary for union with the eternal. These are deep puzzles, and ones that are not subject to any tidy answer now that the spiritually most evolved of the Solar Templars have orchestrated their own deaths, along with those of certain of their enemies. With the third Transit at the spring equinox of 1997, perhaps all their closest followers have now departed.

The difficulty in squaring the Transit with either pure mysticism or currently predominant kinds of client mysticism on their own suggests that these cultural structures are not adequate to explain the violence. A much more likely cultural source is the Western religious dualism that equates life with temporality, death with eternity and (potentially) transcendence. After all, the Solar Temple operated as a neo-traditional quasi-Catholic organization that both mirrored the client mysticism of the Church itself and embraced the saga of the medieval Knights Templar, who reputedly died martyrs because they dared to embrace the true teachings of the gnostic Christ. In these aspects, faced with opposition, the Temple drew from the deep well of the Western tradition that mixes the client mysticism of dispensed salvation with quasi-apocalyptic struggles for the true faith in the death of Jesus, the martyrdom of early Christians, and the burnings at the stake of the Knights Templar who refused to recant their allegiance to the order (Cohn 1993; Williams 1975; Frend 1967; Riddle 1931; Partner 1982). Specifically, Temple theology, in appropriating the idea of Transit from the writings of Jacques Breyer (1959), combined Christian millenarianism with the concept of astrological eras and mystical harmonics of transcendence. In sum, a meaningfully coherent model of mystical mass suicide is difficult to consolidate. When this sociological incoherence is traced in relation to empirical forms of religiosity, its source is to be found in a mysticism colored both by dualism and by connections with Christian apocalyptic martyrdom.

In the Solar Temple, the theology of ecological apocalypse and survival initially did not depend on external opponents for its meaningful coherence within the group. Thus, if the Transit letters had not ranted against the "persecution" that the group alleged, the insistence in one letter that the collective death was "in no way a suicide in the human sense of the term" would have been perfectly plausible. Were it not for the sense of persecution, the deaths would not amount to mass suicide of the sort that we have posited as the potential denouement of conflict between an apocalyptic group and its detractors. Instead, the deaths would be better understood as the product of an idiosyncratic theology made possible by a form of client mysticism that mapped transcendence within a dualistic matrix of life and death. As Mayer has observed, however, Joseph DiMambro was flexible and syncretic in tapping theological sources and principles as occasion required. From what empirical information is available, it seems that the initial Transit in October 1994 was neither the product of a purely mystical theology nor did it stem from mysticism colored only by an ideology of apocalyptic survivalism. Rather, there was a shift from earthly apocalyptic survivalism to passage beyond the earthly apocalypse in the early 1990s, but this theology only became fully elaborated as "departure" in the context of an increased perception of earthly opposition, from February 1993 onward (Mayer 1996, pp. 70–8).

Whether the October 1994 deaths would have been orchestrated without the opposition and ensuing scandals is a counterfactual experiment that cannot be completed. Moreover, it remains unclear whether the second and third Transits would have occurred in the absence of the initial one. The evidence is ambiguous. What does seem plausible as a conclusion about what did happen – especially given the Transit letters' condemnation of the Temple's opponents, and also the murder of the Dutoits – is that opposition was sufficient to push believing Adepts already enamored with mystical transcendence to the initial physical enactment of Transit through death under apocalyptically framed circumstances. Although apocalyptic mass suicide is properly associated with external confrontations, the dialectic between the Solar Temple's theology of mystical consociation with eternity and the play of events on the ground shows that apocalyptic developments of confrontation can be quite powerful, even if the apocalyptic element of theology is initially relatively weak and otherworldly. As for the second and third transits, even though our understanding of them cannot be disentangled from the conditions under which the first transit occurred, at least implicitly, they raise a central question: could there be religious mass suicide in the absence of apocalyptic confrontation?

5

FINDING HEAVEN'S GATE

Astronomers discovered the fiery Hale-Bopp comet, with its icy core twenty-five miles wide, in July 1995. On 22 March of the following year, only a day after the third group of Solar Temple members committed suicide on the spring equinox, and during the week leading up to Passover and Easter, the comet reached its closest point to Earth on its journey through the universe. At a distance of 122 million miles, it was only 29 million miles further away from Earth than the sun. That day or the next, Marshall Herff Applewhite (who called himself "Do") and thirty-eight followers initiated their collective exit from this planet via a death meant as a departure for the Evolutionary Kingdom Level Above Human, conventionally called Heaven. There, they presumed to meet up again with Do's former platonic partner – the deceased "Ti" – Bonnie Lu Trusdale Nettles.

For months, a buzz of discussions on the internet and a radio show had speculated about a spacecraft that some people reported lurking behind the comet. Do and the thirty-eight men and women in what they called his "class" did not know for sure whether there was a spacecraft, but they took the appearance of the comet as a definitive sign confirming their prediction that "the Earth's present 'civilization' is about to be recycled – 'spaded under.'"

The cosmic forces do not always work according to prophecy. Initially, in the 1970s, Do and Ti, known in another couplet as "Bo" and "Peep" (and collectively as "the Two"), had expected conventional society to rise up against their heresy and assassinate them. This event would initiate the Last Days, and during those days, only individuals who had prepared to shed their earthly "vehicles" would be ready to make the transition through Heaven's Gate. Seeking to avoid

Aside from sources cited at specific points in the text, the following account is based on news reports, primarily in the LAT, NYT, IHT, and CT, as well the accounts of two sociologists who conducted research on the group in the mid-1970s: Robert W. Balch and David Taylor (Balch 1980, 1995; Balch and Taylor 1976, 1977). Among news accounts, NYT 28 April 1997 is particularly important for its coverage of Marshall Herff Applewhite, Bonnie Lu Nettles, and the history of the group they founded. Thanks go to Ann-Marie Dunnicliff for gathering and cataloguing research materials, and to Robert Balch for very helpful comments on a draft of this chapter.

initial ridicule as a "UFO cult," and concerned about family members who kept trying to get their relatives away from the group, the Two established what amounted to a small nomadic monastery. After friends tried to prise one member away, the group went underground for nearly seventeen years. Separated from the world at large, they developed their theology and its implications for the purification from bodily desires and the perfection of souls that would be ready to make the transition to the Next Level. After Ti, or Bonnie, died of cancer in 1985, Do carried on, seeking communiques from the "Older Member," and looking for the sign that finally came in the form of a comet. To learn about how they made the attempt to enter Heaven's Gate is to push toward, and perhaps beyond, the outer reaches of the Apocalyptic.

Two became "the Two"

The most important thing that had happened to Marshall Applewhite before he led the class to Heaven's Gate was meeting Bonnie Lu Nettles in March 1972. Applewhite was born in Texas in the early 1930s, the son of a strict southern Presbyterian minister who roved around the state founding churches. Originally, he wanted to follow his father into the ministry, but he had a great baritone voice, and he made his way into the world of music instead. When he attended Austin College in Sherman, Texas, "Herff," as his friends called Applewhite, already showed real talent for singing Negro spirituals and Handel's *Messiah*. After graduating in 1952 with a degree in philosophy, he went on to study religion at the Union Theological Seminary and Presbyterian School of Christian Education in Richmond, Virginia. However, he soon dropped out, and settled into a job as music director at the First Presbyterian Church in the small town of Gastonia, North Carolina, where he lived with his bride, the former Ann Pearce. Applewhite was drafted in 1954, and he and his wife were sent to Austria, and then to White Sands, New Mexico. After receiving an honorable discharge in 1956, the voluble and well dressed singer and choir director earned a master's degree in music at the University of Colorado at Boulder in 1960 and became something of an impresario. He pursued a series of jobs in music, working everywhere from Texas to New York City, in Episcopal and Unitarian churches, the opera, on the music faculty at the University of Alabama, and as music director of the University of Saint Thomas in Houston.

Life somehow changed for Applewhite in the socially turbulent decade of the 1960s. He left his wife in 1965, divorced in 1968, and seldom saw his two children thereafter. According to Robert Balch, a sociologist who studied the group that later became known as Heaven's Gate, Applewhite had a series of homosexual relationships (Balch 1982). By 1970, he had been dismissed from his position at the University of Saint Thomas. "He was behaving somewhat oddly at the time," the then president of the university, Father Thomas Braden, later reported. "Just talking to him, he would mention things that had no connection to the thing he said before." Braden has disputed a flurry of media claims that the university fired Applewhite because he had a sexual relationship with a male student, saying he never knew of such a relationship, and that Applewhite left voluntarily because he had "health problems of an emotional nature." Balch reports that the Saint Thomas relationship was with a female student, not a male one (personal communication, 1999; cf. Balch 1982, p. 32). Some former members of the group have asserted that Herff Applewhite felt guilty about his homosexual affairs, and checked himself into a psychiatric hospital the following year, asking to be "cured" of his impulses. Whether or not this is so, Balch affirms that Applewhite did seek out a therapist at least once because he was experiencing emotional distress (personal communication, 1999). Balch reports that Applewhite "confided to at least one of his lovers his longing for a meaningful, platonic relationship where he could develop his full potential without sexual entanglements" (1995, p. 141). The degree of guilt Applewhite felt about his sexuality, however, is disputed. Some of his gay friends later argued that Applewhite accepted his bisexuality. Balch reports a more complex picture: "At one moment, he could argue that homosexuality represents a higher form of consciousness, yet at another, he could be very sensitive about his 'straight' reputation" (NYT 28 April 1997).

Whatever Applewhite's feelings about his sexuality, he evidently experienced a series of crises. His job at Saint Thomas came to an end, his father died the following year, and he began to borrow money from friends. At some point, Applewhite started the Sunshine Company, a sandwich shop on the plaza in Taos, New Mexico, but he gave it up and returned to Houston in 1971. He started to pursue more focused spiritual questions, studying mystics and going on lone retreats. He also read science fiction authors Robert A. Heinlein and Arthur C. Clarke. Somehow, Herff Applewhite underwent a complete change of persona. Eventually, he stopped at his sister's house in Dallas to bid her farewell. Informed by her brother that he "wasn't going to see us anymore," Louise Winant reports, "I said to him, 'What's the matter with you? That's not the real you.' His response was, 'You just don't know the real me'" (NYT 29 March 1997).

How Applewhite and Bonnie Lu Nettles met in March 1972 is a matter now steeped in myth and memory. A few months earlier, he had experienced an epiphany on a beach in Galveston, Texas. "He said a presence had given him all the knowledge of where the human race had come from and where it was going," a friend named Hayes Parker recalls. "It made you laugh to hear it, but Herff was serious. And he didn't seem crazy" (NYT 28 April 1997). In some accounts, Nettles was a nurse at the psychiatric hospital where Herff Applewhite went to "cure" himself of homosexuality. Applewhite himself later claimed he was visiting a friend in a hospital when Bonnie, a pediatric nurse filling in for someone else, entered the room and their eyes locked into a mutual trance. Mrs. Nettles's daughter says that they met in a drama school, but acknowledges that she was very young at the time (Balch 1982, p. 33; Balch, personal communication, 1999). Applewhite's sister, Louise Winant, says he was hospitalized for heart problems, and Bonnie was his nurse at a point when he had a "near-death experience." "When he came to, Bonnie said God had a purpose for him, and he was going to do all this great work for God" (LAT 30 March 1997). However the encounter occurred, the two became the Two.

Bonnie Lu Nettles was a Texas woman and a Baptist. Born in 1927, she graduated from a Houston nursing school in 1948 and married a businessman soon thereafter. But Nettles's calling eventually overshadowed her job. Her daughter Terrie remembers how different she and her mother felt from other people. "We'd go out and stare into the sky, and we'd swear we had just seen a flying saucer. We thought, 'Wouldn't it be fun if it'd just pick us up and take us away'" (NYT 28 April 1997). By the time Bonnie and her husband divorced, in 1972, she had broken from her Baptist background and become a student of metaphysics and spiritualism in general and Theosophy in particular. She believed in the doctrine of ascended masters and used mediums to contact deceased souls in Wednesday evening seances, where one night they may even have communicated with the spirit of Marilyn Monroe. Bonnie's astrological practice was aided by Brother Francis, a monk who had died in Greece in 1818. "He stands behind me when I interpret the charts," she informed the *Houston Post* shortly after she met Applewhite. "There can be several meanings to them, and if I'm wrong, he will correct me" (Balch 1982, p. 34; LAT 30 March 1997). Assuming that Brother Francis was on the job at the time, he got a chance to oversee Bonnie reading her chart in relation to Herff Applewhite. Astrology affirmed what was to be an intense platonic alignment of two soul seekers. After the two met, they briefly ran an enterprise called the Christian Arts Center where they stocked books on astrology, Theosophy, healing, and non-western religions. In this confluence, Balch and Taylor report, "they first began to suspect their higher purpose on the planet." Bonnie's daughter, twenty years old at the time, witnessed the change: "They had this unbelievable power. Suddenly, I felt privileged to be around them" (Balch and Taylor 1977, p. 858; Balch 1982, pp. 33–9; NYT 28 April 1997).

On the first day of 1973, Bonnie and Herff took to the road, first nosing around the hill country of Texas, then heading out to Las Vegas in a sports car convertible, picking up a little money at odd jobs here and there. Then they went up to Oregon's Rogue River valley, where they took work digging septic tanks. In Oregon, the two received instructions from God that revealed an "overwhelming mission." They hurriedly drove off on a 8,000 mile trip criss-crossing around the United States and Canada, picking up work as they could, even selling blood to blood banks, and writing letters and manuscripts in which they developed their beliefs. As Herff announced from King's Motel ("We treat you royally") in Angola, Indiana, in a letter dated 11 August 1973,

> The time in the "wilderness" has finally ended. During that time I learned the meaning of separation from all attachments, concepts, possessions, passions & even self. Jesus' words and example took on their true meaning, and after much necessary suffering – the "Big

Daddy" revealed to Bonnie and me our mission. We are His 2 lampstands or candlesticks, his 2 olive trees [*sic*].

(NYT 28 April 1997)

Thus, Applewhite invoked Revelation 11: 4–15, "The two witnesses are the two olive trees and the two lamps that stand before the Lord of the earth." In the Bible, the Two would hold immense powers, to stop the rain, and turn rivers to blood. But devastation was to be visited upon them, the good book continues. "The beast that comes out of the abyss will fight against them. He will defeat them and kill them. . . . The people of the earth will be happy because of the death of these two." Their reward would come in reaching Heaven, while the horrors of the Apocalypse unfolded back on Earth. "Look for chaos – fires, shortages, excesses, earthquakes, destruction of all kinds," the Two warned in a letter. The time left before the earth's "expiration" was "desperately short" (Balch 1982, p. 44).

Long ago, psychologist William James noted the thin line that might divide religious vision from insanity. This issue turned out to be a sensitive one for Herff and Bonnie early on, and it continued to be a theme of group life over the years. While they were on their road trip, on 27 August 1973, Bonnie wrote to a friend, "Whenever anyone calls you a witch or implies insanity, feel thankful – you will get to a state where you will feel in the world, but not part of it." The same day, Herff wrote, "By social, psychiatric, medical & religious standards we and you have long since lost our sanity." He also asked the friend to recognize that the course the Two had chosen was not an easy one: "just put yourself in our shoes and imagine what we're up against" (NYT 2 April 1997).

For all their efforts on the road, Bonnie and Herff returned to Houston in May 1974 without a single recruit. But they had succeeded in building up interest among friends to whom they had been writing, and one of them, Sharon Morgan, was in a difficult marriage. She agonized over her choice. Should she stay with her children or walk with the Two who claimed to follow Jesus? After six days she decided to go with the Two on their next roadtrip. During the trip, she might hang around occult bookstores, approach someone who seemed to have the right vibrations, and ask, "Would you be interested in talking to two people who can tell you how to leave this planet and take your body with you?" But Mrs Morgan's discipleship was short lived. She was somewhat nervous about the Two's practice of skipping out on food and motel bills, and after about four weeks she arranged to visit a friend when she and the Two stopped in Dallas. At the rendezvous, Sharon's husband appeared, grabbed her, threatened to have her committed, and brought her home for what would turn out to be only a short-lived reconciliation. Not only did the Two lose their one disciple, her husband filed a legal complaint for credit card fraud. Even though the complaint was eventually dropped, a police check showed that Marshall Applewhite was wanted in St. Louis for stealing a rental car – the Mercury Comet that he was still driving – and police arrested him on 28 August 1974. While serving four months jail time in Missouri, Applewhite claimed divine permission for his crime (Balch 1982, pp. 39–50; NYT 2, 28 April 1997).

Gathering of the flock that became the class

The time in jail offered Herff plenty of opportunity for meditation about theological matters, for puzzling over recent developments, and for planning. Years later, in a *USA Today* advertisement (27 May 1993), he would freely admit shortcomings. "Well, it won't be hard to discredit this group from its leaders down, for prior to and during their 'awakening' and subsequent coming together, they all made many mistakes and learned from them." Apparently, from a strictly legal perspective, the Two played things fairly straight from 1974 onwards; at least they never again seem to have run foul of the authorities. They also gained an object lesson from the departure of Sharon Morgan to reunite with her husband and family. While she was with the Two, Sharon made a strong effort to cut ties, writing a note to her family telling them that they might as well imagine her to have been taken away by God in death. But she did harbor doubts, and her husband retrieved her. After this loss, the Two would redouble their efforts to demand that followers sever all relationships with their families, and they would initiate elaborate procedures to create a migratory monastery, a religious movement that really moved, from national park to state campground, hopscotching around the country, maintaining methods of contact that allowed people intrigued with their message to meet up with them, but kept others away.

The theology also firmed up while Herff was in jail. Although space-age occult ideas deeply permeated the theology, it was increasingly framed in Christian terms strongly influenced by Herff's Presbyterian background; gone were any explicit references to Bonnie's spiritual traditions of occultism, astrology, and Theosophy (Balch 1982, p. 51). Pursuing the idea that he and Bonnie were the Two mentioned in Revelation, Herff wrote that a "Demonstration" would come in which the Two would be killed, and then resurrected in a "cloud of light" that took the form of a UFO or spacecraft (NYT 28 April 1997). After Herff was released from jail in early 1975, he and Bonnie began an intense effort to proselytize. Do (1994) later recounted,

> As the two Older Members put out a "statement" and held public meetings over about a 9-month period in 1975–76 to bring their crew together, the media tagged them the "UFO cult" because of their expectation of leaving aboard a spacecraft ("cloud of light") at the completion of their "overcoming."

This account retrospectively layers in theological language that only came later. However, by the time the Two surfaced in southern California during the spring of 1975, their central ideas were already formulated, and they began the recruitment drive that Do later described.

Sending out letters from the art-colony and hot-springs town of Ojai, they hooked up with Clarence Klug, a mystic in his seventies, and Klug invited them to speak to his students at the home of his friend Joan Culpepper, a psychic who lived in Studio City. This was the Two's big break. On an evening in May 1975, some eighty people jammed into Culpepper's house. The Two, dressed in desert boots and jogging outfits, and sporting short hair, created a sensation. People later recalled Applewhite saying, "God has sent us here as an experiment, so you might call us Guinea and Pig." Joan Culpepper remembers the riveting blue eyes of Applewhite as he engaged the crowd, and how

> they laid it on the line that night. They were very stern. There was not any kind of loving kindness or nurturing. They said they would die, be assassinated, and anyone who followed would travel with them on a spaceship to a higher level, to heaven.

Those who wanted to follow were expected to give up everything from their past: family, possessions, even their identities. For her part, Culpepper did not find the message credible and she did not expect that anyone else would either. But apparently, spaceships or not, people were captivated with the idea that heaven is a physical place that people can actually reach. Some two dozen members of the audience decided to follow the Two, to Heaven they hoped (Balch 1982, pp. 51–4; LAT 30 March 1997; NYT 28 April 1997).

One of the first stops on the long journey was a campground in the Rogue River valley near the Pacific Ocean in southwestern Oregon that the Two marked with a cardboard sheep that played off their nursery-rhyme identity as a duo, Bo and Peep. The Two then began what amounted to a barnstorming tour, a speeded-up version of Herff's father's sojourns to found churches around Texas. Meetings were held in towns and campgrounds across the west. Six weeks after the Studio City meeting, Joan Culpepper and a friend finally parted ways with the group in Sedona, Arizona. Culpepper then spoke out against the group in an interview with the *Los Angeles Times*. Later she asserted that she had operated a halfway house for former members in Topanga Canyon, and followed the group around, questioning their teachings, until they went into seclusion several years after she left (LAT 30 March 1997).

The most successful meeting Bo and Peep ever held, in September 1975, was also one that brought them unwanted public attention. Held in the central Oregon coast just over the mountains from Eugene in the resort town of Waldport, the meeting was publicized from northern California to southern Washington, and in Oregon as far east as the college towns of Corvallis and Eugene. A leaflet with a block to fill in the time and place announced, "UFO's: • Why they are here. • Who they have come for. • When they will leave. *NOT A DISCUSSION of UFO SIGHTINGS or PHENOMENA.*" The hand-printed message went on,

Figure 5.1 Bo and Peep at a meeting that they staged in northern California in the mid-1970s.

Source: Reginald McGovern

> Two individuals say they are about to leave the human level and literally (physically) enter the next evolutionary level in a space craft (UFO) within months. Followers of "THE TWO" will discuss how the transition from the human level to the next level is accomplished, and when this may be done.
>
> This is not a religious or philosophical organization recruiting membership. However, the information already prompted many individuals to devote their total energy to the transitional process. If you have ever entertained the idea that there may be a real, physical level beyond the earth's confines, you will want to attend this meeting.

The local newspaper displayed a photo of the town's mayor throwing a flying saucer, and the Two gathered an audience of around two hundred people at a hall in the Bayshore Inn. Flanked by "buffers" to absorb the negative energy of the hecklers who often showed up at their events, the Two presented their basic message about how the Demonstration was to be followed by UFO transportation to heaven for their followers. The presentation apparently was compelling enough (and during the 1970s many people were not so settled in their lives) that within days some twenty people recruited from the Waldport meeting traveled to Colorado for a gathering of around 400 people who were interested in boarding a flying saucer that would take them to the next physical level beyond human.

But the Waldport event had other repercussions too. After the sudden exodus of converts, there were town meetings, and the Oregon State Police investigated. Late in 1975 CBS *Evening News* anchor Walter Cronkite reported one evening that the couple expected to be martyred "within weeks." They had told listeners they would be resurrected, perform miracles, and be "beamed up" to the "Next Evolutionary Kingdom" in the Demonstration that would prove they were who they claimed to be (Balch 1980: 137). "A score of persons from a small Oregon town have disappeared," Cronkite observed. "It's a mystery whether they've been taken on a so-called trip to eternity – or simply been taken" (quoted in NYT 28 April 1997: 9). Whatever the solution to that mystery, the authorities could not determine that any crime had been committed and they quickly closed their investigation (NYT 30 March 1997). Soon after, while Bo and Peep were seeking followers in Illinois, two men infiltrated the group in order to locate a friend who had joined them in Oregon. The two men were found out, and Bo and Peep abruptly canceled plans for a public meeting in Chicago. Assassination and the Demonstration might come too soon, they feared, before they could "harvest" all the "ripe fruit" (Balch 1995, p. 144).

A month after the Oregon meeting, the group, now with some 200 followers, completely dropped out of sight. Bo and Peep parted from their followers in Oklahoma, dividing them into living units of around fourteen people. Within each subgroup, the Two proposed a structure of platonic relationships of the sort that had proved so important to their own spiritual development. Each person was to be paired with a "partner," a sort of designated significant other, typically of the opposite sex, and they were to pass day and night together. In these relationships, individuals were expected to encounter the "frictions" through which they could identify their "hangups" and addictions, thereby determining what they had to overcome in order to move on to the next plane of reality.

Bo and Peep instructed that each subgroup was to be headed by one partnership, but as followers moved around the American west the families tended toward more democratic, consensual, or anarchic organization. At camping spots, they spread word about Bo and Peep, the anticipated assassinations, the Demonstration, and the imminent departure of followers on UFOs. Sometimes they were able to recruit new members. A handful of people joined in northern Arizona, and perhaps twenty more at a meeting in the Bay area of northern California. However, the diaspora after Oregon also created substantial logistical problems. The itinerant subgroups sometimes fell completely out of contact with other subgroups or Bo and Peep. Following the example of their leaders, they tried to "tune in" to cosmic messages that might surface in their minds, but this process sometimes only yielded garbled or contradictory information. Rumors circulated, creating waves of excitement and disappointment, and a high degree of disarray (Balch and Taylor 1976, 1977; Balch 1980; NYT 30 March, 28 April 1997).

Perhaps the nomadic flocks approximated the "freely formed groups" of wandering seekers in the times of the New Testament dispensation. Followers of Bo and Peep came from many walks of life, rich, poor, but mostly middling. Certainly some who followed had reached crisis points in their lives, the loss of a lover, divorce, a death in the family. A number of the youths who fell in with the movement already lived at the fringes of society. Often they were already steeped in a "far-out" countercultural milieu where the claims of Bo and Peep did not seem completely outlandish. Other people, older, seem to have been solidly planted in family and community life, but many of them had already dabbled in mystic or UFO subcultures (Balch 1995, p. 145). Whichever direction they came from, most followers seem to have been intelligent and relatively effective human beings. One recruit was a former missile-launching officer in the US Navy. Another, David Geoffrey Moore, was an unemployed nineteen-year-old son of a psychology professor and an English teacher. Kicking around California in the Santa Cruz area, he met up with the group; a few days later, his mother later recalled, he told her, "Mom, I don't know if this is for me, but it's something I want to go check out." Another young man, David Van Sinderen, the twenty-four-year-old son of an east-coast telephone company executive, joined up in Oregon, telling his friends, "It's a once-in-a-lifetime opportunity."

In 1997, the people who died at Rancho Santa Fe were mostly whites, along with a few Blacks and Latinos. Initially, because of their short haircuts, investigators thought all of them were males in their twenties and thirties. Closer investigation revealed that the deceased included twenty-one woman and eighteen men, ranging in age from their twenties to their sixties, with one seventy-two-year-old woman, and the greatest number, twenty-one, in their forties. No children died, but families were broken. There was a postal worker who had left five children behind, and a grandmother who had parted ways with her family back in Iowa. A daughter of a federal corrections worker from Missouri joined, and so did a former oysterman, a nurse from New England, an accountant born in Canada, and a local television personality from Tulsa, Oklahoma. One young woman was born on a farm; another, Susan Frances Strom, the daughter of a Federal district judge, left Oregon State University just before graduating to follow the Two. A member from Colorado, John Craig, once had it all. A tall cowboy-style real estate developer in Durango, friends saw him as a man with a loving wife and six children, active in the Chamber of Commerce and the Republican party. But in August 1975, Craig secretly signed over power-of-attorney to his wife and his lawyer, and then told his wife he was off to Denver on business. An old college friend had heard the Two talk when they were in the Los Angeles area, and he had arranged for Craig to meet them at the Denver airport. The man who would become Brother Logan never returned home (NYT, 30 March, 31 March, 28 April 1997).

Of the thirty-three dead at Rancho Santa Fe whose background is known, eighteen or so had joined hundreds of others in following Bo and Peep during their UFO revival and camping tours of 1975 and 1976. One boy was only fourteen when he joined with his parents; a girl who joined in 1975 was sixteen (Balch, personal communication 1999). Eight were in their twenties when they joined, some of them just finishing college, and eight more were in their thirties or older. Some were into New-Age spirituality, others followed the television-program *Star Trek*, and still others had conventional Protestant or Catholic upbringings.

The recruits in 1975 and 1976 almost all entered the group by coming to hear Bo and Peep or their surrogates at the public talks they advertised at places of high countercultural energy like college campuses, "head" shops, and organic food stores and restaurants. The two sociologists who conducted covert participant-observation research at that time, Robert Balch and David Taylor, describe a routine albeit unconventional process. Contact with the outside world was carefully orchestrated and narrowly focused on the agenda of Bo and Peep. In public talks, the Two (or at times when the group split up, their surrogates) offered up the same message that the group would maintain all the way through 1997. Human individuals, they affirmed, could change in ways that would prepare them for redemption from physical death through UFO flight to the next evolutionary level. After a presentation of fifteen to twenty minutes, there would be a question-and-answer period. People who showed sincere interest were given the location of a secret follow-up meeting, usually held the next day. At that less formal meeting, they could ask further questions. If they wanted to join, they only had a brief window of opportunity: they were informed of steps they would have to take to meet up with other new members at a "buffer camp." Just getting to the camp required effort, and it would thus be an initial test of interest and commitment. Prospective members often had to drive as long as a day to reach the camp, and in one case, they had "four days to reach a post office 800 miles away, where they found directions to the buffer camp scribbled in the Zip Code book." At a buffer camp meeting, prospective members would meet Bo and Peep and undergo what Balch and Taylor describe as a relatively low-key, non-coercive group socialization, spending long hours around a campfire, baking potatoes, gazing at the stars, feeling the vast silence, and "tuning in," seeking to experience the bolt of enlightenment that had struck the Two themselves (Balch and Taylor 1977, p. 845–6).

New-Age Puritans

By the early months of 1976, Bo and Peep decided to stop recruiting and withdraw from the world altogether. Over the cries of hecklers in Manhattan, Kansas, they proclaimed that "the harvest" was closed. In this phase, the Two made efforts to gather together the remnants of their by then far-flung flock. At a meeting in Spokane, sociologist Robert Balch received information about how to reach the Two through a mailbox in Gulfport, Mississippi (Balch 1995, p. 153). In their own account, after leaving Kansas, the Two drove to a campground near Medicine Bow, Wyoming (LAT 30 March 1997).

Those who stayed with Bo and Peep after the harvest are marked not by their similarity, but by their diversity. What they share, by definition, is a willingness to "drop out" of their previous lives. From the outset, the group established a community of goods, initially with a strong base in David Van Sinderen's trust fund of perhaps $500,000. In this communal world, participants undertook the project of undergoing what sociologist Max Weber called "metanoia," a more or less complete change in their cognitive understandings of the world, moving beyond their personal pasts and becoming "new" people, with new names, beliefs, and activities (Hall 1978, pp. 68–9). By the time of the deaths in 1997, they often had fictional names, and their drivers' licenses might list churches, KOA campgrounds, or other fictional addresses (LAT 29 March 1997). The fundamentalist Christian process of becoming "born again" pales by comparison with what the Two expected of their followers after they got to Medicine Bow. The group set about pursuing the Two's project of "Human Individual Metamorphosis" on a much more organized basis than the loosely structured living units of the previous year.

In the mature theology of the group recounted in its 27 May 1993 USA Today advertisement, human bodies are vehicles that can be inhabited by three major kinds of entities. There are, of course, conventional beings from the human level of existence, trying to pursue the normal things that people want out of life. But human bodies are sometimes inhabited by a second type of being – "Luciferians" – "space alien races" that try to dominate others by using "religion and increased sexual behavior to keep humans 'drugged' and ignorant (in darkness)." Third, Older Members, from the Evolutionary Level Above Human, occasionally come to Earth with an "away team," to provide information to human beings about how they can reach the higher evolutionary level. The task of moving on to the next level requires the individual to shed the trappings of human existence, eventually including the vehicle itself.

Getting to Heaven was not going to be so easy, the recruits in the 1970s found soon enough. At first, the wandering entourages connected to Bo and Peep waited for the Demonstration to come at any time. But once the Two reached Medicine Bow in June 1976, the theological premise of the group underwent an important shift. The much-heralded Demonstration was not going to come quickly; rather, the media branding of the group as a "UFO cult" the previous year had already demonstrated the incapacity of society at large to entertain the truth that Bo and Peep had to reveal. The Two stopped talking about the Demonstration in 1976 and set about institutionalizing the activities of their group, in the first instance by asserting the priority of their own relationship with the Next Level as what they came to call "Older Members." Despite this lofty status, Bo and Peep did not become authoritarians. "They were more like parental figures or that cool high school teacher you thought so much of," recalled Dick Joslyn, "not quite your buddy, but someone you could talk to." Still, once followers got to Medicine Bow, they could no longer hope just to "tune in" and connect with cosmic revelation. They needed to go through channels. Bo and Peep did not profess to know exactly how and when the journey to the physical location of the higher evolutionary level would occur, but they took it as their mission to prepare their class for the event. In practice, this goal required the accomplishment of two fundamental tasks: the shedding of previous ties to family and friends, and the renunciation of human forms of gratification. Do and Ti promoted an asceticism so extreme that it would presumably have impressed even the Puritans.

Robert Balch later wrote that park rangers consistently regarded the group as "model campers." Perhaps they were even a little obsessive. Reports are that the group experimented will all kinds of games and procedures for living that would accelerate what they called "the Process" of human metamorphosis. For a while they restricted bathing water to one gallon for each camper, to be used during a six-minute shower. At other points, they took up a regimen in which partners would appear for twelve-minute appointments at a "service desk" where they received work assignments. Sometimes members of the class spent hours listening to tuning forks, perhaps seeking to transcend human thought and enter into the pure energy of sound. At a Wyoming camp, people wore gloves at all times, one former member reported, and by use of written messages, they cut verbal communication down to "yes," "no," and "I don't know." Sometimes, it seems, they managed to go for days without speaking. The Two and their followers did not lose their capacity for fun, but they regulated fun like everything else. They played games like "Clue" and Yahtzee, and watched approved television programs (using a generator). They gazed at the stars at night out in the dark of the wilderness, far away from the lights of civilization, recording every satellite or shooting star that they observed (Balch 1995, pp. 155–6; NYT 29 March 1997; LAT 30 March 1997).

The program of self-purification in preparation for space travel was demanding and rigorous. The world and its attachments had to be renounced. As a Heaven's Gate web site talk by Do explained this requirement years later, members of the class

> don't like their human vehicles. . . . But they have to wear them, because the task of overcoming the human kingdom requires that they overcome human flesh – the genetic vibrations, the lust of the flesh, the desire to reproduce, the desire to cling to offspring, or spouse, or parents, or house, or money, or fame, or job, or, or – that could go on and on – overcoming the human flesh and its desires – even religious desires.
>
> (Do 1996b)

In the first instance, members of the class were expected to cut themselves off from families and previous friends. Children, the Two emphasized, had to be left behind, because they lacked the cognitive development to make informed, rational decisions about joining. But as for adults, the Two wrote in a mimeographed statement,

> Each true seeker must at one time walk out of the door of his life, leaving behind career, security, every loved one, and every single

161

attachment in order to go through the remaining needed experiences necessary to totally wean him from his needs at the human level.

(Balch and Taylor 1976, pp. 61 [quote], 66)

On this point, Do later suggested that people read the red-letter edition of the book containing the words of a Representative who had come two thousand earlier:

> He told His followers, "Go tell the good news that the Kingdom of Heaven is here." Meaning, "This is your chance, I'm here. I can take you out of here. I can lead you into that Kingdom Level Above Human." But He also said, "That can't happen unless you leave the human world that you are in and come and follow Me." That didn't mean on Sundays, it didn't mean part-time. It meant totally – "Leave everything and come and follow Me."

(Do 1996a)

In practice, this is what people had done from the beginning. As any number of friends and relatives recounted in 1997, the followers of the Two left abruptly, and limited their contacts with their families to the occasional card or letter saying they were happy, occasionally making brief visits that seemed, as much as anything, gauged to determine whether anyone in their families was interested in joining the group waiting for the spacecraft.

Bo and Peep seem to have recognized that the actual appearance of any spacecraft to transport them and their followers to the next level was not a certainty. Even believing it would happen, the question of *when* was difficult to answer. The failure of any craft to sweep down led to waves of anticipation and disappointment. One evening in south Texas, Peep became aware of what she thought was a message from the next level. The UFO was about to arrive and carry them off in the proverbial cloud of light. In a flurry of activity, everyone got ready to depart, and they waited through the night in high expectation. When the day dawned and it seemed evident that no landing was imminent, Peep admitted, "Well, I feel like I have egg on my face."

Earlier in the twentieth century, when airplanes first began flying over Melanesia in the Pacific, some islanders thought they might be the fulfillment of old prophecies about the arrival of ships from the heavens that would deliver something akin to the milk and honey of a promised land or, in modern terms, the goods and machines from afar that European colonists seemed to acquire by magical means through no discernible work of their own. Once the immense airships appeared, the problem was how to get them to land. Learning that the airships sometimes touched down on purpose-built runways, a few among the islanders who formed what anthropologists called "cargo cults" constructed ritualistic imitations of an airstrip, complete with makeshift control tower and hanger, to attract a flying ship. No plane ever landed, but each sighting was enough to keep hope alive, and sometimes, to produce further ritual action to attract the wondrous sky vessels (Worsley 1968). The accounts of cargo cults are now criticized for the ways they adopted the colonialist-tinged anthropological worldview after the Second World War, but some landing strips were indeed constructed (Lindstrom 1993).

The craze of anticipation that surrounded the Two's UFO claims bears a family resemblance to the eruption of cargo-cult expectations in Melanesia. The Two and their followers did not build landing pads, but neither did they take the occasional disappointment when a spaceship failed to appear as cause to lose hope. Instead, like both cargo cultists and earlier believers in flying saucers (Festinger, Riecken, and Schachter 1964), the Two took absence of confirmation as an impetus to deepen faith. Specifically, they entertained the notion that they and their flock were not yet prepared to make the journey. Perhaps this was why no ship yet touched down: it would be a wasted trip.

Theologically, self-perfection became the precondition necessary to obtain the salvation marked by the arrival of transportation to the next level. In November 1976, the Two provided their followers with "the 17 steps," posed as a series of questions. In part, the questions focus on obedience ("1. Can you follow instructions without adding your own interpretation?"). But beyond questions relevant to authority and social control, there are interesting queries about matters of personal and moral development. The Two were concerned about "inconsiderate conversation," sensitivity toward others, "defensiveness and its flip side, martyrdom," and people who "needlessly ask a question when the answer is obvious or a moment of silent observation would quickly reveal the answer." They asked followers to consider whether they were "physically clumsy," and whether they tended to "half way complete a task" or "procrastinate." Did they engage in wasteful practices like using an "excessively high cooking flame, more toothpaste than necessary, etc.?" In all this, self-control was a predominant theme:

12 Are you pushy, aggressive, interfering, or demanding in any way?
13 Has familiarity caused you to become so relaxed with your partners or others that your actions or words don't hold enough restraint?
14 Are you gentle, simple, cautious, and thoughtfully restrained in your steps and all other physical actions or words?

The standard by which all these matters were to be judged was simple. Followers were asked to "understand and review in your mind all the ways in which members of the Next Level are sensitive." Having done this, "you have no excuse for not working on improving in these areas at all times" (Bo and Peep 1976).

Overall, the followers of the Two were expected to enter into a project of self-perfection and extreme asceticism. As the 27 May 1993, USA Today advertisement put it,

A "student" or prospective "child" of a member of the true Kingdom of God can, with the help of an Older Member, overcome or rise out of all human mammalian behavior – sexuality and gender consciousness – and all other addictions and desires of the human kingdom. He must complete this change to the point of abhorring human behavior before his soul can become a "match" with a biological body of the true Kingdom of God – for that new body is genderless and incapable of functioning at a human level.

Long before, beginning in the sixteenth century, Calvinist Protestant reformers had sought to make this world the object of a rationalized self-discipline in the conduct of their followers. In their program of radical reconstruction, the Two exceeded the Puritan agenda. They expected their followers to reach a standard of self-discipline that was beyond human. Yet, again, like the Puritans, self-regulation had to be freely chosen.

As the heady days of the counterculture faded during the mid-1970s, not everyone who wanted to go to the Next Evolutionary Level Above Human wanted to give up everything necessary to make the trip. For those who wanted to travel in a different direction, back toward the world, it does not seem to have been difficult to leave. In the diaspora that the Two orchestrated from 1975 to early 1976, many people left soon after joining, and others set personal deadlines for the arrival of the UFOs, departing when they failed to appear. By the time the nomadic families reached Medicine Bow in June 1976, only around ninety people remained of the perhaps 200 seekers who had travelled with the group. The Two got the numbers down even further, insisting that anyone who stayed submit to the perfectionist project. Hippies would have to cut off their long hair and give up marijuana. Everyone would have to give up sex. People would need to analyze what their own attachments were – alcohol? diet? favorite expressions? – and struggle to rise above them. The Two staged one event where they drew a line on the ground and asked those who wanted to stay to cross over it. With its increasingly ascetic emphasis, the class quickly dwindled down to around seventy. Toward the end of 1976 they identified nineteen people of less than adequate commitment, and sent them off to Phoenix, Arizona, eventually to be "cooled out" of the group altogether. Over the years from then until 1979, as the group continued camping in the west, other followers peeled off as well (Balch and Taylor 1976; Balch 1980, 1995; NYT 28 April 1997).

"Metanoia," that decisive change in self demanded by charismatic prophets, may yield a sharp and unambiguous commitment that initiates the turn to a new worldview, but the personality change supposed to accompany the commitment doesn't "take" for everyone, and even those individuals committed to the path may find themselves struggling to move along it. As the numbers of people leaving the Two suggest, the socialization process was far too open to individual choice, doubt, and freedom of departure to be characterized as "brainwashing" or "coercive persuasion."

Robert Balch found in the earliest phases of group life a disorganized situation in which many people improvised their affirmations of identities as participants by imitating the language and demeanor of the followers around them. They did not necessarily fully believe in the message that the Two put before them, especially the part about going to Heaven in space crafts. Even the basic program, of "tuning in" to the higher levels, could prove frustrating. Balch's partner confessed to him one time, "When I try to tune in all I do is think about tuning in. I tune in and think about tuning in, and think about thinking about tuning in, but nothing ever happens." Some camp members maintained inward doubts or even complete disbelief, yet soldiered on. Others were not so good at following the process: one couple who were supposed to be preparing for a lecture by getting "in tune," took the opportunity to go to a Robert Redford movie. Still others maintained "side bets" just in case the Demonstration did not take place. Thus, one man kept his piano-tuning tools in the trunk of his car, in case he should need them back in the world some time (Balch 1980, p. 141).

To be sure, Bo and Peep organized the group and its mores in ways that tended to promote identification with the group and prevent backsliding. The very process of joining up with the group was a test of commitment. Contact with the outside world was defined as evidence of backsliding toward lingering human attachments, and it was thus something that the sincere seeker would want to avoid. In addition, the structuring of relationships via the partner system meant that each person was socially intimate with another person whose ultimate identification was supposed to be with the group as a whole. One man recruited in Waldport, Robert Rubin, later recounted, "The partner was there, if you were falling out of what you had to do, so you wouldn't fall out. It was part of the mind control." However, as with most efforts at social control, the results were considerably less than totalistic. The problem was simple: there was no assurance what partners would talk about, and how they would respond to one another. Just as Balch found his partner openly confiding doubts, if there were any efforts at mind control, they failed to work on Rubin. After five months in which his major distraction was reading the red-letter edition of the Bible, he left (NYT 29 March 1997).

Bo and Peep changed their names around the time of the Medicine Bow camp, to the scale notes Do and Ti, but they never seem to have changed their emphasis on free-will association within the group. Not only was anyone free to leave, but people could also return. Some did so, either immediately or years later. One night in 1977 Dick Joslyn walked away from a campsite down a long road, arriving back in the earthly world as manifested in an all-nite truckstop near Cheyenne, Wyoming. Looking at the waitresses and the truckers chowing down breakfast, he decided that the world did not have much to offer, hitched back to the campsite the same morning, and stayed for twelve more years. Others really did decide to leave, however, and the Two helped them with bus tickets, or even a ride to the airport; typically they also provided money to get reestablished: up to $1,000 (NYT 29 March, 28 April 1997; Balch, personal communication, 1999).

A sharp wall divided the world from those preparing to move to the next evolutionary level, but those who wanted to turn back found it easy enough to do so. The consequence, of course, was that the people who remained could be counted as ever more committed to perfecting themselves in preparation for their voyage. The process would take years. After the initial wave of recruiting in 1975 to 1976, as the *USA Today* advertisement later recounted,

> The two Older Members then went into seclusion with their crew (students), "lifting them out" of the world for almost 17 years (not accepting any new students), making Earth's surface their classroom. This isolation was absolutely necessary. The degree of their overcoming of sexuality, addictions, and ties to the human environment had to be taken to the point of matching the behavior and consciousness of the Evolutionary Kingdom Above Human.

For the first three years, they stayed very close to the Earth, by camping. But in 1978, the group moved into houses, first in the Denver suburb of Wheat Ridge, then in cities and towns around the west, from Dallas to Rancho Santa Fe. The community of goods that depended on the donated wealth of members eventually began to diminish, and the group underwent a certain "routinization" of their previous life of spoils communism, shifting to a more conventional communal economy based on the money from outside work of employable members and the internal labor of communal work (and eventually, the internal business of web page design). At first, to protect the group's isolation, people took only menial jobs well outside their own previously known skills. Eventually, members began to work at relatively high paying jobs, in auto repair, technical writing, and computers. The income from the outside jobs of a dozen or so yielded income after taxes of around $300,000 to $400,000 per year. Like other communal living groups (Hall 1978, chapter 5), the "UFO cult" could achieve significant economies of scale and efficiency, and they could put the skills of participants to good use both by generating income from outside jobs, and by negotiating the organization's dealings with the wider world in effective ways. Brother Logan was particularly important for his skill at negotiating leases, because the group moved often to stay out of reach of certain families that hired detectives to try to track them down.

Information about the years after 1979 is sketchy, but the defectors whom Robert Balch interviewed reveal a life in a world apart. The group kept all the windows covered in the houses where they lived, and they began to dress in similar clothing. At one point they wore uniforms that sometimes included hoods completely covering their heads, with just two holes for the eyes (Balch, personal communication, 1999). In this cloistered world, you could feel like you were in a different place, completely losing track of the earthly flow of external events. The projects of experimentation with perfecting the self for space travel continued, however, and partly they depended on an extreme rationalization of time. As Balch recounts the schedule of one woman who lived in a Denver house,

Her first of four daily rest periods began at 3:36 p.m. and ended exactly two hours later. At 5:57 she bathed. Twenty-four minutes later she took a vitamin pill, one of thirty-two consumed every twenty-four hours. At 6:36 she drank a liquid protein formula, and one hour later she ate a cinnamon roll. By 9:54 she was back in bed for another two hours.

(1995, p. 157)

Money was equally a matter to be treated with extreme rationality. Accounting went down to the penny, and this practice was followed right up to the days before the collective suicide at Rancho Santa Fe. One accounting entry records the $417.27 that the group spent at a local pizza joint seven days before their deaths; the last entry notes that two members of the class found six cents and turned it over to be entered in the books, leaving a final earthly balance of $12,183.21, plus some $5,400 in cash (LAT 3 April 1997). In his famous *Protestant Ethic and the Spirit of Capitalism*, Max Weber could have been describing the class, rather than the Puritans, when he wrote, "Man is only a trustee of the goods which have come to him through God's grace. He must, like the servant in the parable, give an account of every last penny entrusted to him" (1958, p. 170). Much the same rationalized precision ruled the class more widely. A schedule determined who would take out the garbage, how people who worked outside would be transported to their jobs, and when the peeling of carrots would take place. The group developed proper methods for dealing with every situation, from shaving to establishing the perimeters of pancakes on the griddle, and they meticulously logged all the protocols into one or another of their enormous Procedures Books like those of large business, government, or university organizations, but dealing with the minutiae of everyday life.

Rationality, in short, was the order of the day, on all fronts. Preparation to travel to the Next Evolutionary Level Above Human required nothing less. The Shakers, the nineteenth-century communalist followers of Mother Ann Lee, had built beautiful furniture and houses, developed labor-saving inventions, and established thriving businesses in this world, despite feeling no need to procreate, since the Apocalypse was at hand. Equally certain of the End, the group around Do and Ti went even further in the direction of self-discipline. In a way like the cargo cult devotees who built the landing strips to attract the big airships in Melanesia, the Two and their followers organized their lives as though they were living in a highly rationalized Next Level of extra-terrestrial space, hoping that their ritualized demonstration of readiness would make it so.

After Ti: Do, the class, and the final offer

Despite the fact that the Demonstration had once been depicted as an assassination of the Two, Ti died on her own, and not as a martyr to the Earth's rejection of the Next Level, but from the earthly disease of cancer, which spread from one eye, removed in 1983, to her liver. Perhaps in theological anticipation of Ti's death, the group came to the view that the human vehicle is gradually displaced by a Next Level vehicle, as the person grows ready to make that voyage. Ti had not needed her body anymore. In the summer of 1985, she died under an assumed name, Shelly West, in Dallas's Parkland Hospital. Her ashes were spread across a Texas lake. Do later reflected,

> Ti experienced no symptoms prior to the week she left her vehicle, and for the most part, her vehicle slept through the transition. We're not exactly sure how many days it might have taken her to return to the Next Level.
>
> (quoted in NYT 28 April 1997, p. 10)

For all the emphasis the Two gave to denial of earthly attachments, Do was filled with grief, and at a loss as to understand what he was to do with the class. He sent a tape recording to Ti's daughter, telling about her mother, and he could be heard seemingly sobbing as he talked (Balch 1995, p. 164). For several years after Ti's death, Do groped for answers about what course of action to take. He openly spoke of the possibility that he was crazy and should simply tell everyone to go home. But apparently the encapsulated reality that the Two and their followers had created was strong enough to carry Do through the crisis, and he eventually reached the clear understanding that the Older Members wanted his mission to continue, even though Ti had returned. If anything, the ever increasing public fascination with space travel, marked by popular movies like *Star Wars*, showed that the world was catching up. What people outside the class needed was the information that the Older Members had passed on from the Next Evolutionary Level.

In 1992, the group ended the seventeen years of seclusion during which, as a student named Jwnody put it in a 1996 mission statement, "we were very much 'lifted out' of this world – literally." In 1988, the group had begun efforts to update their thinking and "set the record straight" by "refuting many of the false reports and outright lies" that had been circulated back in 1975. They distributed the "'88 Update" "far and wide," Jwnody recounted, "But it was clearly part of the Next Level's design to keep us protected and secluded a while longer." Then things changed. "In the early 1990s, we began to get clear signals that our 'classroom time' *per se* was nearly over, but that some involvement with the public was about to begin." The group put out a satellite television broadcast series, "Beyond Human – The Last Call," and invited viewers to contact them (Jwnody 1996).

Of all the people on planet Earth, those who most wanted to connect, it seems, were the group's own "lost sheep." Gary Jordan St Louis had been one of the participants asked to leave the group in the 1970s. He had taken a job in computers at the Denver airport, and become involved in relationships with two different women. But apparently in the struggle between worldly attachments and the Higher Level, the attachments lost. In February 1992, St Louis told his girlfriend that he "wanted to join my heavenly father and my classmates." Convincing his half-sister Dana Tracey Abreo to come with him, Gary went back to the group. A trickle of others returned as well. One, Darwin Lee Johnson, had not lived up to the group's standards during a brief time with them in the 1970s, but he continued to be a UFO believer. While he was playing in a Utah rock band called Dharma Combat in 1994, he suddenly left after seeing an advertisement for a Heaven's Gate seminar. Others who returned did so after their earthly associations seemed to close down on them, through the deaths of relatives, divorce, or both (Hewitt *et al.* 1997). By whatever route they arrived, Jwnody recounted, these "returnees" were given "a period of time to readapt to the ways of the classroom/Next Level."

The class had not changed a great deal over the years, although they had intensified, clarified and developed basic ideas and practices. In the spring of 1988, they had adopted "additional guidelines for learning control and restraint – a self-examination exercise." Displayed on the Heaven's Gate website in 1997, the guidelines listed three major offenses: "deceit" (including doing something "on the sly"); "sensuality" of all kinds, including not only actions, but also thoughts; and third, "breaking any instruction knowingly." The "Lesser Offenses" reveal the ideal of a world guided by civility and appropriate conduct. Students were not to take actions "without using my check partner." "Trusting my own judgment – or using my own mind," or "twisting procedures for my own benefit" were minor offenses too. The list also included defensiveness, criticism, negativity, aggression, jealousy, selfishness, rebelliousness, laziness, procrastination, familiarity, impatience, intolerance, vanity, "inappropriate curiosity," and "having private thoughts." Beyond these offenses, the student primed to travel to the Next Level would not fall into "exaggerating vehicular symptoms," "having likes or dislikes," "using inadequate restraint," seeking "attention or approval," or "permitting lack of control over emotions to the point that it interferes with my work or rest or is a distraction to others."

Life at the Next Level clearly required a person who submitted to authority, someone who had transcended desires for ego gratification, who could be counted on to do things properly, a person freed from any irrational drives or emotions, ready to proceed in an even, deliberate way, attuned to the matters at hand. This would be a new Puritan ready to participate in the close coordination necessary for space travel.

For the most part, the class participants who persisted seem to have embraced these expectations freely and in good faith, and without chafing under the strict regimen. Do, after all, was not a tyrant. The sticking point evidently was the major offense of sensuality. Since Sigmund Freud, the importance of sexual desire in shaping human conduct has become widely understood. Even long before Freud, communal religious groups sought to regulate sexual thought and conduct, both to prevent coupled relationships that might threaten group solidarity, and to channel sexual energies so as to promote enlightenment. The strategies have been diverse, ranging from celibacy to polygamy (Foster 1991).

In Do's class, the effort to eliminate sexual libido was unrelenting. Using discrete language, people were expected to confess their lapses openly to the group. Clothing deemphasized the body; class participants had an androgynous style of haircut. Sleeping arrangements were organized to segregate class participants – straight or gay – from the objects of their desire. With the help of these arrangements, one woman in her twenties, Gail Maeder, known as Renée in the group, could write her family in 1995, "It may comfort you to know I am still not participating in any sexual acts" (NYT 30 March 1997). Nonetheless, some participants, apparently men in particular, found sexual arousal nearly impossible to curb. Even though he did not want to, one man sometimes had an orgasm while the group watched movies. Another could not seem to avoid fantasies with sexual themes.

The most obvious solution, some members thought, was castration. At first Do recoiled from the idea. Over the years, however, class members, including a man known only as Sawyer, continued to raise the issue. As Sawyer later recounted the argument, "This was really no different than olden days when menservants to the queen would be castrated so they couldn't try anything." Initially, Do apparently worried that someone would complain to the police about such a bizarre practice, and he felt an obligation not to take a wrong step with the members of his class. Finally, he agreed to let members explore the options, and they located a surgeon's assistant in Mexico who was willing to perform the operation. Unfortunately, after the first castration, the patient's scrotum failed to drain properly, and he had to receive further hospital treatment. But even this shaky beginning did not deter the group. Over the next few years, Do and seven other members underwent the same procedure (NYT 28 April 1997).

Over the same period of time, the class redoubled its efforts at outreach, continuing to grapple with the question of how to connect with people in the world at large "who rightfully despise the hypocrisy of what religions have become." On 27 May 1993 they placed their advertisement in USA Today. "UFO cult resurfaces with final offer," they announced, extending the "last call" they had made in 1992. At the beginning of the following year, Jwnody recounted, they sold most of their possessions and went on a barnstorming tour again, travelling coast to coast with their "last chance" offer "to advance beyond human" (Jwnody 1996; Do 1994). At the time when members of the class came through Robert Balch's home town, they had split into three crews to spread the message. A couple of days before the meeting, two members of the class, Sawyer and Gary St Louis's sister Dana, visited Balch. The sociologist had kept up with the group at a distance, staying in touch with parents and the broader network of former members, and he had seen the 1993 USA Today advertisement. Although the group's basic ideas had changed little, Balch wrote later, with its talk about the Earth being "recycled – spaded under," the advertisement "had an apocalyptic tone that was much more dramatic than anything I had heard in 1975" (Balch 1995, p. 163).

The meeting that Balch attended was much like the ones nearly two decades earlier. The group members simply presented information, answered questions, and left people in the audience to make up their own minds. No one joined at the meeting Balch attended, but the nine members present didn't seem discouraged. Apparently they were used to rejection. In Jwnody's account, the group adopted the view that

> our primary purpose for being out there at this particular time, was not to relate to the public in general, but to locate our additional crew members. . . . Once again we realized that this was all part of a greater plan that was unfolding according to the design of those in the Next Level responsible for this current civilization 'experiment.'
>
> (Jwnody 1996)

Overall, the extended last offer beginning in the early 1990s must have netted around twenty recruits. Around half of these, however, were "lost sheep" who decided to rejoin, and the group also lost some members while they intensified recruitment.

Do continued to puzzle over their circumstances, and he ran through a number of possibilities with the class. The group bought some rifles and pistols, with the thought that perhaps they should provoke an attack by government forces. A number of members felt uncomfortable with this scenario, and the guns ended up in a rental storage unit in Escondido, thirty miles northeast of San Diego, California. In September 1994, Sawyer later recalled, Do first raised the possibility of suicide in an office in a warehouse near San Clemente, California, where the group had relocated. When Do asked whether anyone had reservations about dying by a painless potion, "A few actually said they did, though they were newcomers," Sawyer recounted. "There were a couple of others who said that while they'd do it, it was a fearful thought" (NYT 28 April 1997).

Do and his class put more extended offers of the "last chance" out on the internet in September and October 1995. Always looking for clues about providence, convinced that "nothing is predetermined," they found a definitive sign in the "extremely animated and somewhat mixed" response to the web pages headed "Undercover 'Jesus' Surfaces Before Departure," and "95 Statement by an E.T. Presently Incarnate." As Jwnody put it, "the loudest voices were those expressing ridicule, hostility, or both – so quick to judge that which they could not comprehend. This was the signal to us to begin our preparations to return 'home'" (Jwnody 1996). Yet, Jwnody emphasized by way of conclusion in April 1996,

> Nothing is predetermined. The response of the world to the Next Level will be monitored very carefully. What happens next remains in the balance. It has been given that what you do with this – how you respond to us – is strictly up to you.

On to Heaven's Gate

Over the next year, members of the class appeared in many places. From September 1995 to the middle of 1996, some could be found in Paradise Valley, near Phoenix, Arizona, where they pursued a venture that the group had initiated in the 1970s, writing a screenplay called "Beyond Human." Over the same period, members rented offices for their computer work in Manzano, New Mexico, and lived on a nearby ranch, experimenting with constructing "Earth Ship" shelters from recycled rubber tires. Some people who met class members later remembered them as people with practical skills, intelligent, and knowledgeable about computers. However Mike Dew, a preacher from a local fundamentalist church called Prophetic Voices in the Wilderness, had a different recollection. He engaged in a theological debate with Brother Logan, and became convinced that the man was under sinister influences. "It was a pervading form of darkness, not a red devil with horns," the preacher later reported: Brother Logan "would look over his shoulder as if he were consulting with a physical entity and then he would speak to me as if he were taking the words from this being" (NYT 31 March, 1 April 1997).

Apparently, the group became concerned that something might go awry with the visitors they anticipated from space. On 10 October 1996, they paid $1,000 to take out an insurance policy against alien abduction, impregnation, or murder by aliens. Each member's beneficiaries stood to collect $1 million, but, as the managing director of the London insurance broker that wrote the policy pointed out, "they would have to prove that they were abducted." None of the firm's other 4,000 abduction policy holders had ever mounted a successful claim. Around the same time, the class relocated to southern California, where they resided in a series of properties that were up for sale. At a yard sale when they were leaving one such house in the fall of 1996, a neighbor talked to one of the members. "He said they were preparing to take a long journey," the neighbor later recalled. "They didn't want to get tied up in a lease" (LAT 28 March, 31 March 1997; IHT 3 April 1997).

The group's next stop was a nine-bedroom, seven-bath, 9,200 square foot house on a three-acre lot at 18241 Colina Norte, a cul-de-sac a few miles from the Pacific Ocean in Rancho Santa Fe, some thirty miles north of San Diego. Originally, the Santa Fe railroad had used the land to produce eucalyptus wood for railroad ties, but after the railroad expansion played out, the company developed the land as an exclusive community near the Del Mar race track. Rancho Santa Fe claimed such residents as the 1950s singer Patti Page, San Diego Padre owner John Moores, former astronaut Wally Schirra, and the founder of the Taco Bell chain, Glenn Bell. Befitting this sort of clientele, the house on Colina Norte had tennis courts, a putting green, a sauna, and an indoor elevator. Its owner, Sam Koutchesfahani, had run foul of the law for bribing college instructors to certify that foreigners were students enrolled in the San Diego area so that they could live illegally in the United States. The scheme netted Mr

Koutchesfahani up to $350,000, but when he was caught, he pleaded guilty to tax evasion and fraud, and put the house for rent while it was up for sale.

In New Mexico, the computer workers in the group had called themselves "Computer Knowmad," but in Rancho Santa Fe they became the "Higher Source." Beginning in the fall of 1996, they rented the Colina Norte property for $7,000 per month, agreeing to allow realtors to show the house at specified times. Realtors were required to wear surgical booties inside, where they found furnishings with a southwestern motif, computer workstations in the room behind the grand double staircase, and bedrooms fitted out with bunk beds for eight people. The men and women all had crew cuts and called each other "brother" and "sister" as they worked at the banks of computers. Agents for one webpage client, the San Diego Polo Club, later remembered the Higher Source people as "impeccable professionals" who "knew the computer industry backward and forward." Nevertheless, they seemed a little strange what with their homestyle buzzcuts, and the club's general manager, Tom Goodspeed, offered to connect them with a professional marketing company to help "overcome the strangeness of their impression as business people." But they refused, telling him they were "members of a monastery" (LAT 27 March, 28 March 1997; NYT 29 March 1997).

The monastic life required an unearthly schedule of sleep and work. Members of the group seem to have taken a main communal meal ("fuel") at 5 a.m., supplementing it at other times of the day with snacks of fruit and a lemon drink seasoned with cayenne. But they also scheduled time for orderly fun, sitting in assigned seats facing a seventy-two-inch screen Mitsubishi television set to view *Star Trek*, a PBS documentary about Thomas Jefferson, Keanu Reeves in *Chain Reaction*, and *Eddie* with Whoopi Goldberg.

The sign of the Hale-Bopp comet probably came to the group first through radio signals or the internet. On *Coast to Coast with Art Bell*, a radio show heard on nearly 350 stations, stories about the comet surfaced in November 1996. On the program, Chuck Shramek, an amateur astronomer from Houston, Texas, talked of an "unexplainable" anomaly shown near the comet in a photograph that he posted on the internet. A tenured professor of political science at Emory University, Courtney Brown, appeared on the same program promoting his book *Cosmic Voyage*. Brown claimed to be in touch with psychics who employed "remote viewing" to see the enormous alien space craft that was following behind the comet. Clearly a person with an affinity for Higher Level ideas, the Emory professor wanted to make one thing clear. "The purpose is galactic evolution," he said on the show. "It is not an invasion." UFO reports had once been taken quite seriously, even by the government. Beginning in 1947, the US Air Force investigated claims of sightings, but they stopped in 1969 because none of the 12,618 reports they had received led to any evidence of extraterrestrials, or even any kind of unusual aircraft. After the controversy erupted over Hale-Bopp, the co-discoverer of the comet, Alan Hale, wrote in the magazine *Skeptical Inquirer* that the supposed space craft was merely a star overexposed in a photograph of the comet. But true believers accused him of covering up the sighting of a real alien ship, and when professional astronomers announced revisions in their calculations of the comet's trajectory, rumors spread that the UFO was undergoing "course corrections" (SFC 28 March 1997; NYT 2 April 1997).

Whatever the route by which the group around Do found out about the comet, they were very interested. On 30 January 1997, they went to Oceanside Photo and Telescope and purchased an LX200 Schmidt-Cassegrain computerized telescope for $3,645, charging the cost to Brother Logan's credit card. But little over a week later, on 7 February, they brought the telescope back and demanded a refund. The manager of the store later reported, "They said, 'Well, you know, we didn't see the spaceship, so, of course, this instrument is not going to suit our needs.'" They then went down to Scope City in San Diego and bought some binoculars instead. At 4 a.m., they would go out and look up at the sky to the northeast. As the class became ever more oriented toward the comet, one member decided that he was not ready to take his life, and he dropped out (CT 2 April 1997; LAT 28 March, 1 April 1997).

Do and his followers passed their last days on Earth preparing for their journey and enjoying themselves a bit. A group visited Sea World on 12 March, and went to San Diego's Animal World. Some members played slot machines at the Stratosphere Hotel in Las Vegas, winning over $20. Four of them took a last bus trip through some of their old stomping grounds around the town of Gold Beach in southern Oregon, passing through Santa Rosa and Sacramento, California en route. In the early weeks of March, several members paid to have their teeth cleaned; they also took care of a $2.50 library fine.

Do and the class sought to project great joy and excitement about their impending departure from earthly life, and they impressed others who met them as "peaceful" and "loving." During the third week of March, they asked that the house not be shown to prospective buyers, since it was their holy week. On Wednesday 19 March, they videotaped their farewells. The class members appeared two by two on camera, making personal statements that seem neither coerced nor much rehearsed. One woman freely acknowledged, "Maybe they're crazy, for all I know. But I don't have any choice but to go for it, because I've been on this planet for thirty-one years and there's nothing here for me." Concerning her anticipated death, she remarked, "If that's what it takes, that's better than being around here with absolutely nothing to do." Another woman affirmed, "I think everyone in this class wanted something more than this human world had to offer." And a man insisted, "I am doing this of my own free will. . . . It is not something someone brainwashed me into or convinced me of or did a con job on." He went on, "If anybody feels bad about that, that's just their problem." Another man expected "just the happiest day in my life." After making the tape, the group all went out for pizza and then saw the movie *Secrets and Lies*. Two days later, around 2 p.m. on Friday March 21, they again surfaced, eating at the Marie Calender's restaurant in Carlsbad, ordering turkey pot pies and iced tea, staying around forty-five minutes, and paying the $350 tab in cash (LAT 27 March, 29 March, 3 April 1997; NYT 29 March 1997).

The class packed for a trip. As always, each member had a suitcase packed, ready to leave the house at a moment's notice. They all carried a birth certificate, passport, or driver's license, and money in both pockets: a $5 bill and some quarters. They also packed some necessities of life, lip balm, facial tissue, pens and pencils. In waves of fifteen members assisted by eight others, they followed a procedure that had been carefully laid out on little pieces of note paper: "Proc.#1. (maybe dramamine) tea & toast, 1 hr. before alco. & med. (10 or 12) choc. Pudding (4 oz. And powder) more alcohol." The alcohol was vodka, and the "med" was phenobarbital. Apparently, the assistants placed plastic bags over the heads of the others after they had followed the procedure, and removed the bags later. Five of the group, including Do, also took the narcotic painkiller Vicodin. Death came from a combination of the alcohol, the drugs, and asphyxiation.

Three women in their forties and early fifties in earth years were the last to die – Susan Strom, Julie La Montagne, and Judy Rowland. Two had bags over their heads. The third had pulled hers off. All the other plastic bags had been placed in the trash; the house was immaculately clean; and the garbage had been taken out, ready for pickup. The bodies all were stretched out in the bunk beds, dressed in dark shirts and pants, all wearing clean black Nike shoes, with four-foot square purple cloths draped diagonally over their heads and bodies, leaving only the legs of their dark pants uncovered.

Police came upon the scene the following Wednesday, after being tipped off by a former member who had received a copy of the videotape in the mail. Once the officers got past the putrid odor that hit them as the entered the side door, they found all the bodies lying in the beds. "It was a very calm, serene setting," said Deputy Laura Bacek. "Surreal." To the San Diego County sheriff's department commander, the people on the beds looked "as if they had fallen asleep." The medical examiner described the event as "very planned, sort of immaculately carried out." There were no signs of trauma or struggle, and the authorities quickly closed the case for lack of any evidence that a crime had been committed by any living person (SFC 27 March 1997; WP 28 March 1997; NYT 29 March, 30 March 1997; LAT 1 April, 12 April 1997).

The new demonstration

Other people in the community of Rancho Santa Fe lived in their own space crafts, more grounded. When the inevitable hordes of media personnel descended with their satellite dishes and helicopters, neighbors told them that people chose to live in Rancho Santa Fe in order to be left alone. "These houses are very private," a maid for a neighboring family, Miriam Larios, told reporters in Spanish, "Nobody knows anybody." Out on the golf course, a man identified one common factor between the followers of the Two and the other people who lived in Rancho Santa Fe: "This is a place where people live in denial of the rest

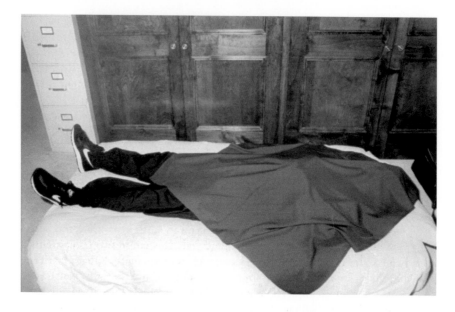

Figure 5.2 One of thirty-nine bodies found in a house in Rancho Santa Fe, California, as photographed by the San Diego County Sheriff's Department on 26 March 1997. Followers of Do – and the previously deceased Ti – had prepared for years to reach the Next Evolutionary Level Above Human.

Source: AP/WORLDWIDE PHOTOS/San Diego Sheriff's Department

of the world." But another resident, interviewed on television, insisted on one point about the Heaven's Gate group: "They were renters. They weren't Rancho Santa Fe people." As if to underscore that point, two local businessmen soon announced plans to buy the house on Colina Norte and raze it, so as to protect property values from the stigma of its association with collective suicide (LAT 31 March, 4 April 1997).

Some families of the deceased reacted with understandable outrage at what had happened to their relatives. One mother, whose husband had hired a detective to search for their daughter three years earlier, told reporters, "If a person is looking for a purpose in life and looking for spiritual life, then go to the mainstream religions but don't go to cults. That's the worst thing that could happen." But others were surprisingly more stoic. Nancy Brown said that she took "some comfort in knowing they died happy. The coroner said David looked very calm." And the family of David Van Sinderen issued a statement that read in part:

> While we did not completely understand or agree with David's beliefs, it was apparent to us that he was happy, healthy, and acting under his own volition. It seemed to us that the group members were a supportive family unit, and David was spiritually fulfilled in his life with them.

The Van Sinderens' statement studiously avoided using the word "cult": "It implies coercion or brainwashing," David's sister explained. "This wasn't true in his case." Others took a position of profound ambivalence. The sister of one man who had returned to the group after years away from it blamed Do for the deaths, saying, "I can't believe somebody could abuse control and power and suck somebody up like that." But then she reflected, "I don't want to be judgmental. Who am I to say what's wrong, what's right? . . . It's between him and God" (NYT 29 March, 30 March 1997; LAT 30 March 1997).

After the deaths of Do and his followers, much was made of the supposed Hale-Bopp spacecraft, but the group's website, located on a server operated by a Minneapolis-based internet company called SpaceStar Communications, took a more complex view. As the millions of people who clicked their way to the group's site could read for themselves:

> Whether Hale-Bopp has a "companion" or not is irrelevant from our perspective. However, its arrival is, joyously, very significant to us at "Heaven's Gate." The joy is that our Older Member in the Evolutionary Level Above Human (the "Kingdom of Heaven") has made it clear to us that Hale-Bopp's approach is the "marker" we've been waiting for – the time for the arrival of the spacecraft from the Level Above Human to take us home to "Their World" – in the literal Heavens.

Because the group had such an effective presence on the web, some of the early moral outrage about the deaths focused on the question of whether the internet was fostering a fringe fanaticism. Later, it turned out that most of the dead had joined years earlier, and very few of them had first learned of the group by way of the internet. Nor, despite breathless media reports on the subject of alien abduction conspiracies, does it seem that the group centrally acted on the basis of this motif. To be sure, they were quite concerned about the contemporary accounts by people who claimed to be victims of space aliens who had subjected them to painful experiences such as medical examinations. Do and the class, however, took these accounts as the inspiration for developing their own Luciferian explanation of certain negative higher entities, thus producing a more nuanced theology of the struggle between good and evil. As for early speculations by scholars of religion and self-appointed experts on cults, a number offered the opinion that Heaven's Gate represented some sort of neo-gnostic religion, updated for the age of space exploration (SFC 28 March 1997; LAT 27 March, 31 March 1997; Balch, personal communication, 1999).

Gnostic traditions, based as they are in positive yet intuitive knowledge, are diverse. The label thus does little to help explain the departure of Do and the thirty-eight members of his class. True, in certain structural characteristics the group around the Two comes closer to the form of the mystical association than to the other-worldly apocalyptic sect (Hall 1978). Especially at the beginning, Bo and Peep eschewed any strong spiritual hierarchy, and they presented themselves as teachers with information to provide (granted, not just any teachers, but individuals who had come from elsewhere to inhabit earthly vehicles). Moreover, the Two made no claim to establishing a heaven-on-earth after the model of the other-worldly sect. Instead, they claimed to provide information and guidance to help members of the class make the journey to the physical Next Evolutionary Level Above Human. In 1975, a follower expressed this orientation in terms that clearly identified partici-pants as engaged in a freely formed mystical association rather than estab-lishing a collective other-worldly apocalyptic sect. "This isn't group metamorphosis," he insisted at a meeting of several subgroups of the Two's followers, "and the organization isn't going to Heaven" (Balch and Taylor 1976, p. 106).

In a quasi-mystical vein influenced by Bonnie's early involvement in the occult movement, the Two and their followers entertained metaphysical ideas about the relation between earthly temporal existence and a timeless eternity that was nevertheless a physical place. Much like members of the Solar Temple, they embraced the idea that certain moments provided rare opportunities of access to the Next Level, and they asserted that the Two were representatives from eternity who had come to Earth. The Templars regarded their "walk-ins" as entities like Saint Bernard, Moses, and Osirus, who moved relatively freely back and forth between eternity and history. Bonnie's early ideas were quite similar (Balch 1982).

By contrast, in the space-age neo-Christian doctrine promulgated by the Two, the Next Level representatives were far more selective in their appearances. Once he reached adulthood, Jesus had become inhabited by a being from the Next Level. Now, Do was "in the same position to today's society as was the One that was in Jesus" two thousand years earlier (Do 1997). In the Solar Temple, Joseph DiMambro acted as a mystagogue who claimed the capacity to harness the peak waves of cosmic energy. In contrast Do and Ti took on the roles of savior-teachers offering students who received their information the opportunity to travel to Heaven. In the end, however, like the leaders of the Solar Temple, Do offered his followers a more select opportunity than has conventionally come to be associated with the mission of Jesus. Even though Jesus himself preached that the gate was narrow and salvation considerably less than universal, the Christian martyrdom on the cross has historically been understood to provide salvation to all (Weber 1978, p. 632; Williams 1975). By contrast, those who wanted to go through Heaven's Gate to the Next Evolutionary Level would have to leave with an Older Member, or very soon thereafter. As the front page "Red Alert" of the Heaven's Gate website put it, "If you study the material on this website you will hopefully understand our joy and what our purpose here on Earth has been. You may even find your 'boarding pass' to leave with us during this brief 'window.'"

Despite the trappings of a mystical association, and notwithstanding the metaphysical aspects of Heaven's Gate doctrines, it is worth remembering that even distinctly non-gnostic prophets have made claims like Do's about their own incarnated divinity, announcing as Jim Jones did, "someone will set themselves in the messiah's chair and declare the unsearchable riches. . . . I have come in the person of Christ the Revolution!" (Hall 1987, p. 31). Moreover, for all that Do and Ti and their class entertained metaphysical ideas, they also embarked on a thoroughgoing program of asceticism and self-regulation distant in motivation from any gnostic or other mystical project of arriving at deep inner truths. Nor are gnostics, or mystics more generally – either in this age or others – known for seeking out martyrdom, or even an early death.

Initial speculation after the collective suicide suggested that Do thought he was going to die, and decided to take his followers with him. An autopsy on the vehicle that Do had inhabited showed no signs of cancer, only a certain degree of coronary restriction, common to men of his age. However, before his death, Do did tell some members he thought he might have prostrate cancer (LAT 31 March, 12 April 1997; Balch, personal communication, 1999). Clearly, Do and the group were concerned about his possible death, but any notion that he took the lives of others simply does not square with the evidence. What seems to have happened is that Do and his followers puzzled over the departure for the Next Evolutionary Level for several years. They anticipated that something would happen, but they were not sure what. In one web site posting, "Our position against suicide," they reviewed several possibilities. In one scenario, "before that spacecraft comes, one or more of us could lose our physical vehicles (bodies) due to 'recall,' accident, or at the hands of some irate individual," but they did not expect that to happen. Another possibility was that the group's information could produce a hostile reaction in the wider society, so that "we could find so much disfavor with the powers that control this world that there could be attempts to incarcerate us or to subject us to some sort of psychological or physical torture (such as occurred at both Ruby Ridge and Waco)."

There had been an apocalyptic side to the teachings of the Two from the days in the 1970s they came to understand themselves as the two candlesticks mentioned in Revelation. Once they became concerned about space aliens who might engage in nefarious acts, their theology incorporated ideas about a quasi-apocalyptic struggle between Luciferians who control this world and the beings of a Higher Level who offer information to those on this planet seeking salvation from that control. Clearly, when Do and the class faced "ridicule" and "hostility" while offering their "last chance," they took their rejection in the wider world as a sign that "the weeds have taken over the garden." Like the Solar Temple's believers, they expressed frustration that their message was not being taken seriously. Nevertheless, they had fulfilled their mission, making the offer to those who would receive it. Having completed their earthly task, Heaven's Gate would depict their departure as a trip to another world, a physical Heaven, just not a heaven located on Earth.

Yet despite these apocalyptic elements, the Two and their class never engaged in anything remotely like the cultural struggle that unfolded between Peoples Temple and the Concerned Relatives, or between the Branch Davidians and their "cultbusters." They certainly did not take on a warring posture like the leaders of Aum Shinrikyō. Nor were they even the object of any sting operation or media savaging of the sort that the Solar Temple encountered.

To be sure, the group was hardly immune from external opposition. From the May 1975 meeting at Joan Culpepper's house in the Los Angles area onwards, there were plenty of hecklers and naysayers at meetings, and even some detractors who followed the group around to denounce it. The group also received a good deal of negative media attention as the "UFO cult" after the highly successful September 1975 meeting in Waldport, Oregon. And from Waldport onward, families and friends tried to retrieve people, hired detectives to try to track their loved ones down, and formed loose networks to share news of members and pool information that might help them determine the group's latest location. For the most part, however, the group seems to have headed off conflict in advance. They kept on the move, frustrating families that might try to locate their relatives, and since followers did not bring any children when they joined, they stayed clear of the emotional custody struggles that animated much of the conflict between Peoples Temple and the Concerned Relatives.

They even seem to have learned something about how to manage family relations. Once in 1983, the mother of David Geoffrey Brown organized a weekend conference about the group at Berkeley. The response from the group was quick, but less than promising. Her son called and announced, "Our group is not comfortable with you drawing attention to us. We don't want this attention. We want to stay removed from the world." "Fine," his mother remembers telling him, "We just want the occasional contact. We want to know you're all right." Perhaps the conference had some effect, for many members did keep better contact with relatives thereafter. Sometimes the families managed to send letters to their relatives in the group, and occasionally they would get a card, a brief phone call, or a short visit. The followers of the Two always assured their families that they were happy where they were, and more than one family concluded of relatives in the group, as did the father of Susan Strom, that "she had plenty of opportunity to come home." In any primary social group, from families to small religious sects, individuals live under considerable pressures to remain within the group. In Heaven's Gate, members no doubt felt solidarity with their peers, and they would have to think long and hard about giving up their one big chance for salvation. These pressures were no doubt real and formidable. However, the followers of Do and Ti were not being held against their will (NYT 29, 30, 31 March 1997; LAT 30 March 1997; Hewitt *et al.* 1997, p. 50).

In short, Do and Ti successfully avoided the apocalypse of earthly struggle with cultural opponents, the mass media, and the state. They did so, however, by recognizing the potential for such a struggle. Early on, they learned to stay one step ahead of pursuing families, simultaneously assuring their followers complete freedom to return to the world, and eventually allowing enough contact to reassure most families of their relatives' wellbeing. By these devices that anticipated the potential for conflict, the Two headed off any apocalyptic struggle. Yet they clearly regarded the Apocalypse as a reality, both in prosaic terms concerned with maintaining the freedom to pursue their religious ideas without external interference from a hostile world, and in the more theological sense of believing the world to be a place of struggle between forces of the Higher Level and the Luciferians.

The very success of the Two at establishing a world that floated near our own but just out of anyone else's reach created an anomalous theological situation. By anticipating the Apocalypse, the Two finessed its Demonstration, thus undermining their own prophecies. In the end, Do and the class were left to discern the Higher Level message in the absence of the Demonstration they had anticipated at the group's inception. Finally, they took the world's general indifference toward the information they were providing as sign enough that their work on Earth had been completed.

The group's push toward rational reconstruction operated in theology as on all other fronts. If Do really were taken back to the Higher Level, those who remained would have been faced with waiting for the spacecraft that had been promised to take them away, but without the guidance of an Older Member. By comparison, the collective suicide that they orchestrated was an affirmation of faith. Yet it was not the faith of individual human beings, each possessing the information necessary to depart to the Next Level in a spacecraft. At one point, when the group stated "Our position against suicide" (Heaven's Gate 1997), they had invoked Masada, where, around 73 AD,

> a devout Jewish sect, after holding out against a siege by the Romans,
> to the best of their ability, and seeing that the murder, rape, and torture
> of their community was inevitable, determined that it was permissible
> for them to evacuate their bodies by a more dignified, and less agonizing
> method.

They went on, "We have thoroughly discussed this topic (of willful exit of the body under such conditions), and have mentally prepared ourselves for this possibility." Affirming that "this act certainly does not need serious consideration at this time," they nevertheless offered a different twist to the idea of revolutionary suicide that Jim Jones had borrowed from Black Panther Huey Newton. At Heaven's Gate, "The true meaning of 'suicide' is to turn against the Next Level when it is being offered."

Do and his followers never encountered anything like the situation that the Jews faced at Masada, but they took their lives anyway, not as individuals, but collectively. This collective suicide cannot be understood as the outcome of apocalyptic struggle. Instead, Do and his followers created a different kind of Demonstration, years after the Two had stopped using the term. They took their

lives as an affirmation of faith that by this act they would be physically transported to Heaven. "I wish I had the strength to have remained," one former
member later told CBS's *60 Minutes*. "I believe they are on a craft somewhere,
whether it's behind the comet or not, I really don't know." That those individuals who remained in the group believed seems absurd from the outside, but it is
also incontrovertible. People who did not believe had every opportunity to forgo
the deaths of their earthly vehicles. For many years, longstanding opponent
Joan Culpepper thought Bo and Peep were charlatans. "But in retrospect," she
said after the deaths, "I think they believed their message to the end, with all
their hearts. They thought they were going to that spaceship" (LAT 30 March,
31 March 1997). In the seventeenth century, the Rosicrucian heresy promised,
as a French poster put it, to "rescue our fellow men from the error of death."
Do and his followers trafficked in religious ideas more appropriate to the
subjectivist emphasis on self-fulfillment in our era: their faith had reached the
point where they had conquered their *fear* of death. To demonstrate this, they
killed themselves.

EPILOGUE

There is a paradox in the claim of Francis Fukayama (1992), that we have reached the end of history. For beyond human history is only the eternity of physical time or the timelessness of eternity. Yet these states cannot lie in the future, for that would imply more history. In our world there is neither an end to history nor heaven on Earth, only what we make of past, present, and future. Perhaps, as postmodern theorist Jean Baudrillard has it, the end is the illusion borne of linear history. Nevertheless, like Fukayama, Baudrillard posits an end of history, though in his case it occurs through the systematic obliteration of the past. True to form, Baudrillard suggests that messianic hopes are dashed because our Apocalypse has become virtual, an illusion (1994, p. 119).

A central illusion of modern thought held that, as we moved toward the future, reason would bring a world where past illusions would fade away, where "non-rational" ties of kin, ethnicity, and religion would be superseded by rational principles of social organization that were to establish a world of democracy, justice, equality, and freedom for all. The contemporary currency of the word "postmodern" suggests, at the least, how elusive the modern project has become, how divided people now are about both the ideology of progress and its current prospects.

If modernist social theories were correct, the books of religions would have closed. In the most emphatic versions of secularization theory, the march of science would continually erode persisting areas of ignorance to the point where belief, faith, and religion would play ever smaller roles in public and personal life. At the onset of the third millennium, however, this theory has been contradicted by events on the ground. World religions thrive. Sects enter a free-for-all seeking converts in the former Soviet bloc. Differences over religion mark seemingly intractable cultural conflicts, between Hindus and Muslims in India and Pakistan, between Zionists and their opponents in the Levant, between secularists and strict Muslims in Turkey, and between Catholic and Protestant Christians living a shaky peace in Northern Ireland. Even where secular forces continue to wax most strongly, in the developed nation-states of Europe, Japan, and North America, charisma is still a potent force (Roth 1975). The realm of faith, belief, ritual, and religious action has not dissolved, nor have we reached the end of religion.

Explaining apocalyptic violence

Clearly religious ferment continues in these times. How, then, are we to understand the sad episodes of extreme violence involving the five religious movements that we have considered in this book? Despite the bizarre and tragic outcomes, no one can be quick to conclude that the people who participated in these groups were radically different in persona and outlook from other people in the societies where they lived. People of all sorts joined, men and women, young and old, from diverse ethnic backgrounds and walks of life. There were some who hadn't finished high school and others with doctoral degrees. Some were raised within strong religious traditions; others had none. Some were poor to the point of destitution; others lived in fabulous opulence. Many were at points of transition in their lives, but others were solidly planted in community and family life; indeed, some of the groups they joined promoted civic participation, albeit within sectarian frameworks. The one thing they shared was a religious need that had apparently been left unfulfilled within conventional religious channels.

We may all hope that the wave of apocalyptic violence connected with marginal religious movements does not continue. Yet René Girard (1977) reminds us that the association of violence and the sacred has a long history; the connection derives not just from the conflicts between peoples of different religious persuasions, but from the core ritual power of religion itself. We would thus be well served to understand what is at stake in the violence at Jonestown and Mount Carmel, in Japan, Switzerland, and Québec, and at the mansion in Rancho Santa Fe. If nothing else, the violence demonstrates the continuing power that religion holds to bring ordinary people to extreme steps that lift them out of everyday life.

The millennialist thesis

One explanation, a reductionist one, is that the eruptions of religious violence occurred because of heightened eschatological expectations at the end of the second millennium. However, this explanation encounters difficulties. Although Peoples Temple and the Branch Davidians were both apocalyptic in their orientations, rationalized calendrical time played no significant role in either group's narrative. The other three groups did indeed invoke the end of the millennium as a reason for heightened apocalyptic expectations, but in none of them was the calendrical shift as important as it has been in other groups that have made prophecies about specific dates. In Aum Shinrikyō, the generalized apocalyptic orientation became infused with millenarian themes only as the significant date loomed nearer. In the group that came to be called Heaven's Gate, the millennial shift was not yet an object of popular cultural fascination when the group began in the 1970s, and it played no role in the group's early ideas about salvation through space travel. Only in the Solar Temple did calendrical ideas about eras of time come to be strongly emphasized. Yet even there, the metaphysics of Jacques Breyer left plenty of room for recalculating exactly when the New Age would dawn. In short, calendrical millennialism was neither a necessary nor a sufficient condition for the occurrence of extreme religious violence.

Because a millennialist thesis does not hold up very well, the problem of accounting for religious violence remains. Those who regard the historical specificity of human events as crucial will be reluctant to explain multiple cases on the basis of a single theory, for they will see all initial conditions as unique. On the other hand, social scientists will want to examine instances in which extreme violence did occur and ones in which it did not, so as to discern factors which differentiate the most violent instances from other instances resolved more peacefully.

Why is it, they will ask, that the Church of Scientology – long subjected to state repression and anticult opposition – has never become caught up in the extreme violence that marks the groups discussed in this book? How has the Hare Krishna movement, with its other-worldly apocalypticism, avoided the worst sorts of apocalyptic confrontations? Or, given the longstanding hostilities between the communal settlement called Rasjneeshpuram and the people and government of the state of Oregon, what prevented the eruption of extreme violence when the group collapsed in 1985? And how did peaceable settlements end the confrontations of FBI agents with the Freemen in Montana during 1996, and earlier, with the Covenant, the Sword, and the Arm of the Lord (CSA) on the Arkansas–Missouri border in 1985?

Social scientists have much to teach authorities and the public about their dealings with apocalyptic countercultural groups, for example, through the study of "standoffs" (Wagner–Pacifici 2000). These discussions can be informed by interpretive attention to two issues: first, whether and how episodes of apocalyptic violence are connected with one another, and, second, whether the violence to be explained is the same in all cases. It is these issues that we now address.

The genealogy of Apocalypse

A basic requirement of generalizing social science is to assume independence of cases from mutual influence. This assumption, however, cannot be sustained for the cases we have considered here. On the contrary, a historical *genealogy* of apocalypse connected the episodes of violence. Transported by the "cultbusters" who opposed David Koresh, concerns about mass suicide deriving from Jonestown decisively influenced the trajectory of violence at Mount Carmel. For their parts, Do and his Heaven's Gate class invoked memories of previous confrontations between religious groups and the authorities, as did participants on both sides of the earlier conflicts in the Solar Temple and Aum Shinrikyō. As these connections suggest, apocalypticism sometimes feeds upon earlier apocalyptic events. With enough cultural amplification, a climate of generalized apocalyptic expectations can take hold. Whether or not this occurs, when what happens in one case affects others, it is impossible to meet the scientific standard for generalization on the basis of multiple cases: that each dramatic apocalyptic event be independent. Still, channels of influence on particular apocalyptic events can sometimes be identified. Such analysis suggests that none of the religious movements examined here simply copied another group's "mass suicide." Rather, the genetic thread, insofar as it exists, has to do mostly with the cultural learning on the parts of new religious movements, apostates, other cultural opponents, news reporters, and state authorities.

For example, Jim Jones and his staff knew about at least one violent confrontation involving a revolutionary quasi-communal movement: the Symbionese Liberation Army, the revolutionary cell group that kidnapped newspaper heiress Patricia Hearst. Indeed, Jones offered a eulogy to the fiery deaths of SLA members at the hands of a Los Angeles Police Department SWAT team that attacked their "safe house" on 17 May 1974.[1] Jones also followed the confrontation between Philadelphia authorities and the anomalous black-power group, MOVE (Hall 1987, p. 237), even though the 1978 murders and mass suicide at Jonestown came well before 1985, when MOVE members were wiped out in a fire started by the Philadelphia police, who managed to burn down several blocks of a Philadelphia neighborhood in the process (Wagner–Pacifici 1994). Jones and his followers thus recognized the possibilities for confrontation between counter-cultural movements and law enforcement authorities, and their siege mentality emerged in the context of this knowledge. Other religious movements, from the militant Aum Shinrikyō to the quietistic group that sought to reach Heaven's Gate, similarly followed wider controversies about religious sects.

As for opponents of religious movements, they too developed distinctive historical memories, and from the 1970s onwards anticult activists refined a general *modus operandi* that they brought into play in confrontations with religious movements. In a number of instances, "deprogrammers" kidnapped sect members and attempted to purge them of their "programmed" beliefs. Opponents of sects also pursued family custody issues in relation to a number of groups, and they found that child welfare agencies could claim jurisdiction and arouse public concern in matters that lay beyond the reach of more conventional law enforcement authorities. Documents passed to law enforcement authorities during the Waco standoff ("How many Jonestowns will it take?" and a "white paper" on cults) show what leaders of the dominant US anticult group at the time, the Cult Awareness Network (CAN), would freely admit: that they coordinated opposition to cults they considered dangerous. Under such circumstances, a religious group might well confront not only its local cultural opponents, but also the accumulated expertise and engaged consultation of a generalized opposition movement.[2]

The state, the third major institutional complex concerned with religious violence, does not have interests and agendas as unequivocal as those of religious movements or their organized cultural opponents (especially not in nation-states with clear constitutional limits on state regulation of religion). Instead, the state seems better understood as an arena where multiple laws, policies, and political interventions come into play. The relatively autonomous nature of state institutions with separate agendas, legal remedies, and definitions of situations – differing between child welfare agencies and firearms control authorities, for example, or between elected officials and hostage negotiators – ensure that state learning is unevenly gained and applied. Nevertheless, it does occur. Initial government reviews of the debacle of state intervention at Waco and the armed confrontation at Ruby Ridge, Idaho, yielded some rethinking of strategy. During the FBI's next big countercultural confrontation – the 1996 standoff with the Montana Freemen – it attempted far less coercion than it had applied against the Branch Davidians, and it managed to apprehend the Freemen without extreme violence. But institutions have selective and fragile memories at best. After all, one of the federal agents involved in the planning of the raid against the Branch Davidians had participated in the successful negotiated settlement with the Covenant, the Sword, and the Arm of the Lord in the 1980s, and this seems to have counted for little, except perhaps hubris.

Overall, beneath any diffuse culture of Apocalypse that may take hold in a particular historical period, religious movements, their cultural opponents, and state authorities often develop specific organizational memories and rubrics of cultural knowledge that shape their subsequent actions. These cultural mediations may weave genealogical threads into a fabric that connects distinctive episodes to other episodes, thereby yielding a substructure of the apocalyptic history that is experienced superficially only as a mood or *zeitgeist*. Given the possibility of cultural mediations, the dynamics of any given case of extreme apocalyptic religious violence cannot be assumed to occur in a vacuum, isolated from prior events. Yet neither do past events work like some contagious cultural virus, replicating themselves in the passage from one group to another. Rather, the genealogies, to the extent that they are significant, come into play for religious social movements within specific conjunctures that must be examined in their own terms.

Cultural meanings and cultural structures

Here, however, an enduring problem of social science arises, namely, how to decide when two cases are the same or different on a given dimension. The present inquiry suggests that "mass suicide" is not really a coherent "thing." Rather, there is complex variety to extreme apocalyptic religious violence.

Under these analytic circumstances, close comparative examination of the major recent cases where significant violence occurred offers an alternative to both historicist refusal of generalizations and general social theorizing that fails to acknowledge interdependence and social complexity. This approach, which explores what Arthur Stinchcombe (1978) has called "deep analogies" between cases, is necessarily tentative in its conclusions. However, it allows analysis of multiple discrete processes – potentially parallel and often divergent – at work in various episodes, while it avoids generalizing from single instances or cases that have mutually influenced one another.[3] Taking this tack, the present study has moved inexorably toward an important conclusion about the religious violence that we have examined, one that would prove elusive to any general analysis that hypostatized "violence" versus "absence of violence" as the "dependent variable" and compared violent to non-violent outcomes. Even though the five cases of extreme religious violence – four of them ending in collective suicides – bear a superficial resemblance to one another, there seem to be two different processes at work rather than one.

Recently, social scientists have made much of what historians have long known, that social processes are "contingent" and "path dependent": what happens at any given point affects the range of future possibilities. Often "culture" is invoked as influential in the play of contingency. It is important to avoid the old-fashioned notion of Culture as some sort of primordial essence that can be invoked in reductionist cultural explanations (that substitute for reductionist structuralist ones). There is, however, more to culture than idiosyncratic contingency or reductionist explanation.

Culture can be theorized at two different "levels": concrete cultural meanings and generic "cultural structures" (Hall 1988; Hall and Neitz 1993 p, 11; cf. Kane 1991). Concrete *cultural meanings* are the invented, received, synthesized, reworked and otherwise improvised idea patterns by which individuals and social groups attach significance to their actions. In a social group, such cultural meanings are neither monolithic nor immutable, and they are specific in their content and sources. The idea of "revolutionary suicide" invoked at Jonestown, for instance, was neither an invention of Peoples Temple nor a generic construct available from some Storehouse of Western Culture. It had a specific genealogy that traced from the Black Panther Party of the 1960s.

Beyond the specifics of situated cultural meanings, it is possible to ask whether events such as the mass suicide of Peoples Temple involved generic *cultural structures* that undergird the specific meanings at work. When we focus on the range of cultural meanings associated with the Apocalypse and with mysticism, it becomes apparent that certain "cultural logics" are associated with religious violence. Culture is not simply contingent historicity, much less random. Nor is it primordial essence. As Max Weber (1958) argued nearly a century ago, coherent patterns of culture can have causal social significance. When these patterned logics have identifiable generic features that encompass diverse situated cultural meanings, we can call them "cultural structures." In culturally structured situations where meanings parallel one another, events play out in enacted dramas with remarkably similar plots.

Two cultural structures of apocalyptic violence

We initiated this investigation by proposing a general model that explained mass suicide as the outcome of an escalating conflict between, on the one hand, a religious sect already organized internally on the basis of apocalyptic ideas that yield a high degree of solidarity and, on the other, an alliance of ideological detractors of "cults" within the society-at-large. In this scenario, the autonomy and legitimacy of an apocalyptic sect is seriously threatened as a consequence of escalating conflict with external opponents. Once we acknowledge that violence may take many forms, not always resulting in physical injury (Jackman, forthcoming), it becomes obvious that opponents sometimes act violently themselves, occasionally threatening the very existence of the religious movement. Under these conditions, the sect unleashes a response of deadly violence.

This model comes close to a generic description of what happened at Jonestown, in the conflagration at Mount Carmel and, in a somewhat different way, with Aum Shinrikyō in Japan. It also brings to light important factors necessary to any explanation of the initial murders and collective suicide of the Solar Temple in Québec and Switzerland. Of course, we have also noted genealogical connections among these episodes, as well as striking differences. Most notable among the differences, in Aum Shinrikyō there was a considerable lapse of time between the initial violence toward opponents and the police efforts to apprehend the group for its crimes. Moreover, Aum directed its violence only toward internal dissenters and external opponents, never pursuing an act of collective suicide. Another important variation came in the case of the Solar Temple, where the murders and collective suicide occurred more than a year after a dramatic confrontation between the group and external opponents. These are all important differences. They seem, however, ones of degree rather than kind. Jonestown, Mount Carmel, Aum Shinrikyō, and the initial murders and ritual suicide of the Solar Temple are all analogic variations on one cultural structure: the *warring apocalypse of religious conflict*.

The different ways in which the warring Apocalypse played out in these episodes has a great deal to do with how these groups construed the meanings of their relationships to the Apocalypse. For Peoples Temple, Jonestown was to have been their heaven-on-earth, where they could develop their socialist utopia without the direct interference of a capitalist state. Yet this post-apocalyptic tableau was never established and free of conflicts with their opponents. In effect, the leadership at Jonestown finally unleashed a murderous act against those opponents, carried out in the pre-apocalyptic time of war. Then they departed from their promised land in collective death.

The scenario for the Branch Davidians at Mount Carmel was similar, but the Davidians never presumed to escape the Apocalypse. Rather, they intended to survive it, defending themselves against enemies during the last days if necessary, so that they could inherit the earthly kingdom of God and replenish it with His chosen people. Like Peoples Temple, the Davidians mobilized for apocalyptic struggle, but in this struggle their direct opponents – the BATF and the FBI – unleashed what really did look like a holy war against them. In the minds of many people, the Branch Davidians were victims as well as perpetrators of extreme violence.

As for Aum Shinrikyō, although they had a broad stratum of members who expected to achieve a post-apocalyptic state of grace, the central leadership of the organization took a far more militant approach to apocalyptic war than either Peoples Temple or the Branch Davidians. Rather than entertaining the conceit that they had escaped the Apocalypse or were simply preparing to survive it, the principals of Aum covered up a death, and took the first sign of opposition as the basis for initiating apocalyptic war themselves. What at first was aimed against any opponents who stood in their way eventually became a grotesquely quixotic attempt to create a societal disaster on an apocalyptic scale.

By comparison with any of these episodes, the Solar Temple embarked on its original "Departure" under a more complex hybrid of meanings than the line connecting pre-apocalyptic war and post-apocalyptic grace. On the one hand, their theology of soul migration had long prepared them for the possibility of a "Transit" to eternity that had a mystical cast. On the other hand, this Transit was framed in millennialist and apocalyptic terms, keyed both to surviving the end of the second millennium and to the ecological Apocalypse of the planet. Yet beyond mystical Transit and apocalyptic survivalism, there were specific incidents of conflict with opponents: the gun sting operation, media exposés, and subsequent government investigations, and the Solar Templars clearly undertook murder and collective suicide in October 1994 in relation to these conflicts.

Despite important differences in timing, intensity, and nuance of circumstance, all of these four episodes in one way or another approximate warring apocalyptic religious conflict, marked by an internal apocalyptic ideology and external conflict with cultural opponents, hostile media, and the state. The definitive trait of such conflict can be found by contrasting these cases with the two subsequent collective suicides of Solar Templars – at the winter solstice of 1995 and the spring equinox of 1997 – and the 1997 deaths of Do and his Heaven's Gate followers at Rancho Santa Fe. In neither the second or third Solar Temple collective suicide nor Heaven's Gate was any violence directed outward. Thus, *outward* extreme violence, typically followed by collective suicide, can be taken as the hallmark of the first four incidents, of apocalyptic religious conflict.

What, then, of the second and third Solar Temple suicides and the Heaven's Gate deaths? These episodes hardly lacked apocalyptic elements, and all of them resulted in unnatural death. But the elements were composed in a different constellation than apocalyptic religious conflict. What was it?

As we have shown, the mystical theology of the Solar Temple suggested the possibility of journeying back and forth between eternity and the temporal world, and it theorized that doing so depended on aligning with key universal forces of energy, themselves mapped onto earthly temporal cycles marked by the Apocalypse as the moment of a critical shift between one earthly temporal era and another. However, there was nothing in this theology that required a war either to survive the onslaught of civilization's decay or to produce the triumph of good. Cosmic forces assured the transition, and those who harnessed those forces through ritual could transcend any merely human apocalypse. The only earthly problem that believers faced was escaping the clutches of the wider society. And this, indeed, was a central motif during the days and months after the initial Solar Temple transit in October 1994. In reflecting on the second and third transits in June 1997, Vivienne Giacobino, the former wife of one of the people murdered at Cheiry, speculated that the participants in the second and third transits might have taken their own lives both because, with the stigma of the first transit, after October 1994 there was no place for them in the wider society, and further, because, amidst rumors about more suicides, they felt hemmed in by police surveillance of the sect and occasional round-ups of members. Pursued by adversaries who might interfere, the participants in the second and third transits did not engage in any outwardly directed violence. Instead, they acted out a narrative of escape, making the ritual voyage that they had been taught would take them across the barrier from this world to eternity.

The parallels between the Solar Temple and Heaven's Gate are striking. In effect, both offered space-age versions of a salvation story dominant in the Western cultural tradition, in which a prophet appears to redeem believers by showing them the path to rebirth into a promised land beyond the travails of this world. Both groups invoked the possibility of moving beyond earthly existence into an eternal transcendence, and both settled on a space voyage as the device of transition. Both groups offered metaphysical notions of the relationship between time and eternity, but in neither case did they pursue a program of meditation within a mystical association that transcends this world through enlightenment while remaining physically in it. Instead, in both groups, the mystical idea of transcendence was mapped onto apocalyptic motifs of passage from this world to the beyond. Redemption required departure from Earth by beings whose consciousness was alien to it. In both groups, believers received information about the windows of opportunity for making this journey beyond the fallen world, in the Solar Temple from a redeeming mystagogue and in Heaven's Gate from a savior-teacher.

Finally, in both groups, there was an apocalyptic narrative of escape. This motif is obvious in the second and third Solar Temple departures, whose participants took elaborate steps to elude the efforts of authorities and other outsiders seeking to prevent further ritual Transit deaths. The same motif of flight operated over a much more extended time in the group around the Two. Early on, Bo and Peep had feared that the assassination and Demonstration might come too soon, before they could "harvest" all the "ripe fruit." The subsequent *modus operandi* over the entire history of the group was to act out a departure from this world based on extreme ascetic self-perfection as a demonstration of readiness. As the followers worked to prepare themselves for the voyage, they kept moving, avoiding any entanglements with the world, staying one step ahead of any pursuit that might interfere with their religious quest. Their final flight came, like the first Solar Temple Transit, at a time when the world was deemed unreceptive to their message, leaving them no further work to accomplish on Earth. Travelling to the Next Evolutionary Level Above Human, they left behind their human "containers" and the world dominated by the Luciferians.

We began this study thinking that such acts of religious violence as murder and collective suicide were so extreme that they would only occur in a countercultural sect that lashed out in an apocalyptic holy war against the putative forces of evil, namely, their own opponents. It is now apparent, however, that neither the later Solar Temple Transits nor the voyage to Heaven's Gate fits this model. Instead, these episodes involved a *mystical Apocalypse of deathly transcendence* in which flight from the Apocalypse on Earth through the ritualized practice of collective suicide would supposedly achieve other-worldly grace. As these events show, flight from external opposition can become a strong fixation within a group, even when real opponents are lacking, or ineffectual. These cases of minimal or merely imaginary opposition are not apocalyptic conflicts. Rather, they chart a second pathway of religious violence. In this cultural structure – mystical apocalyptic death – ideas of transcendence through ecstasy or inner illumination become mediated by an apocalyptic theology of time. Themes of escape from pursuit and escape from this world bear apocalyptic overtones that align mystical transcendence with death in this life and rebirth in another.

Cultural structures, causalities, and contingencies

Collective religious suicide is not a singular social phenomenon with parallel dynamics in all cases. Rather, two alternative cultural structures mark different social processes that result in the "same" outcome of collective death. To be sure, not all apocalyptically tinged mysticism ends in suicidal escape, any more than conflict between an apocalyptic group, cultural opponents, media, and the state necessarily spirals into murder and suicidal martyrdom. In this light, the two apocalyptic cultural structures are interpretive models rather than causal explanations. Nevertheless, the commonalities among the episodes of religious violence that we have examined are striking. All five of them approximate one or the other (or both) of the cultural structures, the warring Apocalypse of religious conflict and the mystical Apocalypse of deathly transcendence. By its own distinctive pathway, each heightens the potential for extreme religious violence.

Once the cultural structures of social processes are theorized, it is easier to analyse actual episodes of religious violence in causal terms. As Weber (1978) showed when he theorized phenomena such as bureaucracy and the routinization of charisma, the concept of a "cultural structure" implies that culture does not operate as a *geist* in some material vacuum. Rather, the play of events in relation to cultural structures is in part shaped by realities such as the social career interests of individuals, the instability of extraordinary social demands in the face of daily human needs and interests, and the passing of generations. Sociologists of religion – notably Thomas Robbins and Dick Anthony (1995), Robbins (1997), and David Bromley, Gordon Melton, and their associates (forthcoming) – suggest that a number of internal and external conditions and factors are associated with extreme religious violence.

For example, Robbins notes the variation among groups – even with strong apocalyptic theologies – in their capacities to withstand the "rough-and-tumble" of public scrutiny and controversy in what he calls a "media democracy" (Robbins 1997; 1997 personal communication).[4] Following a parallel line of thought on the other side, it is obvious that even highly committed cultural opponents do not necessarily seek – and only rarely precipitate – dramatic confrontations of the sort that occurred at Jonestown and Mount Carmel. Nor does a state always develop an elective affinity of interests with mobilized cultural opponents. As the failed US government campaign against the Church of Scientology suggests: states may operate largely independently of cultural opponents; even a highly committed state is not necessarily effective in a campaign of repression against a religious social movement; and intense conflict (albeit with a non-apocalyptic group) does not inevitably spiral into extreme religious violence.

For the groups considered in the present book, Robbins also argues that factors such as internal dissension, declining health, or threats to the wellbeing of leaders may contribute to impulses to seek a dénouement (1997 personal communication). This is certainly plausible. As our own research has shown, conflicts surfaced in Jonestown and among the Solar templars *within* the groups themselves; internal and external conflicts became connected with one another so that the group experienced a generally beleaguered circumstance. Indeed, for all of the groups other than Heaven's Gate, external conflict was to a significant degree the product of apostates whose conflicts originated on the inside of the various groups. And Robbins is also right to emphasize that matters of health (or, for Koresh, a gunshot wound) influence issues of charismatic instability and group survival. Yet just as clearly, internal conflicts and charismatic instability are features of a much wider array of religious social movements that do not undertake extremely violent acts.

All scholars who research these complex matters recognize that we have not yet found the philosopher's stone that would help us transform our base understandings into refined essences of knowledge. Trying to explain rare events is a difficult enterprise. Extreme religious violence is a highly unlikely outcome, and no doubt there are episodes approximating apocalyptic cultural structures that do not result in extreme violence, even for groups that share many circumstances with those structures.

Indeed, the vast majority of religious sects are completely peaceful in their existences. Any number of small post-apocalyptic groups manage to hold to vivid ideas about their position in relation to the end times, yet they achieve their transcendence in life, not death. And on the pre-apocalyptic side of time's divide, Jehovah's Witnesses seem like an eternal tableau of the modern landscape, perennially knocking on people's doors to distribute *The Watchtower* and warn people to convert before the inevitable end, shown to be close at hand by exact signs prophesied in Revelation, which always mirror current events.

The Apocalypse thus is not always violent, and most of social life transpires far beyond its channels. Given these simple facts, what is the cultural significance of the apocalyptic religious violence that erupted over the final quarter-century of the second millennium? Some people will identify with Time–Warner vice-chair Ted Turner, who commented after the Heaven's Gates suicides that the attempted space voyage was "a good way to get rid of a few nuts." In Turner's view, "They did it peacefully. At least they didn't go in like those SOBs who go in a McDonald's or the post office and shoot a lot of innocent people, then shoot themselves. At least they just did it to themselves" (LAT 30 March 1997). These comments seem cynical, even callous, yet they raise a serious question about how far the social order should go to protect individuals against their own beliefs, and at what cost to the freedoms of wider populations.

Turner at least implies that even not all extreme religious violence is equivalent, a point confirmed by the divergent cultural structures of religious violence found among the cases examined here. This suggests that we should not expect a single lesson from the present inquiry. Rather, we should look to different frames of significance. The episodes we have described seem especially relevant to two issues concerning religion and contemporary society: first, tensions over "cultural legitimacy" between an established social order and deviant religious social movements and, second, the content of emergent countercultural ethics of salvation. These two issues are implicated in a broad cultural transformation from a modern world where economic life, authority, and social organization were packaged together under a cultural ethic of *de facto* Puritanism to an era in which uncertainties and anxieties create the impetus to search for some new dispensation.

Cultural legitimacy, paranoia, and religious deviance

In his well known book, *The Cultural Contradictions of Capitalism* (1976), Daniel Bell identified the contemporary cultural transformation as the consequence of a growing disjuncture between a sober modern bourgeois capitalist ethic of *work* and a more hedonistic ethic of *consumption*. Yet how do people respond to the cultural tensions of this disjuncture? To answer this question, John Carroll (1977) charted a series of cultural identity complexes that move from, first, the Puritan, through, second, the Paranoid, and potentially, third, to the establishment of a new cultural persona: the Remissive, who is freed from past burdens of individual and collective sins to pursue a hedonistic life of self-fulfillment.

At the onset of the third millennium, nearly a quarter-century after Bell and Carroll wrote, Puritanism has for some time lacked much appeal, even to fundamentalists. Since the mid-twentieth century, evangelical Christians have relaxed their attitudes toward card games and social dancing. However, any rise of a Remissive ethic of self-fulfillment remains very much contested in what have come to be called the "culture wars" (Hunter 1987, 1991). Especially in the United States, a series of controversies – over topics such as recreational drug use, homosexuality, abortion, and sex education in high schools (Powers 1998) – manifest the very uncertainties and anxieties that Carroll identified. More widely, Western culture and an increasingly hegemonic world capitalism no longer depend upon the unrelenting discipline of Puritanism for their spirit, but no compelling new ethic – remissive or otherwise – has arisen.

Living between the faded Puritan and the anticipated Remissive dispensations, we inhabit an intermediate zone of cultural Paranoia. Although paranoia conventionally is regarded as an affliction of the individual person, sociologists

Stanford Lyman and Marvin Scott have reviewed a body of research that examines the social conditions of individual paranoia. In their analysis, individuals are especially prone to becoming paranoid under specific circumstances of social interaction which have been modelled by game theorists, where other people are conspiring against them behind their backs: "unlike normals, 'paranoids' are more aware of social realities, more alive to contingencies and nuances, more strategic in their responses" (Lyman and Scott 1989, p. 105). Beyond this interpersonal dynamic, Carroll tells us that paranoia can also operate as a general cultural motif. This is hardly an especially novel idea. It is already anticipated by Richard Hofstadter's (1965) famous discussion of the "paranoid style" in American politics, most notably in the McCarthyism of the 1950s. The signs were already strong, in the United States, for example, in the conspiracy-theory culture that arose in the wake of John F. Kennedy's assassination in 1962. Yet modern cultural paranoia is diverse in its contents and it does not only thrive at the fringes. Sometimes it attains a kind of main-stream legitimacy, as in a famous corporate executive's 1996 book, *Only the Paranoid Survive* (Grove 1996). Overall, as a generic social form, paranoia can operate in individual actions, in the social dynamics of individuals and groups, and as a cultural logic.

In our era, cultural paranoia has often become marked in its contents by specifically apocalyptic motifs. Thus, in the cultural imaginary of film we are bombarded with scenes of collective disaster. In the past few years alone, New York City has been blown up by aliens (*Independence Day*), trampled by monsters (*Godzilla*), and pelted by asteroids (*Armageddon*). Meanwhile, in the real world, parallel preparations unfolded for the chaos that a Year-2000 (Y2K) computer meltdown might unleash, and for the random terrorism that a rogue religious, ethnic, or political movement might perpetrate. In this broader climate, religious apocalypticism has a strong claim to represent the quintessential domain of paranoia. Yet the paranoia associated with apoca-lyptic religion is not all of a piece. It operates in diverse ways, and on multiple fronts, individual, social, and cultural.

As Carroll describes paranoia, it reverses the Puritan's strong sense of internal-ized personal authority. Paranoia fears the outside world and imbues its public authorities with inflated power exercised for clandestine purposes.

> On the one hand, what is external is regarded as threatening and there-fore evil, operating at an uncontrollable distance, beyond mediation. On the other hand, paradoxically, private and public are confused, so that all distance collapses in the projection of the inner world on to external phenomena.
>
> (Carroll 1977, p. 12)

In both of the cultural structures of religious violence that we identified, this collapse of distance creates an Apocalypse that connects the ideological world of the established order with the world of an elect group who claim a special relationship to an emergent new order.

Paranoid communities

The paranoia within the religious movements we have examined is obvious and often remarked, but it tends to be reduced to individual personalities. Carroll challenges us, instead, to recognize paranoia as having social sources. When Puritanism fails, he suggests, "it turns to paranoia. The sense of authority remains equally strong, but the valence is reversed" (1977, p. 62). Charismatic apocalyptic movements need not recapitulate the Puritan reversal that Carroll describes. Puritan derived or not, such movements offer fertile ground for paranoia to take hold, both because claims about the threat posed by society at large can be used to bolster internal solidarity and social control, and because, as Carroll anticipated, external opposition attains a simultaneously highly public and deeply internalized character. The predisposition toward collective paranoia becomes further enhanced if the group really does have something to hide, or imagines that it does. Thus, Lyman and Scott argue that paranoia is often socially located among individuals who are hiding what they or others regard as stigmas, and attempting to "pass" in the wider society (1989, p. 103). If apocalyptic groups approximate this circumstance not just in their individual members, but collectively, the result is what Carroll calls a "paranoid community" (1977, p. 77).

The two cultural structures of apocalyptic violence are alternative pathways arising out of paranoid community. On the one hand, the mystical Apocalypse is marked by elaborate practices of secrecy, permeated with fears of discovery and plans for flight and escape, potentially into mystical death. On the other hand, the warring apocalyptic group carries the secrets of its clandestine deeds, as it plays out the strategic game of conflict against demonic forces of the established order, even to collective martyrdom.

Paranoia and societal repression

Yet it would be mistaken to assume that all paranoia is loaded onto the apocalyptic movements, with none left to operate in the wider societies where they arise. Quite to the contrary, paranoia is also manifested in actions undertaken to defend an established cultural and social order against alien "Others." Peter Gardella's claim (quoted in Anthony and Robbins 1997, p. 266) about the violence of the apocalyptic – that it "derives from projecting rejected aspects of the self onto enemies" – can as easily be applied to apocalyptic defenders of the established order as to apocalyptic religious movements themselves (Hall 1987, pp. 294–311; cf. Girard 1986, 1987; Alexander and Smith 1993). The threats are diverse. Some individuals and organizations that act in the defense of an established order are ever vigilant, and they do not necessarily distinguish

196

between apocalyptic groups and other developments that they deem threatening, religious or otherwise: all moral struggles against external threats become tinged with apocalyptic significance.

Within the domain of religion, the degree of perceived threat may have nothing to do with whether the group holds to an apocalyptic theology. On the other hand, many groups that do hold apocalyptic ideas are not taken to pose a serious moral threat to the established order, and they typically are ignored, tolerated, or treated as exotic novelties. However, when a group becomes construed as posing a threat, this construction can have consequences that do not depend on whether, on some objective basis, the threat might be deemed significant.

As Emile Durkheim (1995) understood, collective representations of a moral order socially define the boundaries of offense by identifying transgressions. The construction of moral boundaries operates in relation to an idealized society, but its efficacy depends on real and public events that affect the moral status of individuals and social groups. Under the logic of public moral ritual, the identification of religious social movements as deviant can be used to cleanse the society of alien influences by ritually marking the group as a "negative cult." The process reflects the same sort of "exemplary dualism" – categorizing social forces on the basis of "moral, eschatological, and cosmic polarities" – that Anthony and Robbins (1997, p. 266) define as characteristic of apocalyptic groups themselves. But the power valence is reversed, and thus the social processes are not symmetric. Among the dominant, legitimated dualists, drawing moral boundaries plays out as a process that amounts to scapegoating. Here, the complexity of human life is reduced to sharp distinctions between good and evil. Evil – whatever its source – is located in the alien cult, and treated as something foreign to the moral sensibilities of the existing order.

Though Carroll traces paranoia as a reaction against Puritanism, the possibilities are more complex. Ritual work that distinguishes an existing social order from alien Others can be undertaken either as a holding action against the rise of modernity or in order to defend modernity. In the Inquisition, the Church of Rome resisted cultural changes *prior* to (indeed, anticipating) the Protestant reformation and the emergence of Puritanism. In turn, as the Salem witch trials evidence, embedded within Puritanism, there is a strong revulsion for magic, uncertainty, and disorder. This revulsion can take the form of a righteous, disciplined, methodical purge that engulfs a community (Erikson 1966). Even more disconcerting, Nazi pursuit of the "final solution" depended on forms of organization and rationalized uses of technology that are the paragon of the modern culture with which the Puritan ethic became aligned. The Holocaust was chillingly disciplined in its implementation (Rubenstein 1978). Notwithstanding the brutal character that repressions of the Other can take, it would thus be mistaken to assume that modern societies have been purged of the techniques of such repression or the capacity and will to use them.

Repression and modernity

From the crucifixion of Jesus and the early Christian Church's struggles for its very survival to present-day efforts to curb sectarian movements around the globe, much religious history could be written onto a metanarrative of religious deviance, societal repression, violent conflict, martyrdom, and escape. The bold claim of theorists of secularization was that with the triumph of modernity during the twentieth century, and consonant with democratic pluralism, religion would become a matter of private faith, no longer a thematic of public culture. Yet this expectation is belied by modern repression of religious "cults," even benign ones.

Just as paranoia is manifested via apocalyptic meanings within certain religious social movements, agents of modernity may find themselves acting out an apocalyptic struggle against the opponents of the modern institutional complex of capitalism, science, and democracy. When this happens, they too participate in a strategic game that can take on paranoid features, especially in efforts to repress alien threats. Here, the threat of "cults" neatly bridges cultural and state anxieties about collective deviance, occasionally with devastating consequences. As one religious observer of the conflict between Peoples Temple and its opponents reflected, "I never got into a situation so paranoid on both sides" (quoted in Hall 1987, p. 234).

Two decades ago, sociologist of religion Peter Berger (1979) argued that modernity universalizes heresy because it opens up possibilities of religious choice. Key questions remain, however, concerning whether social institutions accommodate to religious diversity, and whether, among the many heresies, some get singled out as deviant. Here, repression is not a sign of strength, but of fear, of an anxiety about modernity, its opponents, and its prospects. Modernity triumphant might presumably accommodate religious heresy as an extension of democratic pluralism so long as the heresy did not fundamentally compromise principles of modern society: freedom of association, religious freedom, life and liberty, the capacity to pursue one's own individual vision of happiness. In this light, crusades against religious movements have had a perverse consequence for modernity: they have blurred the liberal vision of a social order by overlaying universalistic concerns for freedom with cultural concerns about moral boundaries.

There are two tacks among cultural opponents of religious social movements. Often their opposition is animated by the threat that such a group's religious ethos, cultural sensibility, or lifestyle poses to the established cultural order and, much more directly, to the social allegiances of family members and friends. Under modern dictates of pluralism, however, resolution of these cultural conflicts would favor the freedom of individuals to pursue happiness, no matter what their lifestyles, no matter what the sentiments of their friends or relatives. Thus, opponents of cults are hard put to give up their "brainwashing" and "mind control" theories and replace them with a potentially more disturbing analysis spelled out by Anthony and Robbins (1997): that individuals might embrace alien ideologies of their own free will. The reason seems straightforward: the moral interests of cultural opponents may be sufficient to mobilize certain reporters and editors within the mass media who use the journalistic enterprise to affirm the moral virtues of the established social order (cf. Gans 1979). However, the alignment of the state with these interests is more problematic, because liberal ideals of religious freedom protect deviant and offensive ideas equally with normative ones, and the thesis of free will would leave cultural opponents with no basis to seek state leverage against "cults."

In the face of modern institutional limits on the actions of states to control the voluntary embrace of morally offensive ideas, sect opponents often have adopted a second strategy to draw the state to their cause, couching their opposition in terms that invoke the modern project of assuring universal human rights. Thus, accusations of brainwashing, mind-control, or psychological manipulation suggest that a religious movement is antidemocratic in that it undermines the free choice of individuals. Similarly, accusations of child abuse invoke basic rights of children, and charges of economic chicanery speak to issues of whether individuals are entering into valid contracts. In effect, an elective affinity becomes established between cultural paranoia and the paranoia of modernity, and this affinity finds its social vehicle in the mobilization of a loose alliance between cultural opponents, the media, and the state (and within the state, among sectors most predisposed to defend against alien threats). In the bargain, the legitimacy of modernity as a normative project is compromised by its contradictory alignment with enforcements of particular moral boundaries and ritual exclusion of cultural Others.

The circumstances of modern religious repression vary by nation-state. To put the matter in the rational-choice terms of Stark and Bainbridge (1997), efforts of repression may amount to attempts to maintain religious monopoly in societies dominated by a single religious organization, or to control competition in a society where religions offer "commodities" in something like a marketplace. But other factors reinforce repressive efforts to control competition. In Germany, memories of the Nazi movement fuel political attempts to curb the Church of Scientology. Across the border, in France, the Catholics and humanists, media and the state that participate in the anticult movement do so in a climate described by James Beckford fifteen years ago, sharing the sentiment that "the country's formerly unitary value-system is under concerted attack" (1985, p. 266; NYT 20 June 1996). In the United States, the cult label has become such a generalized currency of demonization that it sometimes gets applied by members of one Christian group seeking to expose the heretical doctrines of another. Despite the differences, in all these nation-states, state actions of religious repression have on occasion become aligned with cultural efforts to purify the society of an alien threat. Modern Japan is the exception that demonstrates the principle at stake. Longstanding practices of religious repression at the hands of the state were ended with the country's defeat in the Second World War, and religiously based political parties have become influential. Under these complex conditions, the Japanese state has been reluctant to move against religious organizations, even when faced with the devastation unleashed by Aum Shinrikyō.

States and religious violence

By its very nature, the state claims a monopoly of the legitimate use of the means of violence, and on this basis its concerns about terrorism in general and the use of biological and chemical weapons in particular are well placed. As the deadly project of Aum clearly demonstrated, religious movements can sometimes amass significant capabilities of mass destruction that were once presumed to be held only by states. In the United States, a parallel challenge is posed by the right-wing racist Christian Identity movement which, despite its differences from Aum in theology, shares what Barkun (1997, p. 250) calls a merger of "the paramilitary with religious imperatives."

A modern world organized by bounded nation-states, it seems, is giving way to one where a warring sect can become a rogue power, waging a holy war against an established order. Even though contemporary states are maintained through highly sophisticated technological apparatuses of power, actions like the Oklahoma City bombing demonstrate that public transit systems, buildings of commerce, and places of government can never be completely protected from the threat of terrorist attack.

The continuities between sectarian apocalyptic war and political terrorism have gained increasing recognition within state defense and security circles.[5] As they acknowledge, apocalyptic war does not always center on territorially located communities. It can take the form of sporadic and geographically diffuse terrorism legitimated by a sectarian countercultural ideology (Hall 1978; Lamy 1997). The objective may be to create a general climate of terror, or perpetrators of violence may direct their actions toward specific targets, as terrorist opponents of abortion have done in the United States by targeting medical clinics that offer abortion services. States face a delicate situation: they are duty bound to control acts of strategic apocalyptic war, but to the degree that they do so, they become apocalyptic actors themselves. Thus, the problem that states confront is one of acting strategically without feeding images of the state as an actor in an apocalyptic drama.

As Michael Barkun has suggested, the state can become caught up in an extreme version of a process that has come to be called "deviance amplification." In this pattern, first applied to religious movements by Roy Wallis in his study of Scientology, a self-expanding cycle of deviance, external repression, alienation, and further repression spirals into ever more intense conflict (Wallis 1977; Barkun 1997, p. 257). As the murders and mass suicide at Jonestown sadly demonstrated, under apocalyptic circumstances, the result of a deviance amplification process can be extreme violence (Hall 1987). Faced with such a prospect, Barkun argues, the state has two viable options: increasing repression to the point where "the sanctions become so severe that the deviants no longer find it in their interest to continue former patterns of behavior," or lifting repression altogether. Between these extremes, a pattern of "deviance amplification" is the likely dynamic.

Cultural opponents, the media, and the state

The present study may offer some rules of experience concerning how states can pursue their own interests under circumstances in which state actions are deemed within a sectarian religious movement to be the fulfillment of apocalyptic prophecies. The state faces a dilemma if any action to curtail violence itself feeds paranoia. In some cases, a showdown may be inevitable. Aum Shinrikyō, for example, had an inner circle that developed a warring posture very early in the group's existence, and it began to seek terrorist capabilities in the absence of any organized state intervention. There, the state intervened naïvely and too late; rather than forestalling an apocalyptic dénouement, it triggered the most devastating of the incidents which Aum perpetrated. In other cases, states have launched preemptive actions against apocalyptically oriented sects. Thus, in 1993, Ukrainian police are reported to have rounded up some 500 members of a group that they claimed was threatening a mass suicide three weeks later (Robbins and Anthony 1995, p. 253). In early January 1999, Israeli police arrested and deported eight members of a Denver, Colorado, sect called Concerned Christians. Although police did not report finding weapons or other incriminating evidence, according to one official the sect "planned to carry out violent and extreme acts in the streets of Jerusalem at the end of 1999 to start the process of bringing Jesus back to life" (NYT 4 January 1999).

Preemptive actions by a state acting on its own may succeed in heading off violence, but they risk backfiring completely, and unless evidence of planned violence is strong, claims about a deviant group's intentions become a cheap and dangerous basis for curtailing religious freedom. Moreover, preemptive state action is not always undertaken autonomously. Quite to the contrary, the cases of Peoples Temple, the Branch Davidians, and the initial deaths in the Solar Temple all involved the mobilization of a loose coalition of cultural opponents, reporters and editors in the media, and state operatives, and this coalition was a party to escalating conflict that resulted in violence. The strong relationship between state-cultural opposition and outcomes of violence underscores how problematic state action becomes in the view of apocalyptic sectarians when it seems to take the side of cultural opponents under the glare of hostile media coverage.

This is not to say that cultural opponents lack any basis of grievance against religious movements. Families of individuals who join religious social movements may well have legitimate legal rights to pursue. Furthermore, whatever the opposing rights of adult individuals to freedom of association even against the wishes of their families, the emotional trauma that friends and relatives experience can be substantial, and sometimes their concerns about the sectarian convert may be well placed, either because of the particular person involved or because of the group. Yet what are relatives to do? Certainly if religious groups are violating the law, they are subject to the same enforcement at the hands of authorities as other individuals and groups. On the other hand, publicity trials and other highly visible moral campaigns are likely to amplify conflict. Given the volatile character of amplification processes, families and friends of people involved in sects who seek to deal rationally with their situations are probably best served by seeking communication and mediation by way of mechanisms such as those that Eileen Barker (1989) has described.

The role of the mass media in relation to religious violence poses other vexsome problems. Coverage of religious movements that frames them as "cults" tends to exacerbate any polarization that develops between religious movements and their cultural opponents, and the media "spotlight" can transpose conflictual events into nearly mythic drama. Moreover, the line of objective distance dividing media coverage from the subject of its coverage has become blurred; increasingly, news coverage itself reflexively contributes to the play of events that are its subject, as Shupe and Hadden (1995) show for the case of the Branch Davidians. In the 1990s, despite journalistic handwringing over their handling of the O. J. Simpson trial and the impeachment trial of US President Bill Clinton, the mass media showed themselves ever ready to transport news to a narrative register that approximates the soap opera, spinning out endless details revealed only slowly, in day-to-day installments of scandal, crisis, and drama.

The mass media in modern societies, of course, are not subject to much external institutional regulation. But if anyone might expect self-regulation, they would find a disturbing rejection of this possibility in the ethical blindspot of professional journalists concerning the effects of mass media on the violence at Waco (Society of Professional Journalists 1993). Journalists who want to enhance the professional status of their enterprise thus continue to face a significant challenge in considering how to cover incidents of cultural conflict between an established social order and religious social movements.

States may have legitimate concerns about illegal activities in religious social movements, but are best served if they operate independently of cultural opponents and the mass media. It is nevertheless the case that truly paranoid apocalyptic communities will project ever smaller events onto the field of transcendent meaning. Because the Apocalypse collapses the distance between public events and their significance for a group, and does so in a way that an apocalyptic group can align with its own prophetic calculus, non-action by states is not necessarily going to eliminate all acts of apocalyptic violence.

Neither is limiting state intervention likely to lead to a flood of apocalyptic collective suicide, however. On the contrary, when the state does nothing, many apocalyptic groups find their prophecies unfulfilled, and they develop new ones or revise their theologies altogether. Other groups undergo crises of charismatic authority or schism, or they collapse for reasons that have to do with dynamics internal to the group. State intervention stands a strong chance of interrupting these trajectories, and doing so in ways that increase the potential for violence. It shifts collective religious-movement attention away from internal matters and towards an external struggle that can easily be framed in apocalyptic terms. Moreover, to the degree that state intervention results in a public drama, it feeds a generalized apocalyptic culture that can spawn further socially organized actions undertaken under one or another paranoid script. Thus, when a state does intervene, its strategy must be concerned not only with immediate goals, but with gauging the consequences of state action for promoting an apocalyptic *zeitgeist*. Given the alternative dynamics and projections of possible consequences, in the vast majority of cases states are less well served by a pre-apocalyptic policy than by one that is non-interventionist and post-apocalyptic.

Emergent ethics of salvation and cultural change

If John Carroll is correct in identifying contemporary cultural paranoia as a product of cultural shifts and uncertainty, then an apocalyptic mood will not disappear simply because states resist allying themselves with cultural opponents of religious movements, any more than a post-apocalyptic policy of benign neglect will eliminate all apocalyptic religious violence. In Carroll's model, paranoia is the result of a mismatch between the conditions under which people live and available cultural recipes for meaningful participation in social life. The reasons for this mismatch are structural: in Daniel Bell's terms, they have to do with the disjuncture between a highly rationalized world of work versus a world of leisure that promotes opportunities of self-fulfillment through consumption. Beyond this binary opposition, it should be added, many people take up questions of meaning that may emerge from the absence of agency implied by the work–leisure dichotomy. Living in a world at odds with their own value preferences, entertaining doubts about work as a vocation, they will wonder how to make a difference. For the person facing any of these contradictions, religious "salvation" is not simply a theological matter about what happens to the soul after death; in the perspective developed by Emile Durkheim, it is concerned with how life on earth is to be sacralized. Broadly speaking, Bell's problems are "religious" ones. Reconciling the cultural formulae for work, leisure, and meaningful agency becomes a matter of constructing an ethic of life conduct that addresses fundamental questions: "who am I?," "how shall I live?," and "what god shall I serve?" Thus, movement beyond apocalyptic paranoia depends upon the capacity of people to find new religious ethics for life in a new millennium.

The quest for new religious ethics does not happen solely within religious social movements, much less apocalyptic ones that end violently. If anything, groups that self-destruct reduce the chances of their religious ethics spreading through the wider population because they eliminate the one organization best equipped to pursue the project of diffusion. Whether and how the distinctive formulae of salvation advanced by apocalyptic groups become diffused depends on religious practice. It is beyond anyone's nightmare that collective suicide, either as supposed martyrdom or as mystical transcendence, will become a dominant motif. Nevertheless, violence – and martyrdom, if it can be successfully claimed – sometimes produce a perverse attraction to religious ideas, as though death somehow underscores the seriousness of religious commitments rather than the hapless irrationality of the people who embrace them. Perhaps not surprisingly, people at close cultural proximity to the deaths continue to grapple with their significance. Survivors of the Apocalypse at Jonestown and associates of Peoples Temple debate the legacy (Moore 1988, Thrash 1995, Kahalas 1998, Layton 1998).[6] Adventist groups continue to vie for the audience once tapped by the Branch Davidians, Aum Shinrikyō attracts new members, European fascination with templar and rosicrucian gnosis continues unabated, and religious movements oriented to UFO theologies remain a growth industry (Lewis 1995). Moreover, not all religious diffusion occurs through organizational channels, especially in an age of mass media. Religious movements such as Peoples Temple and Heaven's Gate, when they no longer exist in the material world, can continue a shadow life in the zone of the simulacrum called the internet (cf. Bainbridge 1997, chapter 6). Perhaps parallel processes have sustained religious ideas of the dead in the past.

In the view of religion critic Gustav Niebuhr, "mass deaths of small, socially isolated religious groups represent the dark side of the spiritual searching and decline of traditional church structures that mark the last years of the twentieth century"(NYT 27 March 1997). Even if it would be completely inappropriate to generalize from cases of extreme religious violence, social theorists such as Alain Touraine (1981) argue that conflict is strongest at the fault lines of social life. In these terms, the apocalyptic violence of the past quarter-century is suggestive of broader cultural tensions. Given the cultural resistance to religious movements, it is reasonable to wonder what promises of salvation might have attracted the people who joined apocalyptic groups, and whether these attempts to achieve salvation might be harbingers relevant for society more generally.

For all their seemingly exotic character, and despite their tragic ends, the movements considered here dealt with central cultural problems and often reworked cultural formulae of long standing. The followers of Jim Jones drew a theology of the social gospel into alignment with an energetic pentecostalist style of life, tempering them both with a political commitment to communism and the construction of a declassé community where people confronted issues of racial integration in their daily lives. In the wider society, the situation is quite different. Racist hate crimes serve as reminders that, despite progress, a strong ethic of racial integration remains elusive. And comparison with recent approaches to the mission work of religious organizations (Klein 1997) suggests that Peoples Temple was a pioneer in the construction of a social-service congregational model.

If Peoples Temple pursued a radicalized and communalistic ethic of the social gospel, the Branch Davidians followed in a long Adventist tradition of looking for signs to confirm intense expectations about the coming Armageddon. In the current era, the signs often refer to such icons as the World Bank, the United Nations, and the Zionist Occupation Government. Whatever the content, intense anticipation of a final earthly reckoning suggests a culture of resentment which would logically appeal to people who feel left behind, excluded, or betrayed by societal transformations that threaten their presumed status and their religiously formed sense of honor. David Koresh transposed this theology of apocalyptic expectation into militant survivalist preparation for the last days, and initiated the formation of a post-apocalyptic social order through a practice of polygamy meant to establish a new lineage, the "House of David." The Branch Davidians' religious ethic of ascetic apocalyptic anticipation was not particularly novel; rather, what counted was their envisioned organizational trajectory as an expansive proto-ethnic religious movement along the lines of the nineteenth-century Mormons.

The salvation ethic of Aum Shinrikyō parallels that of the Branch Davidians in striking ways, but it is more complex. Certainly the general success of Aum and other "new new" religions in Japan suggests a ready audience for ethics of worldly salvation that transcend the institutionalized formulae that dominate Japanese life. Aum consolidated an ethic that combined mystical Buddhist practices with a doctrine that linked personal salvation to group apocalyptic survival. In turn, the organization established a sort of "shadow state" conceived as a religious empire, infused with echoes of *samurai* military culture. To date, no study provides anything close to a definitive account of these cultural resonances. Such research could yield important clues about the contemporary sources, tensions, and dilemmas of Japanese culture. But it could not yet clarify the import of Aum Shinrikyō; that import remains in flux because Aum continues to operate – and even recruit – in the face of public condemnation. The refusal of Asahara Shōkō and other leaders to recant their crimes creates a volatile circumstance in which people attracted to the group voluntarily take on the mantle of the group's collective stigmatization, thus confronting the Japanese state with a potentially powerful symbolic challenge to its legitimacy.[7] The story of Aum Shinrikyō is not yet over.

By comparison to Peoples Temple, the Branch Davidians, and Aum Shinrikyō, the other two groups – the Solar Temple and Heaven's Gate – were less militant and more mystical in their apocalypticism. In certain respects, the two groups shared a good deal. Both had spiritual leaders who projected the image of a world to which highly evolved spiritual beings could "travel," and they thus both committed a heresy against modern norms by wresting from God and taking into their own hands decisions about when to cross boundaries between life and death, between the world of material being and that of transcendent being. Yet despite their shared logic of escape in a mystical apocalypse of transcendence through biological death, the two groups differed substantially in the ethics of salvation that they promoted.

In the Solar Temple, the boundary that could be transgressed divided the temporality of the material world from a non-material world of eternity (often nevertheless concretized as a distant star or planet). A basic mystagogic theme of harmony suggested that careful action could harness hidden cosmic forces on multiple fronts, from sexuality to time travel. The elect who participated in the group were to be elevated to the status of higher beings who could move back and forth between the material world and eternity. Yet both for daily life activities such as washing the lettuce and for cosmic travel to the planet Sirius, the basic instrument used was ritual. In this emphasis, the Solar Temple appealed almost exclusively to an audience of people who were culturally Catholic in their socialization, and it offered them the very sort of client mysticism and ritualization of life that had been deemphasized by the Church since the reforms of Vatican II in the 1960s.

By comparison with the Solar Temple, the vision of Heaven's Gate held the Next Evolutionary Level Above Human to be located in a real material world, just like Earth, but with inhabitants who differed from those of North America during the "hang-loose" days of the counterculture when the group emerged in the 1970s. And though the deaths at Rancho Santa Fe were carefully ritualized, the emphasis among the class led by Do and Ti was on a relentless rationalization of life that bore no resemblance to the more aristocratic emphasis in the Solar Temple on *l'art de vivre*. Not ritual, but only the shedding of human traits, right down to sexual impulses, could prepare the individual to enter the Kingdom. The members of the class did not completely purge their lives of enjoyment, but they approached even relaxation and pleasure with the kind of disciplined and sober rationality that would have gained the approval of the most demanding Puritan. True to Do's Presbyterian roots, members of their class sought salvation in a limitless project of ascetic self-perfection.

Fundamental religious changes take decades and centuries for their realization. No one yet knows what the new millennium holds in the way of religious ethics of worldly salvation, nor whether the diverse visions advanced within the apocalyptic groups considered here will persist, or be taken up within some new movement. It is evident, however, that they have transported enduring cultural structures – of mysticism, asceticism, and the apocalyptic – into new social circumstances. Moreover, these apocalyptic groups are connected by the vitality of their salvation discourses to a panoply of wider developments: countercultural and fundamentalist religious movements, the institutionalization of New-Age practices ranging from aromatherapy to Zen meditation, feminist and gay engagements of religious issues, environmental and organic-food movements that deal in broadly sacred notions of nature and purity, sightings of spiritualized entities ranging from angels and the blessed Virgin to space aliens, and the freelance reformation of religious practices by individuals who are forging their own notions of the sacred.[8] It is too soon to know whether these developments are simply marginal fads, or, alternatively, whether they are creating foundations on which new religious ethics will be constructed. However, evidence suggests a blurring of the sharp divide that Karl Mannheim (1936) once described between the ideological and the utopian. What used to be countercultural religious movements now exercise an influence disproportionate to the numbers of their followers. And as Penny Becker (1999) has demonstrated, mainstream religions are considerably more diverse in their projects than is conventionally supposed. In an apocalyptic era, religions are undergoing reconstruction.

From Apocalypse to Omega

Motifs of Apocalypse in Western culture trace to ancient Mesopotamia, and they have been cast across the religions of Judaism, Christianity, and Islam

(Cohn 1993). These motifs are rich in their potential for cultural specification, ranging from fearful anticipation, through sober and practical preparation for the End Times, to holy war and the declaration of one or another post-apocalyptic kingdom. They have informed social movements as diverse as the ancient Jews' quest for a promised land, medieval millenarianism, and the Taiping rebellion in nineteenth-century China (Cohn 1970; Jen 1973). Beyond any specific movement, the diffusion of Christianity has made the apocalyptic a widely accessible theme, which by the end of the second millennium had spread beyond religion into secular social movements, films, popular culture about UFOs, and generalized anxiety about the millennial shift. Some day, no doubt, the final Apocalypse will come for the planet Earth. If nothing else, countless millennia from now, the planet's slow axial wobble and its eccentric yearly cycle no longer will sustain its orbit around the Sun. Much sooner, the planet will be enveloped by another ice age (NYT 16 February 1999, p. D1). No doubt other planetary catastrophes await before then, and ecological disaster may come much sooner.

Nevertheless, the apocalyptic anxieties of our era have little to do with the inevitable physical destruction of the planet. They are concerned with the history, fate, and redemption of its people. These anxieties have a modern history as well as an ancient one. The culture of Protestantism posited Rome as the whore of Babylon and the Reformation as the founding of a post-apocalyptic kingdom of heaven, translated for some into a physical place through migration from religious persecution in Europe to the Promised Land of religious freedom in North America. The stronger Calvinist versions of Puritanism advanced the doctrine of predestination in a way that displaced the believer's religious anxiety about salvation onto intensely productive, rationally ordered activity (Weber 1958). In effect, for the believer, Calvinism rendered apocalyptic eschatology moot. But other variants of Protestantism offered believers ways to relieve the salvation anxieties that Calvinism simply sublimated. The courses of these developments were diverse, as Weber showed. Many of them hinged on the seeker's quest for certainty of salvation, but Weber argued that certain alternatives to Calvinism, especially the doctrines of the Baptists and the Quakers "rested above all on the idea of expectant waiting for the Spirit to descend." Pushed in intensity, "this waiting might result in hysterical conditions, prophecy, and, as long as eschatological hopes survived, under certain circumstances even in an outbreak of chiliastic enthusiasm" (Weber 1958, pp. 148–9). In effect, Weber argued, because the promise of salvation through any ritual or magic on the part of the church was foreclosed by the Protestant turn, the quest for salvation became subject to diverse formulations, many of which trafficked in apocalyptic images of hellfire and brimstone and the imminence of Christ's Second Coming.

Here, the major theological issue depended on the difference between "premillennialists" who promote intense expectations that Christ will return soon to usher in the millennium (and save believers from the trauma of Armageddon) versus "post-millennialists" who anticipate Christ's return only at the end of the millennial era (see, e.g., Shupe 1997). For two centuries of industrialization and postindustrialization, Protestant preachers from fundamen-talist, adventist, holiness, and pentecostal churches have operated as something like Gramsci's traditional intellectuals, preaching to people experiencing the dislocations of rapid social change and ministering to those people too poor in spirit to bear the burdens of their times. But there has been a dialectic to the activities of these particular traditional intellectuals: they have both addressed and intensified apocalyptic expectations. In the cultural heyday of Puritanism, the apocalyptic motif took strong root in popular Protestant culture.

John Carroll's (1977) analysis of contemporary culture up to the time of his writ-ing in effect thematizes Weber's allusion about the theological avenue of transition from anti-emotional Calvinism to eschatological anxieties and anticipations. As Carroll saw it, a hegemonic high-culture Puritan ethic was being displaced by cultural Paranoia. However, Carroll regarded the latter as only a transitional forma-tion on the road to a culture of Remission. As he envisioned this dispensation, "at the moral level, remission represents forgiveness of all sins; at the institutional level, release from all controls." In religious terms, Carroll depicted remissive culture as a sort of "secularized Catholicism that returns, substituting an ethic of tolerance and forgiveness for the Puritan ethic of perfection and unredeemable culpability." The contemporary practice that approximated this model was to be found in psycho-analysis, where "to talk honestly is to exorcise all guilt" (1977, p. 19, 21).[9] Yet Carroll did not anticipate any easy development of a remissive ethic, nor did he assume that a remissive culture would result in ecstasy or even self-fulfillment rather than cynicism, boredom, and nihilism. Moreover, there was a tricky problem: on the side of the economic order, the Puritan virtues, or some new variant of them, would remain important.

Carroll wrote at the time when the counterculture was near its high water mark in the developed countries of Europe, North America, and East Asia, before AIDS and before resurgent fundamentalism. He correctly described the emergence of cultural paranoia in the wake of a Puritanism that had been waning for some time. But the consolidation of any viable institutional pattern of remissive culture that would displace paranoia remains elusive. Carroll's account is at present only a sociological prophecy of a post-apocalyptic heaven-on-earth, much like Marx's evocative description in *The German Ideology* of life under communism.

Any attempt to read local and temporally finite signs at the dawn of the third millennium as emblematic of broader cultural dilemmas is fraught with potential for error. Nevertheless, certain signs are suggestive. The unrelenting yet ultimately failed effort to remove US President Bill Clinton from office for covering up his sexual spooning with Monica Lewinsky was certainly the product of a strong Puritanesque morality, and one of the individuals who embraced it reflected on his camp's defeat by adopting the language of cultural contagion. "What steps can we take to make sure that we and our children are not infected?" asked conservative moralist Paul Weyrich. "We need some sort of quarantine" (NYT 21 February 1999, p. wk3). No remission, nor forgiveness, there.

On a different front, among youth, the portents of the New Age, if more remissive, are no less contorted. An advertisement for the internet browser Netscape displays the contradictions in two photographs superimposed on one another in alternating vertical strips. In one, young affluent white men and women gyrate their hip-hop paces in a netherworld of night culture that shadows contemporary life in the outer world. In the other photograph, sober business suits, one with a bow tie, work the floor of a stock market. But, the advertisement tells us, no one has to choose between these two venues. You can simply mouse click across them. "Go from the dance floor to the trading floor in your pajamas," the ad announces (*Wired* February 1999, p. 22). The question remains, who is the person doing the clicking? The advertisement offers an image that will prove appealing to many, of transcending the Puritan and the remissive, or, in the language of Daniel Bell, the ascetic and the hedonistic. Yet the reconciliation is left to the viewer to imagine, and to perform on the internet.

The apocalyptic religious movements – from Jonestown to Heaven's Gate – are vivid cautionary demonstrations that the contradictions have not yet been transcended. Yet, however obscurely, their shards suggest the erosion not only of Puritanism but of the broader modern culture that it initially supported. No longer does modernism effectively police once sharp distinctions between the material and the spiritual; reality and illusion; life and death; past, present, and future. The apocalypse lives in people who seek a new dispensation. From Peoples Temple to Heaven's Gate, believers did so through the affirmation of a progressive social ethic, a conservative asceticism, holy war against an established social order, a quasi-aristocratic ritualization of life, and the unrelenting ascetic quest for self-perfection. Others, more widely, explore similar terrains.[10] New hybrid people are emerging, seeking ethics and forms of spirituality that are as yet only dimly understood. In doing so, they unevenly erase modernity.

The apocalyptic calamities have taught many people to beware any prophet who claims to offer a compelling new revelation that speaks to the sensibilities and the needs of the age. But the collective suicides are only the most extreme consequences of an Apocalypse that is much more widely dispersed. The culture of paranoia will persist for those who do not find their ways out. To transcend it, if that is to occur, will take the construction of post-apocalyptic "religious" ethics linked with social practices that defuse the sources of apocalyptic anxieties around us: hunger, ignorance and poverty, war and less intensive but still devastating conflicts, environmental degradation, and the modern and now postmodern tension between lifeworldly existence and the systemic forces that envelop it. The search for religious meaning cannot be repressed. Either people well versed in the inherited traditions will demonstrate the significance of those traditions for new circumstances, or new prophets will gather followers into their own hands. Those who don't want the Apocalypse should work for something else.

NOTES

INTRODUCTION

1 For a compendium of developments, see "God decentralized: a special issue," *New York Times Magazine*, 7 December 1997.

2 These distinctions between the pre-apocalyptic and post-apocalyptic sect are drawn from *The Ways Out* (Hall 1978). The term "apocalyptic sect" was coined there because it seemed more widely relevant than, first, the often used, but strongly Christian-centered empirical distinction between "pre-millennialist" and "post-millennialist" Protestant sects, keyed to specific theological interpretations about the second coming of Christ; second, the generic term "millennialist sect," which, as we argue, theorizes time in too narrow a calendrical way; or third, the "messianic sect," which fails to identify the utopian content of the movement in *temporal* terms, a fundamental desideratum of both Karl Mannheim and phenomenological sociology (Hall 1978, pp. 9–14).

3 This kind of conflict escalation has usefully been theorized by Roy Wallis (1977) by drawing on a model of "deviance amplification" developed in sociological studies of gangs (see the Epilogue). Such a model, however, stops short of explaining violence *per se*.

4 My claim that opposition is cultural links up with Wallis's (1979, pp. 100, 104) borrowing from David Martin of the term "cultural defense," as opposed to "status defense" to describe the basis of moral and symbolic crusades analyzed by Joseph Gusfield and others. To be sure, families of religious movement members pursue status defense; however, if they become aligned with broader campaigns, those campaigns, which Gusfield called "symbolic crusades," are predominantly cultural in their constructions of "cults" as antithetical to established social values and mores.

5 To use the language of statistics, we are not "sampling on the dependent variable." The sample is not drawn from a universe of "all religious movements," those that result in violence and those that do not. It is a (non-random) sample of groups that ended in violence, but there is variation in the kind of violence that seems to have occurred. The commonalities and variations among different outcomes – all of them violent – are what we can seek to explain.

1 THE APOCALYPSE AT JONESTOWN

1 Unless otherwise indicated, information for this chapter is drawn from *Gone From the Promised Land: Jonestown in American Cultural History* (Hall 1987). See also Hall ([1979] 1990), Moore (1985), Chidester (1988), Moore and McGehee (1988), and Maaga (1998).

2 The CIA reportedly has burned its files concerning its operations in Guyana during the 1960s, when socialist Forbes Burnham came to power; see IHT 30 May 1997, pp. 1, 7.

2 FROM JONESTOWN TO WACO

1 *Advent Review and Sabbath Herald*, "Special 'Sealing' Edition." Lincoln, Oregon, undated [post-Mount Carmel fire], 1993.
2 For a comparative analysis of alternative sexual and gender institutions in nineteenth-century communal groups, see Foster 1991.
3 Since the conflagration at Mount Carmel, Ross has been convicted for participating in a "conspiracy to deprive Plaintiff of his civil rights of freedom of religion or freedom of interstate travel" in the case of a 1991 abduction of a then eighteen-year-old Washington state boy whom Ross attempted to "deprogram" from his participation in the United Pentecostal Church International (United States District Court, Western District of Washington at Seattle, "Verdict form," case no. C94-0079C; Seattle *Times*, 30 September, 1995).
4 In June 1984, 112 children were taken by armed state troopers from communal houses of the Northeast Kingdom Community Church in Island Pond, Vermont; later, a judge ruled the raid "grossly unlawful" and ordered the children released. One of the early opponents of the sect was a woman who also had contact with defectors from the Branch Davidian, Priscilla Coates, in 1982 a director of the Citizens Freedom Foundation (NYT 25 December 1987; WP 25 April 1993). More recently, the sect called The Family has been the subject of similar raids in France, Spain, Australia, and Argentina (NYT 26 September 1993, p. A4).
5 By 20 November, Assistant US Attorney Johnston found enough grounds for a "historical search warrant," but only on 15 December did BATF headquarters report that materials shipped to the Mag Bag were "consistent with component parts and accessories for AR-15 rifles or M16 machineguns." Arrest and search warrants were issued on 25 February, 1993. The BATF effort to meet "probable cause" – the standard for search and arrest warrants – depended on evidence and inferences concerning the conversion of legal weapons into illegal automatic weapons. There is room for debate as to whether their evidence met the standard. The Treasury Department review argues that the standard was met, but even several experts tasked by the review used equivocal language concerning the issue (USTD 1993, pp. 122–8; B137–95).
6 Although the Treasury Department cites this event at several junctures, Breault's account seems to have been an embellished version of a story that was recounted in a *Waco Tribune-Herald* article, about how a sleeping guard was startled by the newspaper delivery person, and "jumped up and fired a shotgun into the air" (WTH 1 March 1993, p. 6A).
7 One reviewer (USTD 1993, p. B58) indicated some efforts to cross-check information given by opponents, but even such a system might yield non-independent corroborations, since a number of the opponents had shared their accounts for more than a year prior to their contact with the BATF.
8 At this juncture, the BATF did not have an arrest warrant, and it is possible that they downplayed this option because they did not believe that they had probable cause to detain Koresh.
9 The child was probably Kiri Jewell, who related much the same narrative on national television after the BATF raid (Linedecker 1993, p. 139).
10 The Treasury Department review suggests that the tactical planners' concerns – "especially the fear of mass suicide" – were "validated" (USTD 1993, p. 141). Yet

this is an unreflexive claim of "cult essentialism" that fails to consider the genesis of the conditions under which the final deaths occurred.

11 Compare the alternative argument of Michael Barkun (1993, p. 597), who wrote:

> even if the FBI's account proves correct, "suicide" seems an inadequate label for the group's fiery demise. Unlike Jonestown, where community members took their own lives in an isolated setting, the Waco deaths occurred in the midst of a violent confrontation.
>
> (Barkun 1993, p. 597)

No label is adequate, of course, yet Barkun seems to overlook the degree of confrontational conflict that fueled the mass suicide at Jonestown (see chapter 1). There too, sect leaders followed an open-ended millenarian "script" of the sort that Barkun invokes for the Branch Davidians. However anyone chooses to label the event, the present chapter establishes that it occurred in a context where "mass suicide" was frequently invoked by the Davidians's opponents and law-enforcement authorities.

12 Directly contradicting a factual assertion in the US Treasury Department review (1993, p. 162), the Society report (p. 11) gave no analysis, but "found no concrete evidence" that journalists' actions in any way resulted in Koresh being tipped off about the raid.

13 To be quite clear, we do not propose that members of religious groups should be able to violate the law because of their religion. But neither should people acting in religious venues be held to a different standard of enforcement than other individuals.

3 THE VIOLENT PATH OF AUM SHINRIKYŌ

1 The details of these events are not solid, and whatever occurred cannot easily be separated from the sometimes apparently fictionalized writing style of two accounts, Brackett (1996, pp. 86–7) and Kaplan and Marshall (1996, pp. 35–6); Reader (1996, p. 28) is far more circumspect.

2 The word "satyam" was taken from sanskrit and means "truth."

4 THE MYSTICAL APOCALYPSE OF THE SOLAR TEMPLE

1 The following discussion of the original Knights Templar is based largely on the excellent account by Partner (1982).

2 Guery and Macedo (1982). We thank Jean-François Mayer for bringing this publication to our attention.

EPILOGUE

1 For an initial sociological analysis of the SLA, see Hall (1978). Well before Jones's eulogy, Peoples Temple used a public relations ploy to bask irrelevantly in the media spotlight on the SLA kidnapping by offering to let Temple members stand in for the young heiress as hostages (Hall 1987, p. 148).

2 For a review of anticult organization analyses, see Bromley (1998); for discussions of the anticult movement role in the Waco debacle, see Wright (1995b) and Lewis (1995).

3 There have been other recent cases of collective suicide. One case involved fifty-three members of a Thai minority apocalyptic sect in Vietnam who died on 2 October

1993 in an event orchestrated by their leader, Ca Van Lieng, who predicted a disastrous flood in the year 2000. In another, seven women who belonged to a group called the Friends of Truth died from apparent self-immolation on a beach in Japan shortly after the leader of the group died in a hospital. Such cases would be important to study, but it has not been within our capability to do so here.

4 Robbins (1997) also rightly suggests that the potential of what he calls "the interpretive approach" to explain religious violence is greater than the narrow uses to which it has been put, namely, demonstrating the socially constructed and emergent character of conflictual religious situations such as those at Jonestown and Mount Carmel. However, as chapter 3 details, on our analysis, Robbins (1997, p. 23) underestimates the role of external conflict in the trajectory of Aum Shinrikyō. The present study's delineation of a mystical apocalypse of deathly transcendence uses the interpretive approach in a broader way, called for by Robbins. We agree with him that scholars of religious movements would be mistaken to take the reductionist route of treating all cases of extreme violence (or anything else) as necessarily explicable within a single interpretive frame.

5 Unfortunately, the analyses are sometimes framed in terms that will only impede understanding; see, for example, Hubback's (1996) discussion of cults, filled with breezy exaggerations and outright misinformation.

6 For Peoples Temple, see also the web site established by Rebecca Moore, http://www.und.nodak.edu/dept/philrel/jonestown/.

7 In a potent way, Aum's posture resonates with the founding events of Christianity. Girard (1986) offers a useful analysis by which to pursue this comparison, which would move well beyond the present study.

8 On the latter development, see the special issue of the *New York Times Magazine*, "God decentralized," 7 December 1997. For the relation of contemporary religious movements to nature, see Albanese (1990).

9 In a way, what Harold Bloom calls "the American religion" approximates a paradigmatic Christian version of this friendly psychoanalytic exchange in the image Bloom offers of Southern Baptists walking "alone in the garden with Jesus" (1992, p. 202). But Bloom's American religion, he claims, is some 200 years old; it thus competes with Puritanism and with paranoia, rather than sequentially displacing them. Pursuing the complex relations among these alternatives is a matter for a cultural history of religion in the United States, not for the present study.

10 See, for example, the thought-provoking treatment of the apocalyptic condition by feminist theologian Catherine Keller (1996).

BIBLIOGRAPHY

Chinese and Japanese names are listed by first (i.e. family) name.

Albanese, Catherine L. 1990. *Nature Religion in America*. Chicago: University of Chicago Press.

Alexander, Jeffrey C., and Philip Smith. 1993. "The discourse of civil society: a new proposal for cultural studies." *Theory and Society* 22: 151–207.

Andrews, Edward D. 1971 (1933). *The Community Industries of the Shakers*. Charlestown, Mass.: Emporium.

Anthony, Dick, and Thomas Robbins. 1997. "Religious totalism, exemplary dualism, and the Waco tragedy," pp. 261–84 in Robbins and Palmer, eds, *Millennium, Messiahs, and Mayhem*. New York: Routledge.

Asahara Shōkō. 1992. *Declaring Myself the Christ, Disclosing the True Meanings of Jesus Christ's Gospel*. Tokyo: Aum.

—— 1993. *Beyond Life and Death*. Tokyo: Aum.

Bailey, Brad, and Bob Darden. 1993. *Mad Man in Waco: The Complete Story of the Davidian Cult, David Koresh, and the Waco Massacre*. Waco, Texas: WRS Publishing.

Bainbridge, William Sims. 1997. *The Sociology of Religious Movements*. New York: Routledge.

Balch, Robert W. 1980. "Looking behind the scenes in a religious cult: implications for the study of conversion." *Sociological Analysis* 41: 137–43.

—— 1982. "Bo and Peep: a case study of the origins of messianic leadership," pp. 13–72 in Roy Wallis, ed., *Millennialism and Charisma*. Belfast, Northern Ireland: Queen's University.

—— 1995. "Waiting for the ships: disillusionment and the revitalization of faith in Bo and Peep's UFO cult," pp. 137–66 in James R. Lewis, ed., *The Gods Have Landed: New Religions from Other Worlds*. Albany: State University of New York Press.

Balch, Robert W., and David Taylor. 1976. "Salvation in a UFO." *Psychology Today* 10 (October): 58, 61–62, 66, 106.

—— 1977. "Seekers and saucers: the role of the cultic milieu in joining a UFO cult." *American Behavioral Scientist* 20: 839–60.

Barker, Eileen. 1984. *The Making of a Moonie*. New York: Blackwell.

—— 1989. *New Religious Movements: A Practical Introduction*. London: Her Majesty's Stationery Office.

Barkun, Michael. 1993. "Reflections after Waco: millennialists and the state." *Christian Century* 110, no. 18 (2–9 June): 596–600.

—— 1997. "Millenarians and violence: the case of the Christian Identity movement," pp. 247–60 in Robbins and Palmer, eds, *Millennium, Messiahs, and Mayhem*. New York: Routledge.

Barthes, Roland. 1972 (1957). *Mythologies*. New York: Hill and Wang.

Baudrillard, Jean. 1988. *Selected Writings*. Stanford, Calif.: Stanford University Press.
——1994. *The Illusion of the End*. Cambridge, England: Polity Press.
Becker, Penny. 1999. *Congregations in Conflict*. New York: Cambridge University Press.
Beckford, James. 1985. *Cult Controversies*. London: Tavistock.
Bell, Daniel. 1976. *The Cultural Contradictions of Capitalism*. New York: Basic.
Bellah, Robert. 1970 (1957).*Tokagawa Religion: The Values of Pre-Industrial Japan*. Boston: Beacon Press.
Benjamin, Walter. 1968 (1940). "Theses on the philosophy of history," pp. 153–64 in *Illuminations*. New York: Harcourt, Brace, and World.
Berger, Peter. 1967. *The Sacred Canopy*. Garden City, N.Y.: Doubleday.
—— 1979. *The Heretical Imperative*. New York: Anchor.
Berger, Peter L., Brigitte Berger, and Hansfried Kellner. 1973. *The Homeless Mind: Modernization and Consciousness*. New York: Random House.
Bloom, Harold. 1992. *The American Religion: The Emergence of the Post-Christian Nation*. New York: Simon and Schuster.
Bo and Peep (Marshall Herff Applewhite and Bonnie Truesdale). 1976. "Behavioral guidelines given in the early days of the classroom. November 1976." Distributed via heavensgate.com internet web site, 1997.
Boorstin, Daniel J. 1962. *The Image, or What Happened to the American Dream*. New York: Atheneum.
Boyer, Paul. 1992. *When Time Shall Be No More*. Cambridge: Harvard University Press.
Brackett, D. W. 1996. *Holy Terror: Armageddon in Tokyo*. New York: Weatherhill.
Bragg, Roy. 1993. "Ex-prosecutor laments agent's 'storm trooper' tactics." *Houston Chronicle*, 2 March, 7A.
Breault, Marc, and Martin King. 1993. *Inside the Cult: A Member's Chilling, Exclusive Account of Madness and Depravity in David Koresh's Compound*. New York: Penguin Signet.
Breyer, Jacques. 1959. *Arcanes Solaire; ou, Les Secrets du Temple Solaire*. Paris: La Colombe.
Bromley, David G. 1998. "The social construction of contested exit roles: defectors, whistleblowers, and apostates," pp. 19–48 in David G. Bromley, ed., *The Politics of Religious Apostasy*. Westport, Conn.: Praeger.
Bromley, David G., and Gordon Melton, eds, Forthcoming, 2000. *Dramatic Confrontations: Religion and Violence in Contemporary Society*. New York: Cambridge University Press.
Bromley, David G., and Anson Shupe. 1979. "Moonies" in *America: Cult, Church, and Crusade*. Beverly Hills, Calif.: Sage.
Bromley, David G., and Edward D. Silver. 1995. "The Davidian tradition: from patronal clan to prophetic movement," pp. 43–72 in Stuart A. Wright, ed., *Armageddon in Waco*. Chicago: University of Chicago Press.
Brown, Alexander Douglas. 1996. "Religion and reaction: an anthropological study of Aum Shinrikyō." Oxford: St. Anthony's College M.Phil. thesis.
Carroll, John. 1977. *Puritan, Paranoid, Remissive: A Sociology of Modern Culture*. London: Routledge and Kegan Paul.
Chidester, David. 1988. *Salvation and Suicide: an Interpretation of Jim Jones, the Peoples Temple, and Jonestown*. Bloomington: Indiana University Press.
Cohn, Norman. 1970. *The Pursuit of the Millennium*. New York: Oxford University Press.
—— 1993. *Cosmos, Chaos, and the World to Come: The Ancient Roots of Apocalyptic Faith*. New Haven, Conn.: Yale University Press.
Collins, Randall. 1997. "An Asian route to capitalism: religious economy and the origins of self–transforming growth in Japan." *American Sociological Review* 62: 843–65.
Do (né Marshall Herff Applewhite). 1994. "Crew from the Evolutionary Level Above Human offers – last chance to advance beyond human." Distributed via heavensgate.com internet web site, 1997.

—— 1996a. "Last chance to evacuate Earth before it's recycled." Edited transcript of videotape, 29 September. Distributed via heavensgate.com internet web site, 1997.

—— 1996b. "Planet about to be recycled – Your only chance to survive – leave with us." Edited transcript of videotape, 5 October. Distributed via heavensgate.com internet web site, 1997.

—— 1997. "Do's intro: purpose – belief." Distributed via heavensgate.com internet web site.

Durkheim, Emile. 1961 (1925). *Moral Education.* New York: Free Press.

—— 1995 (1915). *The Elementary Forms of Religious Life.* Translated and with an introduction by Karen E. Fields. New York: Free Press.

Egawa Shōko. 1991. *Kiseisha no yabō* (Ambitions of a Messiah). Tokyo: Kyōiku shiryō shuppankai.

Eliade, Mircea. 1959 (1954). *Cosmos and History.* New York: Harper and Row.

Ellison, Christopher G., and John P. Bartkowski. 1995. "'Babies were being beaten': exploring child-abuse allegations at Ranch Apocalypse," pp. 111–49 in Stuart A. Wright, ed., *Armageddon in Waco.* Chicago: University of Chicago Press.

Erikson, Kai. 1966. *Wayward Puritans.* New York, Wiley.

Festinger, Leon, Henry W. Riecken, and Stanley Schachter. 1964 (1956). *When Prophecy Fails.* New York: Harper and Row.

Foster, Lawrence. 1991. *Women, Family, and Utopia: Communal Experiments of the Shakers, the Oneida community, and the Mormons.* Syracuse, N.Y.: Syracuse University Press.

Frend, W. H. C. 1967. *Martyrdom and Persecution in the Early Church.* Garden City, N.J.: Doubleday.

Fukayama, Francis. 1992. *The End of History and the Last Man.* New York : Free Press.

Gamson, William A., and Andre Modigliani. 1989. "Media discourse and public opinion on nuclear power: a constructionist approach." *American Journal of Sociology* 95: 1–37.

Gamson, William A., David Croteau, William Hoynes, and Theodore Sasson. 1992. "Media images and the social construction of reality." *Annual Review of Sociology* 18: 373–93.

Gans, Herbert. 1979. *Deciding What's News.* New York: Random House.

Garon, Sheldon. 1997. *Molding Japanese Minds: The State in Everyday Life.* Princeton, N.J.: Princeton University Press.

Girard, René. 1977 (1972). *Violence and the Sacred.* Baltimore, Md.: Johns Hopkins University Press.

—— 1986. *The Scapegoat.* Baltimore, Md.: Johns Hopkins University Press.

—— 1987. "Generative scapegoating," pp. 73–105 in William Burkert, René Girard, and Jonathan Z. Smith, *Violent Origins: Ritual Killing and Cultural Formation.* Stanford, Calif.: Stanford University Press.

Grove, Andrew S. 1996. *Only the Paranoid Survive. How to Exploit the Crisis Points that Challenge Every Company and Career.* New York: Doubleday.

Guery, Appel, and Serio Macedo. 1982. *Voyage Intemporel: Terre Ciel Connection.* Grenoble, France: Editons Glénat.

Hall, John R. 1978. *The Ways Out: Utopian Communal Groups in an Age of Babylon.* London: Routledge and Kegan Paul.

—— 1987. *Gone From the Promised Land: Jonestown in American Cultural History.* New Brunswick, N.J.: Transaction.

—— 1988. "Social organization and pathways of commitment: types of communal groups, rational choice theory, and the Kanter thesis." *American Sociological Review* 53: 679–92.

—— 1990. "The apocalypse at Jonestown" (1979) with "Afterword," pp. 269–293 in Thomas Robbins and Dick Anthony, eds, *In Gods We Trust,* 2nd edition. New Brunswick, N.J.: Transaction.

—— 1995. "Public narratives and the apocalyptic sect: from Jonestown to Mount Carmel," pp. 205–35 in Stuart A. Wright, ed., *Armageddon in Waco.* Chicago: University of Chicago Press.

—— 1999. *Cultures of Inquiry: From Epistemology to Discourse in Sociohistorical Research.* Cambridge: Cambridge University Press.

Hall, John R. and Mary Jo Neitz. 1993. *Culture: Sociological Perspectives.* Englewood Cliffs, N.J.: Prentice Hall.

Hawthorn, Geoffrey. 1991. *Plausible Worlds: Possibility and Understanding in History and the Social Sciences.* New York: Cambridge University Press.

Heaven's Gate. 1997 (n.d.). "Our position against suicide." Distributed via heavensgate.com internet web site.

Hechter, Michael. 1987. *Principles of Group Solidarity.* Berkeley: University of California Press.

Herberg, Will. 1983 (1955). *Protestant, Catholic, Jew.* Chicago: University of Chicago Press.

Hewitt, Bill, Thomas Fields-Meyer, Bruce Frankel, Dan Jewel, Pam Lambert, Anne-Marie O'Neill, and William Plummer. 1997. "Who were they?" *People Magazine* 47, no. 14 (14 April): 40–56.

Hobsbawm, Eric J. 1994. *The Age of Extremes.* New York: Pantheon.

Hofstadter, Richard. 1965. *The Paranoid Style in American Politics.* New York: Knopf.

Hubback, Andrew. 1996. *The Prophets of Doom: The Security Threat of Religious Cults.* London: Institute for European Defense and Strategic Studies.

Hunter, James Davison. 1987. *Evangelicalism: The Coming Generation.* Chicago: University of Chicago Press.

—— 1991. *Culture Wars.* New York: Basic Books.

Introvigne, Massimo. 1995. "Ordeal by fire." *Religion* 25: 267–83.

Ikegami, Eiko. 1995. *The Taming of the Samurai: Honorific Individualism and the Making of Modern Japan.* Cambridge, Mass.: Harvard University Press.

Ishii Kenji. 1996. *Religion in Japanese Culture.* Tokyo: Kodansha International.

Jackman, Mary R. Forthcoming. "Violence and legitimacy in expropriative intergroup relations," in John T. Jost and Brenda Major, eds, *The Psychology of Legitimacy.* Cambridge: Cambridge University Press.

James, William. 1929 (1902). *The Varieties of Religious Experience.* New York: Random House.

Jen Yu-wen. 1973. *The Taiping Revolutionary Movement.* New Haven, Conn.: Yale University Press.

Jwnody ("a student"). 1996. "Overview of present mission." April. Distributed via heavensgate.com internet web site, 1997.

Kahalas, Laurie Efrein. 1998. *Snake Dance: Unravelling the Mysteries of Jonestown.* Victoria, B.C., Canada: Trafford, for Red Robin Press, New York.

Kane, Anne. 1991. "Cultural analysis and historical sociology: the analytic and concrete forms of the autonomy of culture." *Sociological Theory* 9: 53–69.

—— 1997. "Theorizing meaning construction in social movements: symbolic structures and interpretation during the Irish Land War, 1879–1882." *Sociological Theory* 15: 249–76.

Kanter, Rosabeth Moss. 1972. *Commitment and Community: Communes and Utopias in Sociological Perspective.* Cambridge: Harvard University Press.

Kaplan, David E., and Andrew Marshall. 1996. *The Cult at the End of the World: The Terrifying Story of the Aum Doomsday Cult, from the Subways of Tokyo to the Nuclear Arsenals of Russia.* New York: Crown.

Keller, Catherine. 1996. *Apocalypse Now and Then: A Feminist Guide to the End of the World.* Boston: Beacon Press.

Klein, Joe. 1997. "In God they trust." *New Yorker* 76, no. 16 (16 June): 40–8.

Lamy, Philip. 1997. "Secularizing the millennium: survivalists, militias, and the new world order," pp. 93–117 in Robbins and Palmer, eds, *Millennium, Messiahs, and Mayhem.* New York: Routledge.

Layton, Deborah. 1998. *Seductive Poison: A Jonestown Survivor's Story of Life and Death in the Peoples Temple.* New York: Doubleday.

Lenski, Gerhard. 1961. *The Religious Factor*. Garden City, N.Y.: Doubleday.

Lewis, James R. 1995. *The Gods Have Landed: New Religions from Other Worlds*. Albany: State University of New York Press.

Lewy, Guenter. 1974. *Religion and Revolution*. New York: Oxford University Press.

Lindstrom, Lamont. 1993. *Cargo Cult: Strange Stories of Desire from Melanesia and Beyond*. Honolulu: University of Hawaii Press.

Linedecker, Clifford L. 1993. *Massacre at Waco, Texas: The Shocking True Story of Cult Leader David Koresh and the Branch Davidians*. New York: St. Martin's Paperbacks.

Lyman, Stanford M., and Marvin B. Scott. 1989. *A Sociology of the Absurd*. Dix Hills, N.Y.: General Hall.

Malcomson, Scott L. 1997. "Keep out." *New Yorker*, 7 April: 39.

Maaga, Mary. 1998. *Hearing the Voices of Jonestown*. Syracuse, N.Y.: Syracuse University Press.

Mannheim, Karl. 1936. *Ideology and Utopia*. New York: Harcourt, Brace and World.

—— 1952 (1927). "The problem of generations," pp. 276–322 in Karl Mannheim, *Essays on the Sociology of Knowledge*. New York: Oxford University Press.

Martin, David. 1978. *A General Theory of Secularization*. New York: Harper and Row.

Mary, Blessed Virgin, Saint (Spirit). 1991. *Mary's Message to the World, as Sent by Mary, the Mother of Jesus*. Received by Annie Kirkwood; compiled by Byron Kirkwood. New York: G. P. Putnam's Sons.

Mayer, Jean-François. 1996. *Les Mythes du Temple Solaire*. Geneva: Georg Editeur.

Meiers, Michael. 1988. *Was Jonestown a CIA Medical Experiment?* Lewiston, N.Y.: Edwin Mellen Press.

Mill, John Stuart. 1950 (1843). *John Stuart Mill's Philosophy of Scientific Method*. New York: Hafner.

Miller, Perry, 1956. *Errand into the Wilderness*. Cambridge: Harvard University Press.

Moore, Rebecca. 1985. *A Sympathetic History of Jonestown*. Lewiston, N.Y.: Edwin Mellen Press.

—— 1988. *In Defense of Peoples Temple*. Lewiston, N.Y.: Edwin Mellen Press.

Moore, Rebecca, and Fielding McGehee III, eds, 1988. *New Religious Movements, Mass Suicide, and Peoples Temple*. Lewiston, N.Y.: Edwin Mellen Press.

Moses, William Jeremiah. 1982. *Black Messiahs and Uncle Toms: Social and Literary Manipulations of a Religious Myth*. University Park: Pennsylvania State University Press.

Mullins, Mark. 1997. "Aum Shinrikyō as an apocalyptic movement," pp. 313–24 in Robbins and Palmer, eds, *Millennium, Messiahs, and Mayhem*. New York: Routledge.

Murakami Shigoyoshi. 1972. "New Religions in Japan." *East Asian Cultural Studies* 11 (March): 1–4.

Nakano Tsuyoshi. 1996. "Religion and State," pp, 115–36 in Noriyoshi Tamaru and David Reid, eds, *Religion in Japanese Culture: Where Living Traditions Meet a Changing World*. Tokyo: Kodansha International.

Partner, Peter. 1982. *The Murdered Magicians: The Templars and their Myth*. New York: Oxford University Press.

Pitts, William R. 1995. "Davidians and Branch Davidians: 1929–1987," pp. 20–42 in Stuart A. Wright, ed., *Armageddon in Waco*. Chicago: University of Chicago Press.

Powers, Rosemary F. 1998. "When the subject is sex: teachers and the sexual construction of the secondary school." Ph.D dissertation in Sociology. Davis, Calif.: University of California.

Reader, Ian. 1996. *A Poisonous Cocktail? Aum Shinrikyō's Path to Violence*. Copenhagen: Nordic Institute of Asian Studies.

Richardson, James T. 1995. "Manufacturing consent about Koresh: a structural analysis of the role of media in the Waco tragedy," pp. 153–76 in Stuart A. Wright, ed., *Armageddon in Waco*. Chicago: University of Chicago Press.

Riddle, Donald W. 1931. *The Martyrs: A Study in Social Control*. Chicago: University of

Chicago Press.

Robbins, Thomas. 1986. "Religious mass suicide before Jonestown: the Russian Old Believers." *Sociological Analysis* 47: 1–20.

—— 1997. "Religious movements and violence: a friendly critique of the interpretive approach." *Novio Religio* 1: 17–33.

Robbins, Thomas, and Dick Anthony. 1995. "Sects and violence: factors affecting the volatility of marginal religious movements," pp. 236–59 in Stuart A. Wright, ed., *Armageddon in Waco*. Chicago: University of Chicago Press.

Robbins, Thomas, and Susan J. Palmer, eds, 1997. *Millennium, Messiahs, and Mayhem*. New York: Routledge.

Roof, Wade Clark, and William McKinney. 1987. *American Mainline Religion: Its Changing Shape and Future*. New Brunswick, N.J.: Rutgers University Press.

Roth, Guenther. 1975. "Socio-historical model and developmental theory: charismatic community, charisma of reason, and the counterculture." *American Sociological Review* 40: 148–57.

Rubenstein, Richard L. 1978. *The Cunning of History: The Holocaust and the American Future*. New York: Harper and Row.

Sayle, Murray. 1996. "Nerve gas and the four noble truths." *New Yorker*, 1 April: 56–71.

Scott, James C. 1985. *Weapons of the Weak: Everyday Forms of Peasant Resistance*. New Haven, Conn.: Yale University Press.

Scruggs, Richard, Steven Zipperstein, Robert Lyon, Victor Gonzalez, Herbert Cousins, and Roderick Beverly. 1993. *Report to the Deputy Attorney General on the Events at Waco, Texas, February 28 to April 19, 1993*. Redacted version. Washington, D.C.: US Department of Justice.

Sewell, William H., Jr. 1992. "A theory of structure: duality, agency, and transformation." *American Journal of Sociology* 98: 1–29.

Shimazono Susumu. 1995. "In the wake of Aum: the formation and transformation of a universe of belief." *Japanese Journal of Religious Studies* 22: 381–415.

Shupe, Anson D. 1997. "Christian reconstructionism and the angry rhetoric of neo-post-millennialism," pp. 195–206 in Robbins and Palmer, eds, *Millennium, Messiahs, and Mayhem*. New York: Routledge.

Shupe, Anson D., David G. Bromley, and Donna L. Oliver. 1984. *The Anti-Cult Movement in America: A Bibliography and Historical Survey*. New York: Garland.

Shupe, Anson D., and Jeffrey K. Hadden. 1995. "Cops, news copy, and public opinion: legitimacy and the social construction of evil in Waco," pp. 175–202 in Stuart A. Wright, ed., *Armageddon in Waco*. Chicago: University of Chicago Press.

Simmel. Georg. 1955 (1908). *"Conflict" and "The Web of Group-Affiliations."* New York: Free Press.

Snow, David A., E. Burke Rochford, Jr., Steven K. Worden, and Robert D. Benford. 1986. "Frame alignment processes, micromobilization, and movement participation." *American Sociological Review* 51: 464–81.

Society of Professional Journalists. 1993. "Waco: what went right, what went wrong." 32 pp. Greencastle, In.: Society of Professional Journalists.

Somers, Margaret R. 1992. "Narrativity, narrative identity, and social action: rethinking English working-class formation." *Social Science History* 16: 591–630.

Stark, Rodney, and William Sims Bainbridge. 1997. *Religion, Deviance, and Social Control*. New York: Routledge.

Stinchcombe, Arthur. 1978. *Theoretical Methods in Social History*. New York: Academic Press.

Strozier, Charles B. 1994. *Apocalypse: On the Psychology of Religious Fundamentalism in America*. Boston: Beacon Press.

Tabor, James D., and J. Phillip Arnold. 1995. "A commentary on the Koresh manuscript

(The Seven Seals of the Book of Revelation)," pp. 205–11 in James D. Tabor and J. Phillip Arnold, *Why Waco?* Berkeley: University of California Press.

Takahashi Hidetoshi. 1996. *Aomu kara kikan* (Return from Aum). Tokyo: Sōshisha.

Takimoto Tarō and Fukushima Mizuho. 1996. *Habōhō to Oumu Shinrikyō* (The Anti-subversive Acts Law and Aum Shinrikyō). Tokyo: Iwanami shoten.

Thrash, Catherine (Hyacinth). 1995. *The Onliest One Alive*, as told to Marian K. Towne. Indianapolis, Ind.: M. K. Towne.

Touraine, Alain. 1981. *The Voice and the Eye: An Analysis of Social Movements.* Cambridge: Cambridge University Press.

Trinh, Sylvaine. 1997. "Aum Shinrikyō: secte et violence," pp. 229–90 in Michel Wieviorka, ed., *Un nouveau paradigme de la violence?* Paris; Montreal, Québec: L'Harmattan.

US Department of the Treasury. 1993. *Report of the Department of the Treasury on the Bureau of Alcohol, Tobacco, and Firearms Investigation of Vernon Wayne Howell, also known as David Koresh.* Washington, D.C.: US Government Printing Office.

US District Court, 1993. "Application and affidavit for search warrant," W93–15M, and "Warrant for arrest, case # W93–17M, USA vs. Vernon Wayne Howell, AKA David Koresh." Western District of Texas, Waco, Texas, filed 26 February, 1993.

Wagner-Pacifici, Robin. 1994. *Discourse and Destruction: The City of Philadelphia versus MOVE.* Chicago: University of Chicago Press.

—— 2000. *Theorizing the Standoff: Contingency in Action.* Cambridge: Cambridge University Press.

Wallis, Roy. 1977. *The Road to Total Freedom: A Sociological Analysis of Scientology.* New York: Columbia University Press.

—— 1979. *Salvation and Protest: Studies of Social and Religious Movements.* New York: St Martin's Press.

Warner, R. Stephen. 1993. "Work in progress toward a new paradigm for the sociological study of religion in the United States." *American Journal of Sociology* 98: 1044–93.

Weber, Max. 1946 [1918]. "Science as a vocation," in Hans Gerth and C. Wright Mills, eds, *From Max Weber: Essays in Sociology*, pp. 129–56. New York: Oxford University Press.

—— 1958 (1905). *The Protestant Ethic and the Spirit of Capitalism.* New York: Schribner's.

—— 1964 (1920–21). *The Religion of China.* New York: Macmillan.

—— 1978 (1922). *Economy and Society*, ed. Guenther Roth and Claus Wittich. Berkeley: University of California Press.

Weisbrot, Robert. 1983. *Father Divine and the Struggle for Racial Equality.* Urbana: University of Illinois Press.

Williams, Sam K. 1975. *Jesus' Death as a Saving Event: The Background and Origin of a Concept.* Harvard Dissertations in Religion, no. 2. Cambridge, Mass.: Harvard Theological Review.

Wilson, Bryan R. 1973. *Magic and the Millennium: A Sociological Study of Religious Movements of Protest among Tribal and Third-World Peoples.* New York: Harper and Row.

Wood, James E., Jr. 1993. "The Branch Davidian standoff: an American tragedy." *Journal of Church and State* 35 (Spring): 1–9.

Worsley, Peter. 1968. *The Trumpet Shall Sound.* Second edition. New York: Schocken Books.

Wright, Stuart A., ed. 1995a. *Armageddon in Waco.* Chicago: University of Chicago Press.

—— 1995b. "Construction and escalation of a cult threat," pp. 75–94 in Wright 1995a.

Wuthnow, Robert. 1988. *The Restructuring of American Religion.* Princeton, N.J.: Princeton University Press.

Zilliox, Larry, Jr., and Larry Kahaner. No date. "How to investigate destructive cults and underground groups." 138 pp. photocopy. (No publisher listed).

INDEX